P9-DMV-840

GARIBALDI
The Revolutionary and his Men

Garibaldi with his General Staff during the expedition of the Thousand.

Andrea Viotti

GARIBALDI

The Revolutionary and his Men

BLANDFORD PRESS

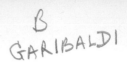

B
GARIBALDI

205988

First published in the U.K. 1979
Copyright © *1979 Andrea Viotti*
Blandford Press Ltd, Link House, West Street,
Poole, Dorset, BH15 1LL
ISBN 0-7137-0942-1

British Library Cataloguing in Publication Data
Viotti, Andrea
  Garibaldi.
  1. Garibaldi, Giuseppe
  2. Revolutionists – Italy – Biography
  945'.08'0924   DG552.8.G2

All rights reserved. No part of this book
may be reproduced or transmitted in any form
or by any means, electronic or mechanical,
including photocopying, recording or any
information storage and retrieval system
without permission from the Publisher.

Printed in Great Britain by
Fletcher & Son Ltd, Norwich
Bound by Richard Clay (The Chaucer Press) Ltd
Bungay, Suffolk

Contents

To Dawne

Acknowledgements

I should like to thank all the people who have helped and advised me during my research and the writing of this book. First and foremost Prof. Alberto Maria Arpino and Miss Stefania Bonnani of the Museo Centrale del Risorgimento in Rome for their constant support. Prof. Lucia Romaniello of the Museo del Risorgimento in Milan. Miss Paola Lombardi for her invaluable assistance with the illustrative research. Prof. John Daley. Her Majesty, Queen Elizabeth II, for kind permission to reproduce part of Queen Victoria's Journal. Prof. Leo Moravito of the Istituto Mazziniano of Genoa. Prof. Bianca Rosa and Prof. Vittorio Parmentola of the Museo del Risorgimento in Turin. Miss Janet Davis of the National Portrait Gallery in London. Mr H. E. Bray of the Photographic Department of the *Illustrated London News*. Mr Gordon Phillips of the *Times* Archives. Mr Krzysztof Barbarski of the Polish Institute in London. The Library staff of the Modern and Contemporary History in Rome.

The extract from Queen Victoria's Diary on page 72, which forms part of the Royal Library at Windsor, is reproduced by Gracious Permission of H.M. The Queen.

The author and publishers wish to acknowledge the following for permission to include the illustrations:

Museo del Risorgimento, Rome
Pages 2–3, 16–17, 18, 19, 22, 24, 46, 51 (above and below), 53, 56, 57, 60–1, 62, 63, 64, 66, 67, 69, 72, 73 (right and left), 75 (left), 84–5, 86, 91, 92, 93 (above and below), 95 (left, centre and right), 97, 100, 102 (above, centre and below), 103, 107 (right), 112 (below), 113 (above and below), 114, 115, 117, 123, 127, 129, 130, 139, 148–9, 150, 157, 163, 166, 168, 169, 178, 179 (above), 187 (above and below), 190–1, 193, 194, 199, 201, 204, 206–7, 210, 212 (below), 213, 214.

Museo del Risorgimento, Milan
Pages 7, 13, 27, 29, 30, 33, 38–9, 43, 49, 50 (below), 55, 70–1, 83, 99, 101, 141, 142, 153 (above), 165, 170–1, 172, 175, 176, 179 (below), 181, 183, 189, 195, 197, 202, 203, 208, 211, 212 (above).

Museo del Risorgimento, Turin
Pages 78–9, 108 (above).

Istituto Mazziniano, Genoa
Pages 75 (right), 89, 107 (left), 110, 167.

Illustrated London News, London
Pages 45, 104, 109, 132–3, 145, 205.

Radio Times – Hulton Picture Library, London
Pages 137, 146.

Victoria and Albert Museum, London
Page 140.

Storia Illustrata (*Archivio Mondadori*) Mondadoripress, Milan
Page 35.

National Portrait Gallery, London
Page 108 (below).

To all the above I renew my thanks and apologize if I have neglected to include any names.

Andrea Viotti

Introduction

This is a book about men who, over an eighty-year period of history and throughout half the world, were the protagonists of revolutions, wars of liberation, and other political and social movements. To write of them without attempting a detailed analysis of their political evolution – or, some might say, involution – may seem superficial. But I find them interesting precisely because they often had no real idea of what they were about: they took up arms against mighty regimes spurred on only by the instinctive knowledge that they were contributing to the struggle for freedom. I have therefore accounted only briefly for the development of their political ideas; I have stressed the actions in which they participated and the effects of these actions in the chancelleries of the European states.

I have not encumbered my narrative with footnotes, but the reader who wishes to know more about the *Garibaldini* will find all the sources from which I have quoted listed in the Bibliography.

Some historians see a continuation of the Garibaldian movement in the Resistance which arose during World War II, and particularly in the Italian partisan groups which took the name of the Hero of Two Worlds. In my view, however, these groups – and others that fought in the Spanish Civil War – have nothing to do with the essential Garibaldian idea, that is, with the struggle for independence or for social liberty. Admirable though their ideals may have been, their use of Garibaldi's name was mere 'public relations'. I have therefore thought best to conclude the story of the *Garibaldini* with World War I when for the last time, in my opinion, they went into battle for libertarian motives but without taking a precise 'political' stand.

WHO THEY WERE

Odd as it may seem, the *Garibaldini* were never called by this name officially. At various times they were designated as the Italian Legion, the *Cacciatori delle Alpi*, the Southern Army, the Italian Volunteer Corps, the Army of the Vosges, and so on. Nor did they always wear the famous Red Shirt: at times they wore white uniforms, blue tunics, grey greatcoats, and even the uniform of the Foreign Legion. And yet it was with the generic name of *Garibaldini* and with the Red Shirt that they came to symbolize men's aspiration to liberty.

They were never an 'army' in the true sense of the word; they may be defined more properly as a political movement which used military means to promote the self-determination of peoples.

They were active above all in Italy, and they made a fundamental contribution to the independence of that country. Their story is inseparable from that of the Italian *Risorgimento*, but Italy was not their only field of operation. Nor were they all Italians. Ricciotti Garibaldi, the General's third-born son and the recognized head of the movement after his father's death, wrote, 'The Red Shirt, symbol of liberty and of the people's cause, is the common property of the human race; its tradition is world-wide.' In fact, the story of the *Garibaldini* began humbly enough in South America, along the coasts of Brazil. And it came to an end quite unromantically, eighty years later, during World War I, among the trenches of the Argonne forest. A world completely taken over by the new ideal of 'nationalism' had relegated the *Garibaldini*, ironically enough, to a military corps which was the very embodiment of oppression and colonialism: the Foreign Legion. Outside Italy, the *Garibaldini* were active in France, in Greece, in Poland, in Spain, in South Africa, in the Balkans – wherever, in short, their intervention might foster the acquisition or the defence of liberty.

On account of these interventions, many non-Italians identified with the movement and took part in it actively. Thus, throughout the eighty years of its history, we find Polish, Hungarian, American, English, French, Swiss and German *Garibaldini*.

Their desire to fight for liberty before all else kept them from acquiring a precise identity as a political party. Throughout most of their history they were republicans with tendencies which we today would call socialist, but this did not prevent them from allying themselves with the monarchy when it came to solving once and for all the problem of Italian unification; many monarchists, in fact, joined their ranks. The one constant in their 'politics' was their anti-clericalism – an attitude which pervaded virtually the entire Italian *Risorgimento*. Their anti-clericalism, be it understood, was not irreligion. It was prompted by the fact that the Church possessed vast territories in central Italy, and maintained them in total backwardness and ignorance. In alliance with the ruling classes in the various other states of the Italian peninsula, the Church did everything in her power to block the process of unification, and elsewhere in Europe she manipulated policy to oppose the Italian cause.

But who were these men whose political credo, in the long run, amounted simply to a dedication to freedom, even when this ideal was expressed in a confused and contradictory manner?

Ordinary men, common citizens. Garibaldi, their charismatic leader, was, for example, a captain in the Merchant Navy; later he became a farmer. Bixio, his right-hand man, was also a sailor. Türr, the organizational brains of the expedition of the Thousand, was a civil engineer. Nullo was an industrialist in the textile trade; Bertani was a surgeon. And in the ranks we find labourers, students, painters, carpenters, lawyers, stock-brokers, deputies and clerks. All the classes possible or imaginable, in short, for whom a 'shirt' symbolized a common ideal.

They were not military men: once a given task was accomplished they returned to their homes and to their old occupations, where they then ran the risk of being kept under surveillance as 'agitators' by the various bourgeois police forces. Strange as it may seem, throughout their history the *Garibaldini*, though they were on the side of freedom (or perhaps for this very reason), were constantly used as support for the regular armies when they were not sent to die at the front lines; in times of peace, however, they were feared and watched closely by the ruling class.

The undisputed leader of these men was Giuseppe Garibaldi: he was invincible on the battlefield, more because of natural instinct than because of his early experiences in South America.

As for his strategy, a curious note which a correspondent – perhaps Ferdinand Eber himself – sent to *The Times* during the expedition of the Thousand sheds much light on it: 'Knowing how impossible it is, with the force he commands, to observe that secrecy which is recommended as the most essential condition of success in military matters, he has adopted the opposite course of doing everything in broad daylight, of announcing his plans long beforehand, thus tiring out all imaginations, and at last doing the very thing he announced, but at the moment when it is least expected. This boldness and scorning of all secrecy have more than once confused his enemies.' But perhaps his ability to win depended principally on his profound understanding of psychology – not only that of his adversary, but also of his own men, from whom he could ask – and obtain – everything. He had the knack, furthermore, of being always present at the key spot on any battlefield, often at great personal risk, so as to spur his men on at the critical moment.

Handling volunteers was not easy – they were men who had gone to war of their own choice. They might take fright at nothing at all during ordinary sentry duty; on the other hand, they could be brave to the point of folly while charging the enemy. Ricciotti defined them to perfection: 'The volunteer is, by nature, extremely intelligent and restless: he wants to know everything, to argue about everything. . . . He will march incredible distances, but beware of making him take the same road twice.'

And yet these were no problems for the General: his men's regard for him always verged on idolatry. At one point a good-naturedly satirical print circulated among the *Garibaldini*, in which Garibaldi was shown standing on an altar amid rifles and cannons, with the inscription: 'Sons of Italy, if you would dry the age-long tears of Rome and Venice, no matter that the priest will not say Mass: these are the candles and this is the Saint.' A version of the Lord's Prayer went, '. . . thy will be done, in the barracks and on the battlefield. Give us this day our daily ammunition ... And lead us not into the temptation of counting our enemy's number, but deliver us from the Austrians and the clergy.' And an unknown *Garibaldino* wrote, in a sort of *Soldiers' Catechism*, 'What does one gain from victory? The sight of Garibaldi in person and all manner of pleasure without pain. Which are the three distinct Persons in Garibaldi? Father of the Nation, Son of the people, and Spirit of Liberty.'

But aside from these rather tasteless examples of the fervour of youthful *Garibaldini*, the General was also a great favourite with the common people, who were attracted by his simple ways. Though he was proud of his own humble origins, he tended to recoil from demonstrations of popular enthusiasm. But in every part of the world he was looked to as a Messiah who would bring freedom. Bakunín wrote, 'Not a few peasants of Great and Little Russia awaited Garibaldi's coming.'

Depicted in a thousand ways – often as Christ – Garibaldi's image occupied the place of honour between the Madonna and the local patron saint. The composers of popular ballads often made extravagant claims – such as, for example, that Saint Rosalia had sent the General a talisman which she had woven in Heaven with her own hands. Garibaldi's alleged semi-divinity also made a vivid impression on his enemies. A Neapolitan soldier expressed himself thus: 'That one is no man. One day the Devil fell in love with a saint. After nine months Garibaldi was born. When he's fighting he takes after his father, but when the battle's over he's like his mother.' Garibaldi was, in fact, quite ruthless in combat: one day he said to the young and inexperienced Ricciotti, 'Don't worry about it if the enemy is weaker than you are.' Away from the battlefield, however, his humanity was unequalled.

When Garibaldi set out on his extraordinary adventure, he certainly had no way of knowing that the handful of men who were with him would one day grow into an army so strong and so numerous that it would not only conquer a kingdom but would overturn the political order of entire nations.

The amazing victories of the *Garibaldini* were not only the work of the General (as he was ordinarily called) but also of the men who assisted him and who organized his volunteers – Anzani, Türr, Cosenz, Bixio, Sirtori, etc. With many of them he came to loggerheads or even, as with Eberhardt, found himself on the opposite side in battle. Others enticed him into sectarian political struggles or involved him in undertakings which failed to produce the desired results.

But Garibaldi remained the unchallenged leader of these men, the catalyst of their ideal. And if many of their political or military decisions did not originate with him, his was the ability, indispensable in a leader, to choose the best of the advice offered.

HOW THEY FOUGHT

Aside from the personal abilities of the General and his highly talented staff, the *Garibaldini* owed their extraordinary victories to various other factors, such as their extremely practical approach to dress and armament, their organization, and their method of fighting.

In a period when most soldiers were weighed down by their equipment, the *Garibaldini* kept their gear to the essential minimum. Their uniform consisted of a rather large and comfortable blouse, which usually had two broad breast-pockets; a short cape (they were issued greatcoats during the Second War of Independence, but on account of the season these were hardly ever used) which they carried rolled up across their chest when they were not wearing it; loose trousers, which were either inserted into coarse canvas gaiters or rolled up at the bottom; a soft hat with a large rectangular visor or, preferably, a broad-brimmed hat. Officers dressed like the troops, except for narrow insignia of rank in gold or silver worn on their caps and sometimes on their sleeves, and for their swords, which were usually their personal property.

Their kit was also practical and light. It consisted of a pouch attached to their belts, containing thirty cartridges (for battles a supplementary thirty were distributed and carried in the haversack), and a haversack which held two shirts and a pair of socks, a tin bowl and a wooden keg containing water, usually mixed with wine or vinegar. The knapsack was completely unknown. Even the officers were required to travel light; they were allowed only a single bag.

The lightness of their equipment enhanced their mobility, and it had a positive effect on their morale. It was perfectly suited to Garibaldi's strategy, which often entailed continued, incessant marches backwards and forwards to confuse the enemy.

Their firearms were of the most disparate sorts, and finding the right sort of ammunition was often a problem. But this never dismayed the *Garibaldini*, whose favourite weapon was and remained the bayonet. Their victories were often the result of its terrifying effect on the enemy. Carlo Romang, a Swiss officer who served with Garibaldi during the expedition of the Thousand, wrote that a bayonet attack was more decisive 'than the four or five hours of gunfire which preceded it'.

The *Garibaldini* organized themselves, for the most part, in battalions of six companies (except during the Second War of Independence, when they adopted the system of regiments comprising two battalions of four companies each). Two or three battalions joined together formed a brigade, and two or three brigades formed a division. But it was only during the expedition of the Thousand that they adopted the idea of brigades. In terms of organization and equipment, therefore, they were to be considered light infantry. This was especially obvious during the expedition of the Thousand, since even when their ranks swelled to 26,000 or more, the artillery and the cavalry remained small units. The cavalry was chiefly assigned scouting duty, although it also took part in furious charges which, if they were relatively ineffectual were so on account of the small number of horses involved.

As light infantry they made use above all of what Romang calls the 'thick chain of carabineers'. He describes it as follows:

'While on the assault, our corps always moved in double rings, holding a formation of four men deployed in a chain. As we advanced each group of four was followed by another group of four at a distance of ten paces. The most intelligent of each group was appointed its leader: he gave orders to his three comrades, showing them where to take cover or grouping them around himself, initiating offensives or resisting cavalry attacks [which were the terror of the *Garibaldini*]. When no cover was available, the last three men always placed themselves behind the first. Thus we could advance to within fifty paces of the enemy, quickly, and virtually unobserved.

'The first advantage of the chain of carabineers lay in its ability to advance under cover, in good order, and rapidly, to a point from which the first round could be fired successfully, thus imposing a sufficiently strong front upon the enemy without exposing itself excessively to their fire. Our attacks rarely failed to produce the desired effect.

'On open battlefields we advanced running until we reached a distance of thirty to a hundred paces from the enemy. ... We never fired from a lesser distance, and when we took the enemy by surprise with dense fire from close range, the effect of this first attack was often such as to decide the entire battle in our favour.

'When we advanced in this manner, that is in groups of four men with a distance of ten paces between each group, a company so deployed could often face fire from an entire battalion without suffering greater damage than the enemy. The chain afforded the enemy much less of a target than an entire column. Furthermore, the fire-power of our hand-weapons was far more effective than that of the enemy's mounted cannon. And our soldiers were already used to manoeuvring in chains, since this was almost the only manoeuvre they had been taught. The rapidity with which we could get close to the enemy was the principal reason for this manoeuvre and the surest means of avoiding casualties. A corps that conducts itself in this manner takes a far lesser risk than another which fires from a distance of 300 or 400 paces and then remains virtually immobile and inactive in this position, within the enemy's range. It often happened that a stray bullet passed over the heads of the men in the forefront and killed or wounded someone who was tarrying in the rear-guard or running about aimlessly behind the lines.'

It is clear that this open order (as we would

Garibaldi at the battle of the Volturno by G. Induno.

call it today) gave the troops great mobility and prevented them from being encircled, or very rarely. In fact, as Romang insists, 'Even when we have been partially defeated, it is not difficult to attack the enemy on one flank or the other. Such a defeat, in fact, is only momentary and certainly does not amount to a retreat. On the contrary, a skilful officer advancing rapidly will soon find a weak point in the enemy front, and will attack repeatedly.'

The skill of the officers was certainly a major factor in the *Garibaldini* victories. They were all experienced men who had earned their stripes on the revolutionary battlefields of Europe: natural selection had had its effect.

In comparison to their colleagues in the regular armies of the time, Garibaldi's officers were allowed great freedom of action on the battlefield. Romang writes,

'Here I must mention a system which Garibaldi used in battle and which is too important and too interesting to be omitted. Many people believe that during a battle the manoeuvres of nearly all the carabineer companies are supervised and directed by the general or by the divisional commander, by means of orders carried by adjutants who run incessantly back and forth. One often reads in reports that a battle ended badly because an adjutant was killed before he could relay an order. This is misleading; a lack of information, or an order gone astray, can cause serious disadvantages, but this was not true in Garibaldi's case. First, he would place himself at the head of a corps of two or three thousand men so as to lead them into battle himself when the right moment should come; and he left the other corps free to execute the duties assigned to them as they chose. [This experiment had already been tried, successfully, during the defence of the Roman Republic.] Each company commander was responsible for the manoeuvres of his own troops, and once the battle had begun he rarely received fresh orders. Even platoon leaders organized and executed their assigned tasks on their own. Free to act according to his judgment, each officer could alter his tactics if circumstances warranted it; the only restriction was that he must never lose sight of his principal objective.'

The relationship between officers and troops among the *Garibaldini* was democratic to the highest degree. Often the officer slept on straw alongside his men, and there was no trace of the formal discipline typical of other armies. Jan Philip Koelman, in his *Roman Memoirs*, recounts Garibaldi's arrival at the convent of San Silvestro in Rome, which the *Garibaldini* had just occupied. His entry into the courtyard produced no effect on the men encamped there: 'Even the sentry stayed where he was, lounging on a bench, and not a single *Garibaldino* budged.' Surprised at this, Koelman asked the officer with whom he was conversing, 'Is it habitual with the *Garibaldini* to show so little respect for their commander?' And in the officer's reply lies the entire explanation of the Garibaldian approach to military life: 'My dear Sir, the General demands discipline on the battlefield, not in the barracks. . . .'

If formal discipline was not imposed on the troops, strictly honest behaviour was required of them. Romang recounts an episode which is confirmed by other witnesses: 'One day Bixio saw two soldiers coming out of a vineyard with their handkerchiefs full of grapes. Without even interrogating them, the General drew his revolver and, with the words 'You are not worthy to serve in Garibaldi's army!' he shot them dead before the eyes of their column.' This was certainly an excessive gesture (and one in keeping with the character of the man who performed it), but there were two important reasons for it. First of all, for the *Garibaldini* even the slightest transgression with respect to the private property of others was absolutely forbidden. And, secondly, because of the ever-present danger that common criminals might be hiding out with the volunteers, the need for 'essential' (as opposed to formal) discipline was even more paramount than in the regular armies. The *Garibaldini* had neither jails nor military police nor the time for this type of organization. Furthermore, in the case of the expedition of the Thousand, the advent of the *Garibaldini* had created a power vacuum in the conquered territories which bandits and other criminals were all too ready to take advantage of: if they were allowed to get the upper hand, the masses would lose faith in the Red-shirts and repent of having supported them.

On the whole, though, there were very few cases of theft. The *Garibaldini*, to be sure, were no plaster saints, but they were fanatical about the ideal for which they were fighting – unlike the regular soldiers, who went to war through no choice of their own. At times their fanaticism drove them to excess: it was not unusual for officers to have to intervene, in the heat of the battle, to save enemy prisoners from their fury.

In my opinion, however, the determining factor behind the victories was the incredible enthusiasm of these men. It was not rare 'for the banker's son to provide the pay for his entire company out of his own pocket for one or two weeks'. And I should like to conclude this note as Romang concludes his:

'The moment they received the order to advance, they thrust themselves forward without the least consideration for their own safety. Indeed, if one had advised them to be cautious, one would certainly have received an indignant reply. Beyond any doubt, the majority of the *Garibaldini* were men who fought for their own convictions.'

The Battle of San Antonio del Salto. In white, Garibaldi is recognizable at the centre, surrounded by his men, curiously dressed in pale blue.

From Pirates to Soldiers

At dawn on 7 May 1837, a *garopera* – a type of South American fishing boat weighing some twenty tons – slipped out of the port of Rio de Janeiro.

She was called the *Mazzini*, and she carried a crew of thirteen. The seamen were Antonio Illama and Giovanni Fiorentino of Capraia, Giovanbattista Caruana of Malta, Maurizio Garibaldi of Genoa, and Giovanni Lamberti of Venice. João Baptista, a Brazilian, was the Master at Arms, and the pilot was a Genoese called Lodola. Luigi Carniglia, from Deiva in Liguria, and Luigi Calia of Malta were the boatswains; the Second Lieutenant was Luigi Rossetti. And the Captain was Giuseppe Garibaldi.

In the hold were fish, smoked meat and flour, and – hidden beneath these provisions – guns. The boat sailed past Sugar Loaf Mountain, then past the fort which dominated the harbour. At the custom house the officials motioned her on. When she had left Guanabara Bay a flag was hoisted to the yard: it had yellow, green and red diagonal stripes. At this moment in Brazilian history it was the symbol of revolution, for it was the ensign of the rebel republic of Rio Grande do Sul.

'Corsairs! Thirteen comrades, sailing the ocean in a *garopera*, we were challenging an empire. We were the first, on those southern shores, to flourish a banner of emancipation! The republican banner of Rio Grande!'

As Garibaldi raised that flag he can hardly have realized that this was the beginning of an adventure which, in only a few years' time, would make his name a synonym for Liberty and a watchword for oppressed peoples everywhere; nor that this motley rabble of a crew (whose physical aspect, he was later to confess, he judged 'none too auspicious') could be the embryo of victorious armies of a military, social and political movement which would bear his name.

Garibaldi was born at Nice on 4 July 1807. His father, who owned a few boats and was a captain in the Sardinian merchant marine, wanted him to be a priest, but his son was not attracted to the contemplative life, preferring the hubbub and bustle of the port. At school he refused to study unless the subject happened to interest him, such topics including Roman history, chivalric poems, and the verse of Ugo Foscolo – an Italian poet who, inflamed by the ideas of the French Revolution, had served in Napoleon's army.

He always loved the sea. When he was twelve he ventured upon the Mediterranean with three companions in a small boat, creating a stir in the port and driving 'Mamma Rosa', his mother, nearly to distraction. In the end his father gave in, and the son on whom the family had pinned its religious hopes was allowed to go to sea as a cabin-boy on a ship bound for the Orient. He rose rapidly in the ranks of the merchant marine, thanks to his innate ability and to the courage which he demonstrated on several occasions when faced with mutiny or pirate attack.

In March 1833 he was serving as second mate on the freighter *Clorinda*, when a group of passengers came aboard at Marseilles. Their leader was an intellectual called Emile Barrault, who had enjoyed some success as a

Giuseppe Mazzini, the great Italian patriot who championed the cause of unity and independence. Garibaldi often found himself at odds with him.

playwright. He had recently become a convert to the socialist ideas of Saint-Simon, and he and his friends were voyaging to the Middle East to found a new community based on equality of the sexes and an absolute disregard for material things.

His encounter with Barrault made an enormous impression upon the twenty-five-year-old Garibaldi: for the first time in his life he heard talk of liberty and social justice. Towards the end of the same voyage he also got to know Giovan Battista Cuneo – otherwise known as 'il Credente di Taranrog' – a young liberal from Liguria who had been driven into exile for his part in a number of conspiracies against Austrian dominion in Italy. In addition to Barrault's social theories Garibaldi now absorbed Cuneo's passionate attachment to the cause of national liberation.

But the decisive meeting – with Giuseppe Mazzini – occurred shortly after Garibaldi's

Giovan Battista Cuneo, the so-called Credente di Taranrog. *After their first encounter in the Black Sea Cuneo collaborated with Garibaldi in South America.*

return to Italy. Mazzini, who was born at Genoa in 1805, was destined to provide moral and psychological inspiration not only for the *Risorgimento* (Italy's 19th-century national revival), but for a number of other European liberal movements as well. Long before the vast majority of his compatriots began to turn their attention to the 'Italian question', Mazzini was a determined and articulate champion of Italian national unity. Garibaldi's acquaintance with Mazzini was not only a determining factor in the evolution of his political ideas; it altered the entire course of his life.

His first step was to join *Giovane Italia* (Young Italy), the secret society which the 'prophet' Mazzini had founded. In 1834 Mazzini attempted to organize an insurrection in Piedmont which would overthrow the Savoy monarchy and establish a republican form of government. A contingent of political exiles was to invade Piedmont while, simultaneously, there was to be a naval mutiny at Genoa. To this purpose Garibaldi had enlisted in the Sardinian Navy the previous December. But he went about recruiting accomplices rather too ingenuously, and the authorities were soon on to the plot. He avoided capture, only to learn from the papers that he had been condemned to death *in absentia*.

Now a political exile himself, Garibaldi went to sea again, under the name of Borel. At first he served in the French merchant marine, and then in the fleet of the Bey of Tunis, who offered to make him its commander. Later, when a cholera epidemic broke out at Marseilles, Garibaldi enrolled in a volunteer nursing corps.

On 16 December 1835, disgusted with a Europe where, it seemed, reactionary regimes were destined to remain in power forever, Garibaldi embarked as second mate on the French brig *Nautonier*, which was bound for South America. He was twenty-eight years old now, shortish but well-built, with blue deep-set eyes and a sober manner of speech. His hair was light and curly, and he had yet to grow a beard. He was disillusioned with politics, and perhaps he regretted the youthful enthusiasm with which he had embraced the liberal cause – on account of which he was now obliged to start life afresh in the New World. He little knew that long years of conflict lay ahead of him, years which would see the maturing of his military genius and the confirmation of his passion for liberty.

He arrived in Rio de Janeiro in January 1836. There he found a thriving community of Italian political exiles, which included Cuneo and Luigi Rossetti, a Genoese revolutionary who had been forced to flee in 1827. Garibaldi, Rossetti, and two other exiles, Giacomo Picasso and Giacomo Griss, bought a *garopera*, christened it the *Mazzini*, and set themselves up in the shipping business. (They never made a success of it; they were too easily swindled by others.)

Garibaldi's natural propensity was for political action, and he was soon led back in this direction by Tito Livio Zambeccari, a Bolognese who had taken part in the abortive Neapolitan revolution of 1821 and had since lived in Spain and in South America. Through Zambeccari Garibaldi came into contact with the revolutionaries of the Brazilian state of Rio Grande do Sul. He soon became their political mentor, and introduced them to the ideas of Mazzini.

Brazil had thrown off Portuguese rule in 1822 and proclaimed itself an empire. But the states which composed it resented the strongly centralized monarchy; most of them would have preferred a federation on the model of the United States. Rio Grande, on the other hand, aspired to complete independence, and its leader was Bento Gonçalves da Silva. Zambeccari was secretary to Gonçalves.

An insurrection in Porto Alegre, the capital of Rio Grande, had driven out the imperial troops in September 1834; war ensued. At first it went well for Rio Grande, but at the battle of the Fanfa (4 October 1836) Gonçalves, his General Staff and Zambeccari were taken prisoner. The rebels, however, would not admit defeat; on 6 November they proclaimed a Republic and elected Gonçalves himself as its president.

Garibaldi and Rossetti visited Zambeccari in prison on several occasions. And during one of these visits the prisoner proposed that they use their boat in the war effort. 'I am weary, God knows, of this utterly useless life as a merchant seaman', wrote Garibaldi to

Cuneo, who had gone to live at Montevideo. The present opportunity seemed too good to miss, and he and Rossetti went to work at once transforming the *Mazzini* into a warship, lightly risking the gallows – their fate if they should fail. 'The hippogriff has taken wing', Garibaldi wrote to Giuseppe Mazzini, by way of announcing his new life as a corsair.

Their first act of piracy was romantic enough, but not very profitable. They seized the cutter *Maribondo*, and the loot amounted to four casks of wine and a silver watch. Garibaldi kept the watch for himself and years later it was to finance his wedding. (Compensation to the crew was paid in the form of dried meat!) Quite aside from the meagre material results of the operation, however, these dilettante pirates did something that day which, in its own way, symbolizes the entire Garibaldian movement as it was to unfold over the decades. Aboard the *Maribondo* was a slave called Antonio, who had been taken captive in his native Africa. For Garibaldi and Rossetti liberty had neither colour or tongues, so they declared Antonio a free man and brought him along aboard the *Mazzini*. Thus as a pirate on the high seas Garibaldi was first to put into practice his ideals of human equality and the emancipation of oppressed peoples.

Business improved as they approached the island of Maricá: they captured the schooner *Luisa* with its cargo of coffee. Since she was a better ship than their *garopera*, Garibaldi and his men sank the *Mazzini* and took the *Luisa* for themselves. They gave her a new name, the *Farroupilha*, derived from *farrapos* – 'ragpickers' – which is what the government forces scornfully called the rebels of Rio Grande. They also liberated four black slaves between the ages of 18 and 30: Luiz, Pedro, Bentura and Manuel, who then joined Garibaldi's crew.

Then they headed south. The crew of the ex-*Luisa* was released on the coast, and João Baptista chose to leave with them: this was the first of four desertions which Garibaldi would have to reckon with during the course of his first South American adventure. On 28 May they arrived at Maldonato (today called Punta del Este) in Uruguay, a country on

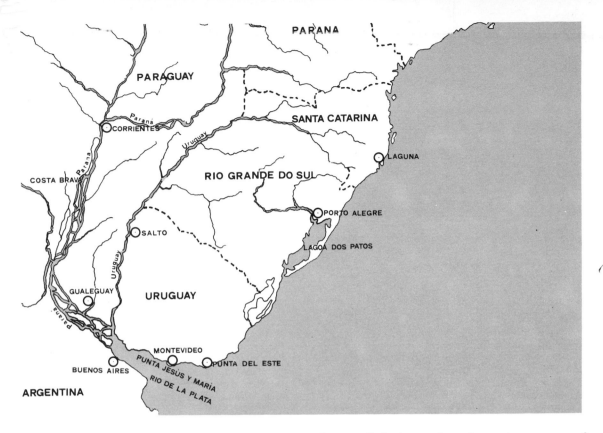

The area of operations of the Garibaldini in South America.

friendly terms with Rio Grande. Rossetti set off for the capital, Montevideo, to recruit more volunteers and to sell the coffee captured with the *Luisa*. But Uruguay suddenly reversed its policy towards Rio Grande, and Garibaldi quickly set sail for Punta Jesús y María, where he had arranged to meet Rossetti. The Uruguayans sent the cutter *Maria* and the schooner *Leba* in pursuit.

At 8 a.m. on 15 June the Uruguayans spotted the pirate ship at Punta Jesús y María. They opened fire, and in the first volley Giovanni Fiorentino was shot in the face – the first of many to die in Garibaldi's service. Garibaldi rushed to take over the helm, but was himself struck down by a second volley, a bullet lodged below his ear. Carniglia took command of the ship, fought back a Uruguayan attempt to board her, and got her to safety.

With Garibaldi on the brink of death, panic seized the crew: three more of them deserted, unhindered by the others. The remainder decided to give themselves up. On 25 June they sailed into the Argentine port of Gualeguay, where they surrendered to the authorities.

The Argentines, who had so far remained neutral in the conflict between Brazil and Rio Grande, found themselves in an embarrassing position: what should they do with these prisoners who, in the course of interrogation, 'never stopped boasting of their extreme democratic principles'. After six months it was decided to transfer Garibaldi to Paraná. Garibaldi heard about this plan and tried to escape, but he was betrayed by his guide, captured, and brought back to Gualeguay, where the military commander Leonard Millán subjected him to gruelling tortures in an attempt to find out his accomplices. Garibaldi gave away nothing, and was transferred to Bajada, the capital of the province, on the intervention of the governor, Don Pascual Echagüe, who was an admirer of his. Here he was given medical treatment, and was released after two months, early in March 1838.

Garibaldi joined Rossetti and Carniglia, and the three went to Piratinim, the seat of the Rio Grande government since Brazilian forces had occupied Porto Alegre. Here they met with Gonçalves, who had escaped from his Brazilian captivity and was in the process of reorganizing the army. Gonçalves appointed Garibaldi commander of the Rio Grande navy and charged him with putting a fleet together (shipbuilding was already underway in a lagoon called the Lagoa dos Patos). Here they encountered John Grigg, an American of good family who was passing his time fighting for Rio Grande while waiting to come into his fortune. (He did not live to see his inheritance.)

Meanwhile the Garibaldian ranks were swelling with volunteers of various nationalities – a large proportion of them North Americans. We cannot be sure to what extent these men were motivated by the pure love of liberty and democracy; Garibaldi himself referred to them as *Frères de la Côte*, an expression which, in America, was a euphemism for pirates. In any event, quite a few of them were to give their lives heroically for the Republic of Rio Grande.

After being tortured, Garibaldi is brought before the Governor of Gualeguay, Millán. It seems that years later, when Millán was taken prisoner by the Garibaldini, *Garibaldi refused to see him. He was afraid that, now their positions were reversed, he might lose his self-control and take his revenge.*

Four cutters were built in a relatively short time, the *Farroupilha II*, the *Republicano*, the *Seival* and the *Rio Pardo*. As soon as they were armed, Garibaldi, Rossetti, Grigg and Carniglia plunged into a running war, while the Brazilian fleet made vain attempts to capture them.

Garibaldi's name soon became associated with these rather disreputable acts of piracy; to capture him, for a Brazilian officer, would mean certain promotion. A Colonel Moringue almost succeeded, but Garibaldi was saved by one of his seamen, a black man called Procopio who wounded Moringue so badly in the arm that it had to be amputated.

In July 1839 Gonçalves ordered Garibaldi to take part, with his fleet, in the invasion of Santa Catarina, the state neighbouring Rio Grande to the north. But his ships were at their base in the Lagoa dos Patos, and the inlet which led from the lagoon to the Atlantic was now commanded by Brazilian cannon. To attempt to sail through it would be to court massacre. So Garibaldi and Grigg mounted the *Rio Pardo* and the *Republicano* on a pair of enormous wagons, each drawn by a hundred oxen, and hauled them fifty-four miles to the sea. Off the coast of Santa Catarina, however, they ran into a violent storm. Grigg's ship

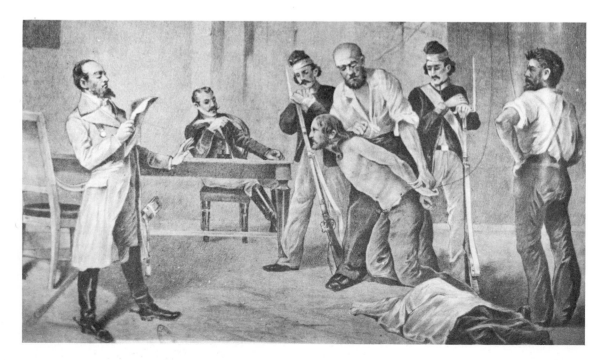

escaped, but Garibaldi's *Rio Pardo* sank. Only fourteen of the thirty men aboard were saved; Carniglia was among those drowned. The survivors joined up with the Rio Grande army and took part in the attack on Laguna, the capital of Santa Catarina, which fell on 23 July. ✓

And it was at Laguna, while Rossetti was lecturing on the principles of democracy, that Garibaldi met the woman who was to remain at his side for the rest of her life and through all manner of peril: the woman he was to call 'the mother of my children'. He was then thirty-two. One morning in October 1839 he was on the quarter-deck of the *Itaparica* (one of the ships captured at Laguna), brooding over the loss of his companions, when through his field-glasses, he saw Anita on the quay.

Anna María de Jesús da Silva, known as Anita, was 'a beauty with large and stupendous eyes, black hair, an oval, slightly freckled face and a proud and haughty manner'. She was about nineteen years old. The information which has come down to us about this woman – dead now for a hundred and thirty years – is incomplete and equivocal. Brazilian historians later recorded the recollections of the fishermen of Laguna, but these do not amount to much. We have her portrait, painted in 1845 in Montevideo. And the size of the dress which she was given by the women of San Marino in 1849 shows that she was tiny in stature. The details of her meeting with Garibaldi are swathed in mystery. He himself is surprisingly reticent on the subject in his memoirs, no doubt because of his sense of having 'wronged an innocent party'. Anita, in fact, was already the wife of a fisherman (or, according to some, a shoemaker) called Emanuel Duarte. They had been married on 30 August 1835, and according to local legend an unlucky omen had occurred on the wedding day. As she entered the church Anita stumbled and lost a satin slipper; this was taken as a sign that she was destined to abandon her husband.

Anita, contrary to what we are told by Garibaldi himself and by many of his biographers, was not in the least interested in the 'sacrosanct cause of Nations', nor had she a taste for war. Her personal courage – which often verged on recklessness – was not ideological in nature. She was motivated only by her immense love for 'José', wanting to be with him wherever he went. She could be insanely jealous – on more than one occasion she came to Garibaldi with two pistols: one, she told him, was meant for him and the other for her suspected rival. Another time she made him cut off his shoulder-length hair: it made him, as she explained, too desirable in the eyes of other women. This little woman was the first of a long list of women who were to don the red shirt, whether in the name of liberty, for the unspoken love of the Hero, or for the love of some other man.

At the end of 1839 the Brazilians again attacked the rebel forces *en masse*. The rebels had not used the two months' respite to make good their positions, and they were forced to retreat. Garibaldi, bottled up in Laguna, was under fire from the enemy fleet. For the Brazilians, it amounted to a simple game of target practice; John Grigg went down with his ship. Seeing that resistance was useless, Garibaldi had no choice but to burn his ships and retreat with the army. Anita went with him, her reputation for valour by now well established.

The next year-and-a-half were spent fighting with the Rio Grande army. The struggle was bloody, and life was grim. It was brightened, however, by the birth of Garibaldi's first son, Menotti, on 16 September 1840. (Menotti was later to become his father's right-hand man.) Menotti was born with a scar on his head caused by his mother's fall from a horse during the battle of Coritibani. At that time Anita was several months pregnant, but still she was unwilling to remain a spectator. So she dedicated herself to overseeing the Rio Grande army's ammunition supply. One day, as she was leading a munitions train from behind the lines to the front, she was surrounded by enemy cavalry. She exhorted the soldiers who were with her to put up a fight although the Brazilians requested her surrender. In reply to their request she jumped on a horse and, riding through the Brazilian troops, fled. But her horse was shot from under her, and she was taken prisoner. She later managed to escape her captors, crossed a no-man's land full of

Garibaldi's first meeting with Anita, in a drawing by Matania. In his memoirs Garibaldi reports his first words to her as 'You must be mine'.

natural perils and man-made snares and, eight days later, rejoined her beloved José.

But not even motherhood brought peace for Anita. Twelve days after Menotti's birth the farm near Saint-Simon where she and Garibaldi were residing was surrounded by Colonel Moringue's troops. (Garibaldi was off on a mission.) Half naked, Anita snatched up her baby, jumped on a horse and fled into the forest, where she remained until Garibaldi went to fetch her.

Towards the end of 1840 the tide of the war had definitely turned against Rio Grande. The rebel forces were retreating everywhere with the Brazilians in hot pursuit. Garibaldi was with a column led by General Canavarro which was retreating through the mountain passes of the Mattos Portugués.

Moringue, relentlessly on the heels of the Republicans, caught up with a rear-guard commanded by Rossetti. Rossetti was un-horsed and wounded but, rather than give up,

he went on fighting until, finally, the Brazilians cut him down. His death was a serious loss, not only to the *Garibaldini* but to the entire international Republican movement, for he was one of its most politically competent supporters.

The retreat through the mountains was rife with horrors. Food was scarce, and many died of malnutrition. Soldiers in South American armies habitually brought their families along with them, and this not only slowed down their movements; it frequently had tragic consequences. Many women and children died of hunger and fatigue; some were actually murdered by their husbands or fathers, who preferred to see them dead rather than prisoners of the Brazilians. Garibaldi and Anita were terrified at the thought of what might become of little Menotti if one of them were to die. It was very cold in the mountains: Garibaldi carried the baby slung around his neck hoping to keep him warm with his own breath and body heat, but this was insufficient. At one point, when Menotti seemed about to succumb from frostbite, the *Garibaldini* had to give up the last of their woollen underclothes. Eventually the survivors of the Rio Grande army came down from the mountains into the plains.

Six years had passed since Garibaldi had taken up arms for Rio Grande. He was weary of war, and the fact that he now had a family brought new problems. He needed a rest, obtained leave of absence from Gonçalves, and set out for Montevideo. As compensation for his years of service he was given a herd of nine hundred oxen. This capital was for the journey and to help him get established in his new place of residence. But Garibaldi was no gaucho, and the *vaqueros* who went with him were no saints. When he arrived at Montevideo only three hundred of the oxen were left, and they were in such a sorry condition that they had to be sold off for a nominal price.

The family arrived at Montevideo in the spring of 1841 and set up housekeeping in two rooms and a kitchen at 14 Calle del Portón. Garibaldi found a job as a salesman, and he also taught mathematics in a school founded by a Corsican priest called Semidei. With his mathematics book under his arm, he would often stroll on the nearby customs quay, dressed in a heavy dark blue coat, and a broad-brimmed hat, beneath which his long blond hair was visible. He would stare at the sea for hours on end. His father had died recently, and his nostalgia for Italy was made the more poignant by the presence in Montevideo of a large colony of Italian political exiles.

He preferred not to be reminded of Rio Grande, partly because the war was now going through a stagnant phase which did not appeal to him as a man of action, but more especially because an episode in which he had been involved was weighing on his conscience. When the Rio Grande forces had invaded the state of Santa Caterina, the population had welcomed them at first. But the excesses of the rebels caused most of them to change sides. General Canavarro, the Rio Grande commander, ordered Garibaldi to recapture the city of Imaruhy, which had rebelled against them and now represented a threat to Canavarro's rear-guard. Garibaldi occupied it with ease, but he was unable or insufficiently willing to prevent his troops from plundering the city 'and worse'. In his memoirs he recalls the scenes of savagery he witnessed there. One vignette will render the general idea: a group of soldiers are described gambling their shares of booty by the light of a candle stuck into the belly of a corpse. Imaruhy was certainly a blot on Garibaldi's name; never again, however, would men

Anita in a miniature by Gallino, made in Montevideo in 1845 and authenticated by Ricciotti Garibaldi.

under his command be permitted to loot a conquered city.

But if Garibaldi had no wish to return to the military life, events in Uruguay were to force his hand. The wars for the independence of the 'East Bank of the River Plate' (the territory more or less coinciding with present-day Uruguay) began on 28 February 1811 with the so-called *Grito de Asencio* and went on until the end of 1830. During this period Uruguay fought Spain, Portugal, and later Brazil, which was seeking to expand at the expense of the other young nations of South America. Besides the leader and national hero José Artigas, two outstanding figures in these wars were Manuel Oribe and Fructuoso Rivera, men who, as fate would have it, held diametrically opposed political philosophies. Throughout newly independent South America there were two rival schools of thought: the 'Unitarians' favoured strong central governments; the 'Federalists' believed in relatively loose associations of autonomous provinces. The conflict between the two parties frequently degenerated into bloodthirsty feuds. In 1830 Rivera, head of the Unitarian faction, was elected president of Uruguay; at the end of his five-year term his rival the Federalist Oribe was elected to succeed him. Directly upon taking office Oribe levelled false charges of corruption at the previous administration. By way of response Rivera's men took up arms against Oribe. The Federalist forces were victorious at the battle of Carpinteria (19 September 1836), and Rivera fled to Brazil. But two years later he re-entered Uruguay at the head of an army. He defeated Oribe at Palmar on 15 June 1838, and Oribe then took refuge in Argentina as a protégé of the Argentine dictator Rosas. Rosas, who had designs of his own upon Uruguay, provided Oribe with an army. This was the beginning of the so-called Great War, which was to last from 1839 to 1851.

At first the war went well for the Unitarians. They managed to foment local revolts within Argentina, and the French navy supported them by blocking the Argentine fleet in the port of Buenos Aires. But the Argentines came to terms with the French diplomatically, and they proceeded to reorganize their own navy under the leadership of British admiral William Brown, who had been a pupil of Nelson. They took possession of the mouth of the River Plate (which separates Argentina from Uruguay) and blockaded Montevideo. In so doing, they cut off their own rebel state of Corrientes, which had opted for union with Uruguay; Uruguay then decided to organize a naval expedition to bring relief to Corrientes.

This expedition can only be described as suicidal. The Uruguayan force was to sail upstream for some four hundred miles through enemy territory, at a time of year when the rivers were low, with no friendly bases along the way. The motive was more propangandist than strategic; other nations – especially Britain and France, whose support was crucial – might be persuaded that Rosas' armies were less than invincible.

Leadership of the operation was entrusted to the only man suitable for the task: a seasoned veteran of guerrilla campaigns who, at this point in his life, could perhaps be better described as a poet of warfare than as a strategist – Giuseppe Garibaldi.

The flotilla for the expedition consisted of two brigs, the *Constitucíon*, and the *Pereyra*, and the schooner *Prócida*. The crews included many veterans of the Rio Grande campaign: Manuel Rodríguez, a Catalan who had saved Garibaldi's life at Laguna, Gaetano Casella, Luigi De Agostini, the Greek Jorge Cardasi, and others. There were also quite a few common criminals and deserters from various armies, of many nationalities, who were hoping to start a new life.

Garibaldi took command of the *Constitucíon*, and Manuel Arana of the *Pereyra*. The little fleet left Montevideo on 27 June 1842. The first obstacle on its route was the fortress of Martín García, which guarded the entrance to the delta where the Paraná and the Uruguay rivers meet to form the River Plate. Heavy cannon-fire produced a few casualties, but little damage to the ships. Three miles from the fortress, however, when – fortunately – she was already out of range of the cannon, *Constitucíon* ran aground. As the crew tried to refloat her, five Argentine warships appeared, under the command of Admiral Brown. This was indeed a serious

turn of events: the *Garibaldini* were inferior in fire-power as well as in number. In order to lighten her load, the *Constitucíon* had moved her cannon on to the *Prócida*, which in the hurry of the departure had not even mounted her own, so only the *Pereyra* was in a fighting condition. But an incredible stroke of luck saved the day for the *Garibaldini*: the Argentine flagship *Belgrano* ran aground, blocking the mouth of the delta, and making it impossible for her sister ships to manoeuvre. Taking advantage of the situation the *Garibaldini* redoubled their efforts and succeeded in refloating *Constitucíon* (which Garibaldi was reluctant to abandon).

A second stroke of luck increased their advantage: a thick fog came up suddenly over the delta, allowing the Uruguayan flotilla to move away unobserved; by the time Admiral Brown had extricated his own ships from their predicament he had no idea of the exact course which the *Garibaldini* had taken. To reach Corrientes one could sail up either the Paraná or the Uruguay rivers. The former flowed entirely through Argentine territory, while the latter formed the boundary between Argentina and Uruguay. According to the most elementary rules of military logic Garibaldi should obviously have chosen the Uruguay river, the left bank of which could at least have provided him with provisions and, if necessary, an escape route. What Brown didn't know was that Garibaldi, characteristically, paid no heed to military logic. He had, in fact, sailed up the Paraná. When at last Brown found this out, he exclaimed, 'Only Garibaldi could be capable of such lunacy!' As the Argentine ships retraced their course they ran aground several times on the shoals of the Uruguay; not until 13 July could they resume their pursuit up the Paraná.

Though they had escaped from Brown, the *Garibaldini* soon found themselves in what might be an even more serious difficulty: there were no guides aboard their ships who knew the Paraná river. The government at Montevideo, in fact, in an attempt to keep the mission secret and to throw spies off the track, had conspicuously hired guides to the Uruguay! And without guides it was virtually impossible to navigate upon this tortuous waterway with its ubiquitous shallows. Then

Battle of Laguna. Realizing that resistance was impossible, Garibaldi ordered the burning of the ships and retreated inland. Anita can be seen at his side with a rifle in her hand.

Garibaldi learned that one of his seamen was in fact reasonably familiar with the Paraná; he had been keeping quiet in the hope that the whole mission would be called off. It took a bit of persuasion – a sabre at his throat – to get him to change his mind. After that the expedition could again proceed.

The first engagement took place near San Nicolas on the right bank of the river, where the *Garibaldini* seized a few Argentine transport-ships and also captured some sailors who knew the Paraná river well. The next obstacle was a well munitioned fort called Bajada del Paraná. To get past it they had to withstand three hours of cannon-fire, but fortunately the Argentine gunners were not remarkable for their proficiency and damages to the ship were slight. On 25 and 26 July they had to pass yet another artillery post, El Cerrito. Here they not only came out unscathed; they actually managed to capture three merchant ships which had sought the protection of the Argentine guns.

In addition to these encounters there were daily skirmishes with the local population and with the Argentine cavalry, which was following them along the river bank. Replenishing food and water supplies was thus extremely difficult; the price of a side of beef was often a veritable massacre.

As they progressed upstream, navigation became slower and more difficult. It took them nineteen days to negotiate the shoals between El Cerrito and Costa Brava, a distance of some eighty miles. At Arroyo Verde the *Garibaldini* were joined by the fleet from Corrientes, commanded by a Lieutenant Villegas, which had moved down the Paraná to meet them. It didn't amount to much: one launch with sails and two with oars. But it was welcome nonetheless, for sooner or later Brown would catch up with the Uruguayan flotilla, and then it would need all the help it could get.

The schooner *Prócida*, with some of Garibaldi's best men aboard (José Napoleon, Carlo Pozzo, Luigi De Agostino, Francisco Blanco) was sent on ahead to Corrientes; the crew were to see to the arming of new ships and then return in reinforcement.

On 14 August, after forty-eight days of hardship and fighting, the fleet was forced to halt near a place called Costa Brava. They were only about twenty miles from their goal, but the water level was now less than 7 ft. Garibaldi could of course have abandoned the *Constitucíon* and gone on his way with the other, lighter vessels. But he and his officers felt that to abandon the flagship would be a betrayal of the propagandist aims of the expedition. It is also quite possible that many of the men were itching for a full-scale conflict with the enemy, who had been dogging them for the entire voyage. Brown, in fact, was approaching fast; he had succeeded in covering in twenty-one days the distance which it had taken the *Garibaldini* forty-eight to cover.

Garibaldi disposed his ships in three lines,

spanning the river from one bank to the other. The first rank consisted of the *Constitución*, the *Pereyra* and two of the captured ships, the *Joven Esteban*, now armed with four cannon, and the *Bella Margarita*, which there had been no time to arm. The second line was made up of the other captured ships: the *Santa Ana*, the *María Luisa*, the small schooner *Uruguay* and the *Mercedes*, which was now equipped as a hospital ship. Villegas' light craft, ready to transport the various crews up the river should flight become necessary, comprised the third line. All the crew members who were not needed to man the cannons were sent ashore, under the command of Lieutenant D. Pedro Rodríguez and Sub-lieutenant Francisco Aycapubi, to head off a possible land attack.

The Argentine fleet arrived on the night of 14 August. At dawn on the 15th the land-troops under Colonel Montaña put ashore and began to attack Garibaldi's ships from the river-bank. Rodríguez counter-attacked. A fierce battle broke out immediately, on both banks of the river. The Uruguayans made up in bravery for their numerical inferiority as they strove to prevent Montaña's troops from advancing. It was a violent, savage scene: for both sides survival would depend on the death or the flight of the enemy. But at night-fall the fighting ceased, and the Argentine troops returned to their ships. During the night Brown's fleet moved forward, in preparation for the battle.

At dawn on Tuesday 16 August the enemies faced each other, each side determined to win a decisive victory. On the one hand, the prestige of a celebrated admiral was at stake: Brown could not afford to be foiled once again by a 'pirate'. On the other, the corsair who had chosen to fight for freedom in this remote corner of South America was also the leader of a gang made up largely of desperados in search of social redemption.

The Argentine fleet consisted of three brigs, four schooners and three smaller ships, and they had fifty-three long-range cannons and seven hundred crew members. The *Garibaldini* had twenty-three cannons and three hundred men in all. The two fleets were nearly a quarter of a mile apart, a distance which could only be traversed by heavy-cali-bre projectiles. And in fact the superiority of the Argentine artillery was immediately evident. Garibaldi's ships were hit in numerous places, even below the water line. The pumps were in continuous operation, while the dead and wounded piled up on the decks.

Evening came, and with it a lull in the hostilities. The *Garibaldini* tried a desperate stratagem: they loaded two small boats with gunpowder and set fire to them, trusting that the current would carry them downstream where they would explode in the midst of the Argentine fleet. But two brave Argentine sailors, B. L. Cordero (who was later made a Rear-admiral) and Luigi Cavassa (a Genoese by birth, who was promoted to the rank of Lieutenant on the spot) succeeded in driving the 'floating bombs' away from the ships.

Subsequently Manuel Arana, the captain of the *Pereyra*, assaulted the Argentine brig *Echagüe* with fifty of his men; but he himself was struck in the forehead by a bullet. Garibaldi was later to write, 'When Arana was killed, I lost the bravest and best of my comrades.' The men panicked, and only a few of them escaped with their lives. At this crucial moment a shameful event took place: the boats from Corrientes deserted, leaving the *Garibaldini* to their fate.

Next day the Argentinians recommenced their bombardment harder than before; Garibaldi's men had now run out of cannon-balls. As a last resort they used links of chain as projectiles, but to little avail. Casualties had been very heavy, and the only options left were retreat or surrender. Garibaldi had the wounded put aboard the last remaining launches, and gave orders to burn his ships, using spirits as fuel. Ten or so of his men decided to drink the spirits instead, and became so incapacitated that they had to be left behind – one can only suppose that they were already out of their minds with fear, otherwise their craving for alcohol would scarcely have prevailed over their instinct for self-preservation.

Those who survived escaped overland, and Brown made no attempt to pursue them. He is reported to have said to his officers, 'Garibaldi is a brave man – let him go, and may God preserve him!' In any event, it is certain that Brown sincerely admired

A portrait in oils of Garibaldi by Malinski (Montevideo 1845).

Little Menotti in her arms, Anita flees on horseback from the farm near San Simon.

Garibaldi. When, in 1847, he resigned from the Argentine navy on orders from the British Admiralty he stopped in Montevideo on his return voyage to England. He specially requested an interview with Garibaldi, and the two had a long and cordial conversation.

The retreating *Garibaldini* were physically exhausted after their three-day battle, and their morale was low. Strict disciplinary measures were necessary to prevent the situation from degenerating completely. It took them three days to march fifteen miles through swamp and forest, with a biscuit a day for rations, before they reached a friendly haven.

Beyond a doubt, the victor·of the Paraná campaign was Admiral Brown – who was showered with exceptional honours on his return to Buenos Aires. Garibaldi, however, had at least attained his goal in demonstrating that Argentine power could be challenged. But this moral victory, such as it was, lost all its value when Oribe defeated Rivera at Arroyo Grande on 6 December 1842. The Federalist leaders could now advance, unopposed, upon Montevideo. The Uruguayan fleet had been destroyed by Brown, and munitions were scarce. But not a soul in the capital felt inclined to surrender.

Luckily for the Uruguayans, a capable and efficient leader, General Paz, took charge of the city's defence, with the co-operation of the new war minister, General Pacheco. He quickly erected a ring of fortifications around Montevideo. Recruiting the gauchos, he created a cavalry where none had existed; he also reorganized the infantry, by trying to co-ordinate the actions of the surviving units scattered throughout the countryside. Munitions factories, cannon foundries and tailors' shops specializing in uniforms were opened. Garibaldi was assigned to assemble another fleet.

On 16 February 1843 Oribe reached the gates of Montevideo with his army of fourteen thousand men. He had already acquired a reputation for cruelty, and now he proclaimed that no one who resisted his conquest of the city would be spared. The foreign residents of Montevideo decided to do their part in defence of the Republic. The French formed a legion of 2,500 men under Colonel Theibaud; the Spaniards formed a legion of their own (which, however, was to change sides a few months later), and the Italians mustered five hundred men under Colonel Mancini. With the constitution of the Italian Legion, on 20 April 1843, the *Garibaldini*, for the first time, obtained official recognition as a military unit. Though Garibaldi was not himself its commander, he belonged to the founding committee together with Cuneo and other exiles.

The Legion's early experiences in battle were disastrous, so Garibaldi decided to take command personally. His first step was to merge the Legion with his own 'sailors'. Thus the 'official' *Garibaldini* and the men who had already been fighting at his side for years – white men and black, Spaniards, Portuguese, North Americans and Brazilians – now, under their natural leader, became the international brigade which it was to remain ever after.

Meanwhile Oribe had encircled Montevideo. He occupied the mountain spurs which overlooked it and advanced as far as the El Cerro fortress, which formed the keystone of the city's defence. On 10 June the Uruguayan army was sent out to dislodge the Argentinians from their position on a hill called El Cerrito.

Oribe's key position was a rise held by his right wing. It was surrounded by a wide ditch, which served as a trench. In front of this trench there was a house being used as an outpost. Garibaldi guessed where the Argentines' weak point was, and obtained permission to attack the position. It was the first time he had led these men in battle, so he gave precise orders: 'We will charge the house there with lowered bayonets, without firing a single shot. Follow me!' The soldiers were impressed by his calm, assured manner, and they assaulted the house and took it. Garibaldi then ordered, 'And now we will charge that ditch in exactly the same way.' The Legion charged, and took the trench without a struggle: the enemy, at the sight of their gleaming bayonets, had taken flight.

This action at El Cerrito was of no military or strategic importance, but it contributed a great deal to the Legion's self-confidence. It also saw the first use of the method of attack which was to become typically Garibaldian: the bayonet charge by troops advancing with their heads lowered, heedless of enemy gun-fire. It was to prove effective; only rarely would the enemy be prepared psychologically to withstand a swift but compact mass of yell-ing soldiers preceded by a thicket of glinting razor-sharp blades. Once such an attack was underway it was nigh on impossible to arrest it with the fire-power available in the mid-19th century.

On the morning following the action, during a review of the troops in the Plaza de la Matriz, General Pacheco, the war minister, publicly congratulated the Italian Legion for its bravery. Although it had greatly improved in the few weeks since its formation, it still was not yet all that Garibaldi desired. Internal discord was rife; a change of cadres was clearly called for. In agreement with the Committee, Garibaldi appointed Francesco Anzani to undertake the task of reorganization.

Anzani was born near Como, to a well-to-do family, on 11 November 1809. He fought in Greece in 1821, in Paris during the revolutionary events of 1832, and in Portugal, with the constitutionalists, in 1833. After that he fought in Spain with the Foreign Legion, a kind of international brigade, in the civil war between the liberals and the clerical legitimists. Here, during a conflict, he was struck in the chest by a large rock heaved by one of the enemy. (This injury was, years later, to be the cause of his death.) In 1838 he returned to Italy and was arrested by the Austrian police, charged with harbouring liberal ideas. Upon his release he requested to leave the country, and received permission to go to America. He landed in Brazil in 1839, and was enrolled as an officer in the Rio Grande infantry.

His first meeting with Garibaldi was rather like a scene in a cowboy film. Garibaldi had heard of this curious character whose physical appearance alone was enough to stop bandits in their tracks, and he decided to make his acquaintance. He travelled to San Gabriel, only to learn that Anzani had gone on business to another town some forty miles away. So he set out, on horseback, to catch up with him. Along the road he came upon a man, stripped to the waist, washing his shirt in a stream. Garibaldi approached him from behind; the man never turned his head, but every muscle in his back visibly tightened. 'You must be Anzani!', said Garibaldi. Still kneeling beside the stream, Anzani now turned, looked at the blond hair and beard, and replied, smiling, 'And you must be Garibaldi!' They became firm friends at once – Anzani was one of the few who ever called Garibaldi by his christian name – and they remained such until Anzani's death.

Anzani arrived in Montevideo in July 1843. He put his excellent organizational abilities to work at once, transforming the Legion by sacking and replacing incompetent officers. He also gave the Legion a uniform and a flag of their own. He realized that while uniforms do not make good soldiers, they are nonetheless necessary. But the Legion lacked funds. This, in fact, would always be a serious problem for the *Garibaldini* – never was an army so ragged, threadbare and dishevelled! Fortunately, a Montevideo firm which manufactured red smocks for the butchers of Buenos Aires was obliged by the war to sell off its stock. These tunics were commodious affairs which reached almost to the knees; there was nothing elegant about them. But they were better than nothing – and perhaps, by stretching the point a little, they could even be considered uniforms. This, then, was the origin of the famous 'red shirts' – a thoroughly prosaic one, and nothing to do with the psychological and political connotations which they were later to acquire. The new flag showed Mount Vesuvius erupting against a black background.

The Legion was now ready to go back into action. Anzani was afraid that the minor victory of El Cerrito had turned the troops' heads a little, and he wanted them 'to learn that war is no joke'. So he drilled them incessantly and put them in the front line wherever the pressure on them would be greatest. Garibaldi and Anzani had, in fact, a secret desire: they wanted to make their Legion into an impeccable military instrument, to be used eventually in Italy when the time should be right.

Meanwhile Rivera had put together a small army of 6,000 men, and with them he roamed the countryside behind the Argentine lines, attacking them whenever he could. Oribe countered the offensive by sending a portion of his troops, commanded by General Urquiza. To do so meant a reduction in the number of troops besieging Montevideo, and the Uruguayans meant to take advantage of this. It was decided that one detachment would storm the Argentine observation post at El Cerro, obliging Oribe to send more reinforcements to that stronghold. Then the Uruguayans would be in a position to come out and attack the Argentines on the open field.

But something went wrong with the plan. Oribe got wind of the Uruguayan manoeuvre, and managed to head it off. He surrounded the 'attack force', which then extricated itself with great difficulty. The *Garibaldini* formed the rear-guard during the retreat. The only way for the detachment to get back to Montevideo was to ford a muddy river called the Bayada. But the enemy had mounted four pieces of artillery on a ridge overlooking the river and they opened fire as soon as the Uruguayans began their crossing.

Garibaldi left some of his men to hold the river bank, and stormed the Argentine battery with the rest. He succeeded in destroying it, and thus made possible an orderly retreat. That day the *Garibaldini* suffered sixty casualties, including dead and wounded, but they had saved the 'attack force' and ensured its return to the city. Such was their valour that President Rivera, in an official document of 30 April 1845, assigned them land and houses as gifts. (The gifts, however, were not accepted.) In fact, the Italian Legion served without pay. Those who needed money hired themselves out, in their spare time, as military surrogates for shopkeepers who thus managed to stay out of the army themselves. They received, for this service, two French livres for each turn of service.

The war went on. Rivera was defeated again at India Muerta; now Oribe could bring all his pressure to bear on Montevideo. In the absence of General Paz (who was directing operations in the countryside) a 'triad' consisting of General Pacheco, Colonel Cerrea and Garibaldi, who had recently been made a colonel, took charge of the city's defences. They did all they could, but it was becoming clear that Montevideo could not hold out much longer. In the end it was France and England (with their important economic interests in the area) who saved the city: unexpectedly the Anglo-French fleet chased the Argentine fleet out of the Plate and imposed a blockade of their own on Buenos Aires.

Seeking to take advantage of their miraculous escape the Uruguayans decided to carry the war into enemy territory. After the defeat at India Muerta, Rivera had fled to Brazil, and his troops had been dispersed. The object of the new campaign was to recover these troops and to rcopen communications with Brazil by occupying certain towns and road junctions. Garibaldi was again placed in charge of the operation.

About seven hundred Legionaries embarked on a small flotilla. Accompanied by the Franco-English fleet they took the same route which Garibaldi had taken years earlier. This time they found the fortress of Martin García deserted. They occupied it, and then the city of Colonia, which the Argentines had also abandoned at the approach of the enemy

The uniforms of the Italian Legion of Montevideo in an idealistic reconstruction by Quinto Cenni.

fleet. Then Garibaldi sailed up the Uruguay river with his fleet; the British and the French turned into the Paraná and, in three days of fighting, they succeeded in destroying all the artillery installations along the river.

Garibaldi occupied the towns along the Uruguay, such as Las Vacas, Mercedes, Gualeguaychú, and met very little resistance from the Argentinians. Finally his flotilla arrived at Salto, a village named from a cataract beyond which the river is no longer navigable. The military commander there was the Argentinian general Lavalleya, who, at the approach of the *Garibaldini*, fled, forcing the inhabitants to accompany him, and camped beside a tributary of the Uruguay called the Tapevi. During the night the *Garibaldini*, together with two hundred newly arrived cavalry under Colonel Baez, moved towards the enemy camp. They attacked at dawn, and

after only a few minutes' fighting they took it, with a hundred prisoners, horses, oxen, and – most important – a piece of artillery.

Garibaldi sent a courier to Brazil to establish contact with the Uruguayan refugees and to get them to join his army. He set up a two-gun battery in Salto. On the morning of 6 December General Urquiza arrived at Salto, with 3,500 cavalry, 800 infantry and a battery of field artillery. Garibaldi sent his ships to safety; but he stationed his men in every nook and cranny of the village, leaving only the main street open. Around 9 a.m. Urquiza's men attacked in several places, but they were met by more fire than they had expected – shots from every direction, and an onslaught from the two cannon. For a moment they wavered, just long enough for Garibaldi to order a bayonet attack by his two reserve companies. The Argentinians were overcome and fled, after suffering heavy losses. Urquiza then laid siege to the village, but after twenty-three days of repeated, futile attacks he gave up and withdrew across the Uruguay river, where he encamped on the Canardia plain.

On 7 February Garibaldi received a message from Rivera: Medina, an officer of the Uruguayan army, was marching on Salto with the vanguard of his army. The next day – a torrid one – Garibaldi went out to join forces with this detachment with 186 men and 100 of Baez's cavalry. At noon they were a few miles from the village, with the river to their left and a low ridge not far to their right. Suddenly 1,200 Argentinians appeared on the crest of the ridge: 900 cavalry and 300 infantry, commanded by Servando Gómez.

Baez wanted to retreat, but there was no time for the manoeuvre. Fortunately there was a ruined farmhouse nearby, and Garibaldi and his soldiers took refuge in the ruins while Baez's men remained in the saddle to confront the enemy charge. The three hundred Argentine infantry advanced upon the farmhouse in a long straight line: singularly easy targets for the *Garibaldini*. The enemy began shooting long before they were within range, whereas Garibaldi had given his men orders not to fire 'until they're right on top of us!' When the Argentinians were thirty yards away the *Garibaldini* opened fire, wreaking havoc in their ranks. They followed up with a series of bayonet charges, and most of the afternoon was spent in fierce hand-to-hand conflict.

Meanwhile Baez's cavalry, under heavy attack, withdrew towards Salto, leaving the *Garibaldini* to their fate; only seventeen Uruguayans turned back to join them at the farmhouse, which was now surrounded by corpses and carcasses of horses. These the *Garibaldini* used to build barricades in the more exposed points of the ruins in order to provide shelter from the ever-increasing enemy fire. Gómez sent an envoy to demand their surrender; by way of reply Garibaldi and the officers sang the Uruguayan national anthem.

Later the Argentine cavalry, which had gone off in pursuit of Baez, returned and the Legion was now completely surrounded. Some of the Argentinians dismounted and joined the repeated infantry attacks; others remained in the saddle. Fortunately no mass attack was mounted and, on the whole, the attackers got the worst of the engagement, but Garibaldi's casualties were mounting; the corpses in themselves an obstacle to the attacking Argentinians. A fourteen-year-old bugle-boy, who had sounded incessantly since the morning, was run through by an Argentine cavalryman's lance. The dying boy threw away his bugle and flung himself upon his adversary's right leg, stabbing it again and again with a knife. When he lost this weapon he continued the assault with his teeth. The horseman broke into a gallop and hacked furiously at the boy with his sabre, but he couldn't shake him off. Finally, a burst of rifle fire put an end to their struggles, but even in death the boy still clung to the horseman.

Towards 8.30 p.m., after nine hours of fighting, Garibaldi decided to attempt a retreat. He and his men were completely surrounded by the enemy, and they would have to cross 800 yards of open terrain before they reached the river, where the thick vegetation would offer some protection. They set out nevertheless, carrying their wounded with them – except for one soldier too badly hurt to be moved. Garibaldi ordered that he be administered the *coup de grâce*: it was a bitter decision to take, but he knew the fate which

The Battle of San Antonio del Salto. Garibaldi can be seen at the centre brandishing his sword. News of the battle – in truth little more than a skirmish – made headlines around the world and brought notoriety to the Garibaldini.

awaited those who became prisoners of this inhuman war.

They had to fight every inch of the way, under fire from Gómez's infantry and charged continually by the cavalry. Finally they reached the river, and could at least slake their thirst, but they still had to fight off Argentine attacks. They headed back towards Salto, with the enemy in hot pursuit. At last Anzani brought reinforcements from Baez's cavalry, and the Argentinians withdrew. It took them four and a half hours to cover just over three miles; not until one-o-clock in the morning did they reach the safety of the village. Of Garibaldi's men's 43 had been killed and 53 wounded; Argentine casualties came to 500 dead and wounded.

Anzani had stayed at Salto that day because of a leg wound, and with him were a few other soldiers who were too sick to fight and the twelve artillerymen who were manning the battery. When the Argentine cavalry had arrived at the village in pursuit of Baez, they sent a messenger to tell Anzani that Garibaldi was dead, and that his own life would be spared if he would surrender. Anzani replied that if they wanted the battery they would have to take it; he would rather blow the whole installation sky high than surrender it to them. The Argentinians did not make the attempt. Medina arrived at Salto during the night, a few hours after Garibaldi. Gómez withdrew in the direction of Paysandu.

Two medical officers from a French gunboat, which had accompanied Garibaldi's flotilla and was anchored at Salto, helped care for the wounded. Two men had legs amputated, without anaesthetic; many died of their wounds within the next few days. Garibaldi returned to the battlefield the next day, to recover the dead. All the bodies, comrades and enemies alike, were brought back to Salto and buried in a common grave adorned with a single cross.

Cuneo sent word of the victory at Salto to Mazzini, living in exile in London. Mazzini wrote a report for *The Times* – which, however, refused to print it. Undaunted, Mazzini printed the news in his own paper, the *Apostolato Popolare*. When this reached Italy, it touched off a great wave of enthusiasm: Garibaldi's name was pronounced at a scientific congress at Genoa, and was greeted by a long ovation; at Florence a subscription was raised to present him with a sword of honour. Garibaldi and the Legion were, of course, the toast of Montevideo. Poems in their honour were published in the press and declaimed in the Teatro de Comercio. Admiral Lainé wrote Garibaldi a letter in which he stated that the victory was worthy of Napoleon's *Grande Armée*. Garibaldi himself said, in praise of his men, 'I would not exchange the honour of belonging to the Legion for all the gold in the world.'

The Uruguayan government, to demonstrate its profound gratitude to the heroic Legion, issued the following decree:

Article 1. General Garibaldi and all those who were with him on that glorious day are Honourable Members of the Republic.
Article 2. On the banner of the Italian Legion, on the upper part of Vesuvius, these words shall be inscribed in letters of gold: Action of February 1846 accomplished by the Italian Legion under the command of Garibaldi.
Article 3. The names of those who fought on that day after the departure of the cavalry shall be engraved upon a tablet, which shall hang in the Government Hall opposite the Arms of the Republic. The list shall begin with the names of those who perished.
Article 4. The families of the dead shall receive double the pension to which they would

ordinarily be entitled.
Article 5. Those who fought on after the departure of the cavalry shall be awarded a commemorative badge, to be worn on the left arm, with the following inscription within a wreath of laurel: Invincible, they fought on 8 February 1846.
Article 6. Until another corps of this army shall achieve an equally glorious feat of arms, the Italian Legion shall have precedence in all parades.
Article 7. A certified copy of the present decree shall be consigned to the Italian Legion. It shall be read in General Orders on every anniversary of the battle.
Article 8. The War Ministry shall be responsible for the execution and regulation of this decree, which shall be presented to the Assembly of Notables. It shall be published and inserted in the Official Gazette.

The war ministry then issued a decree of its own, ordering 'that on 15 February the garrison shall pass on parade before the Italian Legion on the Plaza de la Constitución; the commanding officer of each corps shall give the salute, "Long live the Fatherland, General Garibaldi, and his valorous comrades." '

The *Garibaldini* accepted these public expressions of gratitude, but they refused the appanages and promotions in rank which the government offered them. The only emoluments they would consider were those destined for widows and for disabled veterans; they themselves continued to serve the republican cause without pay. The war minister, Pacheco, later stated in one of his publications that 'General Garibaldi, in Montevideo at the head of a legion, never received a penny from the nation he was defending.' The Legionaries were so poor that they had no candles in their homes, since these were not included in the ration of a Uruguayan soldier, and even Garibaldi and his family lived on an ordinary soldier's ration. One day he encountered a Legionary even poorer than he who, literally, hadn't a shirt to his name; Garibaldi stripped off his own shirt and gave it away. When he went home and asked Anita for another shirt she replied, 'You knew perfectly well that you had only one; if you've given it away, so much the worse for you!' So Garibaldi remained shirtless until Anita made him a present of a new one, imploring him, this time, to keep it for himself.

The war had now entered a period of stagnation, and the political situation in Uruguay had begun to deteriorate. Leaders began to squabble among themselves, largely about the foreign interests which were now preponderant in the nation's affairs. The *Garibaldini* began to feel that their services were no longer essential.

Then, late in 1847, reports from Italy rekindled the nationalist ardour of the political exiles in Montevideo: in various states of the peninsula there was a sudden trend away from reactionary and towards liberal government. Anzani and Garibaldi wrote to the Pope, who seemed to be the guiding spirit of this transformation, to offer him their swords and their Legion. Without waiting for a reply – none, in fact, ever came – they began to make frenzied preparations for the homeward journey. They sensed that the new movement would have to be defended by force against the vested interests which it threatened.

Many Italian residents in South America contributed to a subscription for the fitting out of a new ship, but progress was slow. On 27 December Garibaldi saw his family off on a ship bound for Genoa: besides Anita and Menotti there were now two younger children, Ricciotti and Teresita.

On 2 February 1848 Giacomo Medici was sent ahead to Tuscany, where the expedition intended to land. Medici had just turned thirty-one, and had already acquired a sound military training fighting with the liberals in Spain. A cold and lucid man, he was soon to become a leader of the *Garibaldini* (though one day he would abandon the republican cause for the monarchy, and gain a title).

Anzani, meanwhile, wrote to his brother to authorize the disposal of his property, in the hope of raising 12,000 francs with which to finance the revolution: 'Sell or pawn what little I possess, even for a low price, provided I may satisfy this need.' But Anzani's career was coming to an end. His old chest injury was now causing serious trouble, and the doctors feared that the least attack of sea-sickness might prove fatal. They implored him to remain in Montevideo, but he would not be swayed. 'Even if I die the moment I set foot in Italy', he wrote to a friend, 'I shall die happy. For my part, I shall have accomplished that which I swore to do when I was young and strong and healthy.'

On 15 April a hired brig, paid for out of the subscription funds, sailed out of Montevideo. It was called the *Bifronte*, but the Red-shirts rechristened it *Speranza* (Hope). Seventy-three men were leaving South America behind. Smiling, they contemplated the Atlantic, but their minds were on the struggles for the cause of liberty which, they knew, lay ahead. For most of them, the end would not be long in coming: Anzani, for example, would not survive the voyage. Gaetano Sacchi, on the other hand, who had been one of the original Legionaries of Montevideo and who was still in his early youth, would live – despite a serious shoulder wound – to become a general in the Italian army. Giambattista Culiolo would be present at Anita's deathbed and would follow Garibaldi in his second exile. Tommaso Risso, whose face was arabesqued with scars, was to be killed in a duel with a comrade-in-arms over a senseless question of honour. But most were destined to die beneath the walls of Rome, among them Andrés Aguyar (nicknamed 'Garibaldi's Moor', a Montevidean of Negro blood who would save his general's life on several occasions) and Giacomo Minuto who, at the news of the city's surrender, was to rip off his bandages and bleed to death.

These seventy-three men were bringing their experience as combatants to Italy and to Europe. At their head was a man who had made Liberty his goal in life. Those who were to die would say, like Anzani, 'For my part, I have accomplished what I swore to do.'

Garibaldini *on the ruins of the Roman walls, in a painting by Gerolamo Induno.*

A Dream of Freedom

The four great powers which, in coalition, had defeated Napoleon 1 – Austria, Russia, Great Britain and Prussia – convoked a Congress at Vienna in 1815, with the purpose of partitioning the states which had been allied with the French and of re-establishing the national frontiers which the Napoleonic Wars had altered.

Policy for Poland, Saxony and the Rhineland was the subject of heated discussion; but Italian policy was simply left to the 'discretion' of Austria.

The protagonist of the Congress was Prince Metternich, the Chancellor of the Austrian Empire, who had not forgiven the Italians for their too active participation in the Napoleonic campaigns, or for their opposition to the return of Austrian troops to their soil. With Austrian bayonets firmly in command the old territorial divisions of Italy were restored, with boundaries much as they had been before the French Revolution.

In the North were Piedmont (which, together with the island of Sardinia, constituted the so-called Kingdom of Sardinia), ruled by the House of Savoy, and the Lombardo-Veneto, now a province of the Austrian Empire.

In Central Italy the Duchy of Modena and Reggio was ruled by the Italo-Austrian dynasty of Este-Lorraine; the Duchy of Parma and Piacenza was given to Maria Louisa, daughter of the Austrian Emperor and second wife of Napoleon. The Principality of Lucca was assigned temporarily to the Bourbons, who were to inherit the Duchy of Parma upon the death of Maria Louisa. The Grand Duchy of Tuscany was ruled by Leopold II, a nephew of the Austrian Emperor, while the Pope reigned over the States of the Church sustained in power by the Austrian troops.

In the South the Kingdom of the Two Sicilies was ruled by the Bourbon dynasty of Naples, who were closely allied to the Austrians.

Thus, thanks to dynastic and military ties, all Italy – with the exception of Piedmont – was directly or indirectly under the control of Austria.

When anyone suggested to Metternich that, considering the new-found national aspirations of the Italian people, it was perhaps unwise to insist on maintaining these divisions, the Prince would reply, ' "Italy" is merely a geographical

Italy after the the Vienna Congress

expression': there could be no place in his world for Italian national aspirations. But even though, with his genius for politics, he had been able to re-impose the pre-war *status quo*, Metternich was wrong to suppose that the libertarian ideas which had spread so rapidly in Italy after the French Revolution could easily be forgotten.

Between 1820 and 1845, Italy witnessed a practically unbroken series of rebellions. They were poorly organized and uncoordinated, and resulted only in bloodbaths for the people and exile for their leaders. Here we need mention only the most important of them.

The first revolution, of 1820–1, broke out first at Naples and a little later at Turin. It was led by the army and by the middle-classes; their aim was the democratization of the process of government and the promulgation of a constitution – a written constitution was seen by many as a first step towards the national unity of Italy. In Piedmont even Charles Albert, the heir to the throne, was a party to this movement – though later, rather than lose his right to the succession, he went to Spain to fight the supporters of the very constitution which he had sought to promote.

The revolution was put down through the intervention of the Austrians. It ended with the purge of democratic elements in the army, and many death-sentences were passed.

Austria had previously created, with the co-operation of other authoritarian governments, a kind of Reactionary International, the 'Holy Alliance', set up to combat liberalism in Europe through the exchange of information by police forces and the arrest of everyone suspected of harbouring subversive ideas. A member state could also request the armed intervention of its allies to help repress a local democratic movement.

In 1831 another large-scale rebellion broke out, affecting mainly the Papal States and the Duchy of Modena. As in 1820–1 the main objective of the revolutionaries was to obtain a democratic constitution. This time, however, the military did not take part, and support for the movement came from middle-class republican circles.

The first uprising took place at Bologna on 4 February; on the following day, at Modena, the Duke was deposed and driven into exile. On 7 February the revolt spread to Ferrara, on the 8th to Pesaro, Fossombrone, Fano and Urbino, and on the 13th to Parma, Ascoli, Perugia, Terni, Narni and other towns in the Papal States.

But the repression, once again undertaken by the Austrians, was swift, ferocious and successful. Many patriots lost their lives on the gallows; others were imprisoned, and others still were exiled.

The failure of the two revolutions of 1821 and of 1831 marked the end of old-style 'local' liberalism – which had merely demanded the extension of political power in individual states, through constitutional measures, to social classes which previously had been excluded from it. This form of political consciousness was now being superseded, through the influence of Giuseppe Mazzini, by a new awareness that only by struggling for national unity could Italians hope to combat Austrian-led reaction.

Although they failed, these early revolutions nevertheless forged a new generation of men who were to provide the leadership in future struggles. It was now obvious, furthermore, how fragile and ephemeral were the kingdoms and duchies set up by the Congress of Vienna: only the might of the Austrian army could guarantee their survival.

During these years there were a number of other attempts at revolution in Italy. In 1834 Mazzini himself tried to incite an insurrection in Piedmont, with the support of the youthful Garibaldi. And in 1844 the Bandiera brothers instigated a revolt in the Kingdom of the Two Sicilies. (They died before a firing squad.)

Until 1845 small revolts continued to erupt here and there; all doomed to failure from the start. These were years of fruitful work for the reactionary police forces, which were on the look-out in every city and town in Italy. But the more patriots they arrested, the more they put to death, the more came forward to take their places. As Metternich once admitted, 'Close the door to ideas and they'll come in through the window.'

Soon the 'Italian question' began to arouse interest and sympathy beyond the borders of Italy. Late in 1832 Silvio Pellico's autobiographical book *Le mie prigioni* (Memoirs of my Imprisonments) was published. Pellico had been arrested by the Austrian police for his participation in the revolution of 1821 and had spent ten years in Spielberg prison. His book exposed, in a rather pleasantly off-hand style, the extreme harshness of the Austrian prison system. Thanks to its very simplicity it immediately became a best-seller and was translated into French, English, German, Russian, Spanish and Dutch. International public opinion could no longer ignore the Italian question, and Austria received such a bad press that Metternich called the book 'more catastrophic than a lost battle'.

In 1843 and 1844 two other books were published which focused the Italian people's attention on their political problems: Vincenzo Gioberti's *Del primato morale e civile degli italiani* (On the Moral and Civil Primacy of the Italians) and Cesare Balbo's *Delle speranze d'Italia* (Italy's Hopes). Both books called for the abolition of customs barriers between the various Italian states in the interest of an all-Italian economy, and for the creation of a political 'League' embracing all the states of the peninsula.

Gioberti's and Balbo's arguments touched off a series of public debates. The press took a lively interest, and even the most reactionary court circles were not immune. For the first time Italians from every part of the country began to take stock of their common interests.

A rather original contribution to unity came from the 'Scientific Congresses' which began to burgeon in a number of Italian cities: learned discussions of scientific matters furnished a pretext for intellectuals to come together and exchange their views on Italy and her problems.

All these developments were the work of men whom historians would later classify as 'moderates': middle- or upper-class citizens, progressive in their outlook, devoted to the Italian cause but opposed to revolution as a means of achieving unity. These men – unlike the republicans who had earlier sought to overthrow governments by armed revolt but had failed to enlist the active participation of the masses – actually had an enormous success in creating a public capable of critical reflection on the Italian nation's problems.

Another book which significantly influenced the formation of 'moderate' opinion was Massimo d'Azeglio's *Degli ultimi casi di Romagna* (On Recent Events in Romagna), which sold two thousand copies in one week. D'Azeglio condemned the Papacy for its brutal, repressive methods, but he also repudiated popular insurrection as a form of political struggle. Most important, though, he let it be understood, between the lines, that only the Piedmontese monarchy was suited to lead a possible 'Italian League'. On this point he differed from Gioberti, who tended to think of the Pope as the League's natural leader.

Piedmont was one of the most ancient states in Italy and had been ruled by the House of Savoy for roughly nine hundred years. By the 1840s, thanks to the economic reforms of Charles Albert (who had been King of Sardinia since 1831), Piedmont's middle class had not only grown conspicuously in size and power, but had also converted to its own liberal aspirations a sizeable portion of the aristocracy as well as the more advanced elements of the working class.

After its own failure in the rebellion of 1820–1, Piedmont's middle class no longer believed in revolution. However, Piedmont had always been decidedly anti-Austrian, though this sentiment probably had more to do with the desire to remain independent than with any deep sense of Italian nationalism.

When, in 1846, the cardinals met in conclave following the death of the reactionary Gregory XVI, their choice of his successor astonished all of Italy. It also astonished the Viennese court: Metternich remarked, 'Here's something I thought I'd never live to see – a liberal Pope!'

The new Pope, Pius IX, was in fact no liberal. But he had acquired a kind of liberal reputation as bishop of Imola, by maintaining contacts with progressive circles in that city. As Pope, he chose at first not to clear up the misunderstanding; he enhanced his image, in fact, by appointing a well-known liberal – Monsignor Corboli-Bussi – head of a pontifical commission, and by granting an amnesty to political prisoners.

Very soon, in all the towns of Italy, the cry 'Long live Pius IX' came to express the people's longing for change. Governments were well aware of this, but they were helpless before such 'manifestations of faith' – citizens, after all, could hardly be locked up for cheering the Vicar of Christ. But the longed-for changes failed to materialize. By the end of 1847 Pius IX had not adopted any of the reforms which had been proposed: abolition of censorship, import duties, and the state lottery; expansion of the elementary school system; and a more representational form of government.

In Piedmont, meanwhile, Charles Albert (who, according to the proponents of the Italian League, should have been providing the liberation movement with its military leadership) was on the point of declaring war on Austria over a commercial transaction involving the sale of salt. Torn between his own long-repressed liberal instincts and his mistrust of an increasingly militant populace, he failed to act.

The Austrians brought matters to a head through two colossal blunders of their own: they opted for the preventive occupation of Ferrara, a city in the Papal States, and they presumed to address an open letter to Charles Albert in which they warned him of impending revolution. The letter was not meant as a threat, but the Piedmontese, jealous of their independence, took it as an unacceptable interference in their internal affairs.

Thus the Austrians unwittingly hastened the organization of the Italian League. By

Prince Metternich, Chancellor of the Austrian Empire, the real protagonist of the Congress of Vienna. Although a shrewd and careful politician, he could not comprehend the Italians' aspirations and refused to make democratic concessions contrary to his thinking and background.

November 1847 this little 'Italian Common Market' had become a reality. For the time being it consisted only of Piedmont, Tuscany and the Papal States. But membership was open to all the other Italian states – with the exception of the Lombardy-Veneto (which was barred for as long as it should remain an Austrian province).

The people of Milan, who had not the possibility of petitioning for constitutional guarantees or for democratic liberties, had to be content with frenetically singing *Va, pensiero, sull'ali dorate* along with the chorus at performances of Verdi's *Nabucco* – thus implicitly equating their own condition with that of the ancient Hebrews suffering under the Babylonian yoke. The police tried to stop them. From now on the Milanese ostracized the Austrians completely, and treated anyone who had dealings with them as a collaborationist.

Following the example of the Boston colonists, the Milanese, in early January 1848, decided upon a tobacco boycott which, in forty-eight hours, cost the Austrian administration 3,000 ducats. The police responded by smoking in the streets; fighting broke out, and there were sixty casualties. The Milanese then extended their boycott to the lottery (which was an immense source of revenue for the government) and to La Scala, where an Austrian ballerina happened to be dancing. Only nine tickets were sold for that performance; the empty seats were assigned to soldiers. The ringleaders of the boycott were arrested, and the mood of the people grew increasingly violent. Reinforcements were sent from Austria to Radetzky, the military commander of the Lombardo-Veneto.

But the revolution, when it came, broke out where it was least expected: in Sicily. This island had been exploited for centuries by its rulers in Naples; in the past it had frequently asked for local autonomy and political reform, but the authoritarian Bourbon monarchy's only response to such requests had been cannon-balls. On 12 January 1848 the Sicilians rebelled, led by Giuseppe La Masa (who was later to become a *Garibaldini* chief) and Rosolino Pilo. They declared their independence and drafted a constitution. The expeditionary force sent to put down the revolt retreated in defeat.

On 11 February a popular uprising in Naples itself compelled Ferdinand II to grant a constitution and to join the Italian League. Within a short time Tuscany, Piedmont and the Papal States also acquired constitutions.

Meanwhile, the entire European continent was being shaken by explosions of liberal and democratic fervour. The insurrection of 22 February in Paris overthrew the monarchy of Louis Philippe; in March revolutionary violence erupted in Vienna, Berlin and Budapest.

Venice rebelled against Austrian rule on 17 March, proclaimed herself the Republic of St Mark, and freed political prisoners. On the next day Milan followed suit. After five days of street fighting the 14,000 Austrians were expelled from the city. (The death-toll was 1,200.) On 20 March Parma and Modena deposed their respective dukes.

At this point the territories in revolt were all looking for protection to Piedmont, with its small but efficient army. Charles Albert entered the war – after much indecision – on 23 March. But instead of launching a lightning attack on the disorganized and demoralized Austrians, he moved with his characteristic sluggishness. In the first engagements of the war – at Goito, Monzambano and Valeggio – the Piedmontese failed to win a decisive victory. Their officers, though often courageous in action, could also be irresponsible, and the King, though he took personal command of the operations, remained irresolute and laggard. Incapable of capitalizing on their initial advantage the Piedmontese allowed the Austrians to withdraw into the quadrilateral formed by the fortresses of Mantua, Verona, Peschiera and Legnano. Here Radetzky could reorganize his men in safety – and he was later to admit that had Charles Albert not given him this chance the war would have been over for Austria.

Meanwhile the rest of Italy was clamouring to go to war on the Piedmont side. Troops were dispatched, reluctantly, by the Kingdom of the Two Sicilies, by the Papal States and by Tuscany. But of more importance were the thousands of private citizens – especially university students, more outstanding for their determination than for their military proficiency – who set out from every part of the peninsula as volunteers.

But the war was lost before it started – not only because of Charles Albert's disastrous leadership, but also because of the unreliability of his Italian allies, who were often more concerned with the political aspects of the war than with military contingencies. The allied troops were dispatched too late and without precise orders; often they were more inclined to go home than to stay and fight.

The turning-point came on 29 April 1848, with the news that the Pope had withdrawn his troops and called for an end to the war. This change of heart – if such it was, and not a deliberate betrayal – threw the Italian forces into disarray and contributed substantially to their defeat.

Naples immediately retired from the League, as did Tuscany. By way of reply, Lombardy, the Veneto, Parma and Modena voted in favour of annexation by Piedmont.

But it was too late: the longed-for 'Italian crusade' was over.

Radetzky, pent up in his quadrilateral, had received reinforcements under Marshal Welden, and though the surrender of Peschiera weakened his defences he had nevertheless been able to complete the work of reorganizing his army. On 25 June he inflicted a heavy defeat upon the Piedmontese at Custoza, and forced them to sign an armistice and to withdraw to their own territories.

Venice was encircled by the Austrians, and a siege began which was to last until 30 August 1849. There were a few other pockets of resistance, such as Brescia, which earned for herself the *sobriquet* 'Lioness of Italy'. But the Austrian command's principal worry was now 'that South American', who was roving northern Lombardy with 1,500 men.

Garibaldi had received word of the insurrection in Italy after he passed Gibraltar and, forgetting his rendezvous with Medici in Tuscany, he sailed straight for Genoa, where he landed on 28 June 1848. He and his followers were greeted by an enthusiastic populace. The press had been full of the *Garibaldini*, and now the Genoese flocked to the pier to see for themselves. But the men who came ashore bore little resemblance to the impeccably uniformed soldiers they were portrayed as in the illustrated papers. They looked like a band of brigands in fact: hair over the shoulders and beards to the chest; huge broad-brimmed felt – or even straw – hats, made shapeless by the rain; faded, tattered great-coats; trousers with knee-guards but without stripes or braids and of every imaginable cut and colour; makeshift accoutrements; not a polished button to be seen. Nor were they martial in their bearing; they walked with their hands in their pockets and their rifles slung over their shoulders. Garibaldi himself hardly looked like a military leader, with his unkempt beard, his slouch hat and his gaily striped poncho. But an attentive observer would have noticed that all the weapons, though scarred by use, were in perfect working order.

The joy of the occasion was tempered by sorrow for the death of Anzani. As the doctors had feared, he had not survived the voyage. Thus Rossetti's death was followed by that of another of the founding members of the Garibaldian movement; it was an enormous loss.

Garibaldi was later to say, 'Had he been at our head, surely the whole peninsula would long since be free from the foreign yoke. I have never known a truer gentleman than Anzani, or a finer soldier.'

At Genoa the *Garibaldini* made a choice which was to be of momentous importance for the cause of Italian independence. Republicans, and sworn enemies of monarchy though they were, they now decided to overlook the dissensions of the past and to throw in their lot with the Piedmontese, for the sake of national unity. Charles Albert, however, was not so easily persuaded of the desirability of this alliance.

While Sacchi, despite a serious wound,

began recruiting volunteers for a second Legion, Garibaldi went to Charles Albert's headquarters to offer the King his sword and his men. But the King, mistrustful of whatever savoured of the common people, refused to see 'the man from Montevideo' himself, and ordered that he be sent on to his war minister instead.

Nobody, in fact, wanted the *Garibaldini*. For a whole month they were referred back and forth from one ministry to another, from one committee to the next. Eventually they moved on to Milan, where they found that the Revolutionary Committee was prepared to rely on their experience. Garibaldi was asked to organize a volunteer corps to supplement his 'South Americans'. Despite considerable obstacles he succeeded, with the aid of Sacchi and Medici, in forming a legion of five thousand men. Mazzini himself signed up as a stan-

Garibaldini portrayed in Rome in 1849 by George Thomas of the Illustrated London News. *On the left, one of Angelo Masina's* Lancieri *in the characteristic fez of the corps.*

Pope Pius IX fled from Rome on 24 November 1848. On 9 February 1849 the Republic was proclaimed by the Assembly. Although suffering from a severe attack of arthritis, Garibaldi insisted on being present and was carried in by Ignacio Bueno, one of the South Americans.

dard-bearer. Ironically enough the legion was outfitted in white, with remnants of Austrian uniforms requisitioned from the military stores. 'They look like a regiment of cooks', was Medici's comment. The South American soldiers did not really bear much resemblance to cooks, however, for they had no intention of giving up their famous red shirts.

The column marched on Como, led by Andrés Aguyar with his trusty lance and *bolas*. At Como word reached them of the Piedmont defeat at Custoza. Of the five thousand recruits, the vast majority deserted. With 1,200 men left, Garibaldi, Medici and Sacchi decided to carry on with their campaign. They sent word to the commanders of the other volunteer corps, asking them to join forces. But the others had already withdrawn into Piedmont with the royal army – or had fled to Switzerland. And so the *Garibaldini* advanced upon the Austrian army with a force of 1,500 men.

First they occupied Arona on Lake Maggiore; then, in two captured boats, they

moved on to Luino. On 15 August they were attacked by an Austrian column equal to theirs in strength. Though Garibaldi was suffering an attack of fever which he had contracted in South America, his men succeeded in beating the Austrians. But their position was precarious. They abandoned Luino and set out for Varese. Here they learned that three Austrian columns were advancing on them, consisting of four brigades and several cavalry squadrons, commanded by General d'Aspre. Outnumbered, Garibaldi and Medici decided to divide the men into two columns and retreat to Switzerland.

Along the way, Medici was forced into combat several times. Then at San Matteo, a few miles from the Swiss border, he was surrounded by the enemy troops. In the thick of the fighting he was joined by a party of hunters from the Swiss canton of Ticino, who had been drawn by the sound of gunfire. Using a path known only to the locals, the Ticinese led Medici's column to safety in Switzerland.

Garibaldi, on the other hand, was completely encircled by five thousand Austrians at Morazzone. For the entire day of 26 August he withstood the enemy onslaught. During the night, in a desperate gamble, he launched a furious counter-attack and succeeded in breaking through the Austrian lines. A few miles out of Morazzone the column broke up and the men went their separate ways; it was agreed that they would reassemble at Lugano.

The performance of the *Garibaldini* in these last days of the Lombard campaign – 14–26 August 1848 – was accurately assessed by their adversary, General d'Aspre. Years later, conversing with a Piedmont consul, he remarked, 'The one man who could really have helped you to win your 1848 war was the man you turned your backs on – Garibaldi.'

The whole of Italy, prostrated by the defeat, trembled in anticipation of reactionary measures to follow. But the *Garibaldini* had no intention of giving up. They regrouped at Genoa, and then set out for Tuscany. But the provisional government there wanted no part of them, and ordered them off Tuscan territory. They then headed for Bologna, intending to move on to Venice, which was resisting the Austrian siege. At Bologna, too, it was made clear to them that their presence was unwelcome. Fighting might have broken out, had not the populace demonstrated in favour of the *Garibaldini*. General Zucchi of the Papal army therefore changed his mind, and granted them permission to encamp at Ravenna. But then a piece of news came through which altered the whole situation – the Pope had fled Rome, and the *Garibaldini* were needed there!

Pius IX had aroused the wrath of the masses with his withdrawal of support from the war of liberation on 28 April. He tried to restore peace by appointing Pellegrino Rossi head of his government. Rossi was a Tuscan who had made a career for himself in France and had become Senator under Louis-Philippe. He was also a conservative who liked to think that he could keep the people under control. (Needless to say, he only made matters worse.)

On the afternoon of 15 November 1848, as he was entering the palace of the Cancelleria – the seat of his government – Rossi was surrounded by some sixty veterans of the war against Austria, who felt that the papacy had betrayed the national cause. They raised their arms in unison, and when they drew back Pellegrino Rossi lay dead, a dagger wound in his neck. News of his assassination touched off a series of street demonstrations against Pius IX, which became increasingly violent as time went on.

And on the night of 24 November, disguised as an ordinary priest, the Pope fled to Gaeta, in Neapolitan territory, where he could count on the protection of Ferdinand II. He excommunicated the rebels in Rome, and formally called upon the Catholic powers of Europe to restore him to his throne.

Meanwhile a provisional government was formed in Rome. It appealed to all the volunteer forces in Italy, including the *Garibaldini*, to rally to its defence. But it beseeched them not to enter the city of Rome – because, it was feared, the ladies might be alarmed! And in fact, to judge from the drawings of George Thomas, an artist in the employ of the *Illustrated London News*, their appearance must have been far from reassuring.

The *Garibaldini*, therefore, were obliged to pass the winter in the Appennines, with insufficient food and among a sometimes hostile population. In such conditions the maintenance of discipline was not easy, but maintained it was, through the efforts of Nino Bixio, a tough Genoese who was later to be second in command during the expedition of the 'Thousand'. Besides Bixio, two other men who were to have important roles in the campaign to come joined Garibaldi during the course of that winter: Angelo Masina and Ugo Bassi.

Angelo de Masini, known as Masina, was an Emilian nobleman who was then thirty-four years old. He had previously taken part in the uprisings of 1831 and in the Spanish war. When the 1848 war broke out he organized, at his personal expense, a corps of Lancers known as the 'Death Squadron'. It was made up of local aristocrats and was described as 'arousing the envy of every other militia, for the comeliness of its personnel and the elegance of its uniform'. The latter, of the Hussar type, consisted of a dark blue dolman with black braiding, red trousers with a broad blue stripe, a red kepi with a long horse-hair plume, and a full white mantle, the hood of which had an embroidered skull to one side.

Bassi, on the other hand, was a Bolognese priest of liberal views, already known as a political activist. Now he joined the *Garibaldini* as their chaplain, though his attire was hardly that of a conventional cleric.

In early January 1849 the *Garibaldini* arrived at Rieti, a valley town, where they could rest and change their uniforms. They were issued dark blue great-coats with green collars and green pocket-flaps, dark blue trousers with green stripes, and Calabrian hats with cockerel feathers and bands, the only sign of red in the uniform. Some of the men were reluctant to part with their glorious red shirts, but there was no alternative if they wanted a change of uniform, and the Roman government was anxious to have them look as 'civilized' as possible. The officers kept their red uniforms; they were also recognizable by the ostrich plumes on their caps. Garibaldi, meanwhile, had changed his striped poncho for a white one.

On 20 January Garibaldi was elected deputy from Rieti to the Assembly at Rome. He arrived there on 5 February, arthritic and leaning on the arm of Ignacio Bueno. He eagerly took part in the debate about the form of government to be adopted. Observing the hesitations and the indecision of many of the other delegates, he got to his feet and pronounced an impassioned oration: 'I say to you that this Assembly must not be adjourned. Let not one delegate leave this hall until the expectations of the People shall have been met. The People demand to know, once and for all, the form and nature of the State which shall govern them henceforth.' He then declared himself in favour of a republican constitution. The Republic was proclaimed on 9 February.

Goffredo Mameli (the author of the words of the Italian national anthem) wired Mazzini: 'Rome! Republic! Come!'

Mazzini, who had been elected deputy by universal suffrage, arrived in Rome on 5 March 1849. On the following day he addressed the Assembly, setting forth his programme with a lucidity unprecedented in these deliberations. After many hosannas he was elected Triumvir, together with Aurelio Saffi and Carlo Armellini. The three were to take charge of public affairs until such a time as, circumstances permitting, the infant republic might be endowed with normal governmental structures. Effectively, however, all the power was in Mazzini's hands, and the famous 'visionary' was soon to evince unsuspected realism and efficiency.

Meanwhile, the Pope's call for help had been answered by the most Catholic and the most reactionary nations of Europe – Austria, Spain, and the Kingdom of the Two Sicilies – and, surprisingly, by liberal and republican France. After the 1848 revolution had dethroned the Orléans dynasty, the French had proclaimed the Second Republic and had elected to its presidency Louis Napoleon Bonaparte, the nephew of Napoleon the Great. Louis Napoleon had taken part in the liberal revolution in the Papal States in 1831, and he now professed his sympathy for the cause of Italian liberation – so much so that there were rumours of a possible French intervention on the Piedmontese side. But the forces which supported his presidency were largely Catholic and conservative, and he was counting on their backing for the *coup d'état* which he was already planning to seize for himself the Imperial throne. Pressed by them Louis Napoleon agreed to take action against the Roman Republic and in favour of the Pope – in defiance of Article Six of the French Constitution, which forbade armed interventions in foreign countries.

Many in Europe were alarmed at the prospect of such an intervention. To the British, who were beginning to take a favourable interest in the cause of Italian unity, Louis Napoleon declared that he was going to Rome to make peace between the revolutionary forces and the Pope. He told Piedmont, on the other hand, that he was going there to forestall a possible Austrian attack. He assured the Apostolic Nuncio of full military support for the Pope, while in his own Parliament, where the more progressive forces opposed any interference in the affairs of the Roman Republic, he re-affirmed his support for the Romans and publicly rejected an Austrian proposal for a joint intervention.

The French expeditionary force set out with every intention of playing the protagonist. General Oudinot – Duke of Reggio, commander of the French troops – was under orders to limit the participation of the other armies to token demonstrations in support of the Pope. The French forces consisted of a General Staff, three brigades under the command of Generals Mollière, Levaillant and Chaydeson, three batteries, two companies of Engineers, and two squadrons of the First Regiment of Chasseurs à Cheval: a total of 7,800 men.

Oudinot told his soldiers that they were being sent abroad because France 'would not permit the destiny of the Italian people to be subordinated to the will of a foreign power'; he advised his officers to get themselves new uniforms so that they would look no less elegant than the Austrians they were going to fight. Thus everyone was given the impression that they were flying to the aid of the Roman people threatened by an Austrian invasion.

The French fleet sailed into Civitavecchia

Below the Roman walls by Gerolamo Induno. To the right on horseback is Aguyar.

(in Roman territory) on 25 April 1849. Nobody expected them; there had, in fact, been rumours that a contingent of French volunteers would soon be arriving to fight for the Republic. When they had landed they occupied the port and arrested the garrison of four hundred men – thus showing what their vaunted friendship for the Roman people really amounted to. Next day, Colonel Le Blanc went to Mazzini in Rome and repeated the official version: the invasion was an amicable action. And the Romans, therefore, should open their gates to the French army.

Mazzini convened the Assembly to discuss the French proposal. (His ingenuousness, and that of his colleagues, may surprise us today, but we must remember that they belonged to a generation which had been brought up on the notion that France was the homeland of democracy and liberty. Times had changed, and the liberal Second Republic was at this moment in the process of turning into the reactionary Second Empire.) Mazzini presented the problems thus: the Republic had

Luciano Manara. A veteran of the First War of Independence, the nobleman from Lombardy constituted the prestigious corps of bersaglieri *at his personal expense. (Above)*
Garibaldi's adversary, General Oudinot. (Below)

two options. She could 'resist, resist whatever the cost, resist in the name of independence, in the name of honour and of the right of all states, great or small, strong or weak, to govern themselves as they choose'. Or she could open the gates, trusting that international opinion would induce the French to respect her sovereignty. The Assembly voted in favour of resisting to the bitter end, and conferred absolute powers upon Mazzini. This decison was communicated to the French captain, Fabar. And as Fabar set out for Civitavecchia, the populace demonstrated against the French, to the cry of 'Viva l'Italie!'

Oudinot replied with a proclamation in which he reiterated his assurance of friendship. But – according to Jan Philip Koelman, a Dutch painter living in Rome who later fought for the Republic – the attitude of the Roman people to this move was somewhat sceptical.

The Romans were, in fact, excited by the idea of an armed conflict – a conflict which would prove to the world that their desire for liberty was not merely a matter of public pronouncements. And the contemptuous words spoken by Colonel Le Blanc to Mazzini burned in their ears: 'Les Italiens sont des poltrons, ils ne se battent pas.' Everyone wanted to volunteer for active duty; even the women drilled in the use of arms.

Saffi tells us that seven thousand citizens assembled in Piazza Santi Apostoli:

'... an extraordinary number, considering that most able bodied men had already been called up. Enthusiasm was at its peak. Everybody hoisted his beret on his bayonet and shouted in unison, "No foreigners in Rome!" The *vivas* for the Republic were endless. Deputies from the Assembly in tricolour sashes mingled with the fighting men; everyone kissed and embraced everyone else; weeping for joy and with brotherly love, soldiers, volunteers and representatives swore to fight to the death.'

An anonymous pencil portrait of Garibaldi during the defence of Rome. (Above)
The Caffè delle Arti in a rare drawing of the time. This was a meeting-place for the Italian and foreign artists of Rome. During the defence of the Republic the volunteers would gather there between battles to discuss politics. (Below)

Emotional outbursts were frequent among branches of the military such as the *carabinieri*, who were suspected of harbouring papalist sympathies: weeping, they begged to be sent to the front line, 'so that they might be the first to die'.

Meanwhile, preparations for the defence of Rome were underway. Barricades were set up throughout the city so that, should the French break through the walls, fighting might continue in the streets and alleys. A 'Barricade Commission' took charge of constructing them out of the most disparate materials imaginable. The doors of houses were to be left open, so that street-fighters could enter, if needed, and set up pockets of resistance. All horses were requisitioned, in the city and in the surrounding countryside, except those needed for agriculture. Three auxiliary companies of *butteri* (the cowboys of the Roman *campagna*) were organized. Known as 'Mounted Marksmen', they were armed with lances, pistols and sabres. They wore civilian dress, except for the red ribbons, tricolour cockades, and turkey feathers on their broad-brimmed hats.

Price ceilings were fixed and an austerity programme was imposed. Shops were ordered not to close – but the order was superfluous: public spirit ran so high that everyone remained at his job, even after the bombardment began. Telegraph stations were installed at the highest points of the city: the dome of St Peter's, the palace of the Consulta, the Capitol and the bell-tower of St Mary Major. Military hospitals, flying black flags, were set up in churches and palaces such as St John Lateran, San Giovanni dei Fiorentini, Santa Trinità dei Pellegrini, San Girolamo degli Schiavoni, San Giacomo, the Quirinal Palace and Palazzo Venezia.

To make up for the scarcity of munitions, the people contributed weapons of every description: rapiers, pistols, halberds, daggers, and even old blunderbusses and harquebuses unearthed in museums. Among new weapons invented for the occasion was a variety of hook on a long stick which would serve, it was hoped, to unhorse French cavalrymen: civilians, organized in neighbourhood committees, were armed with them. The smiths fashioned thousands of *triboli* (sharply barbed iron triangles), which could be scattered in the streets to stop the advance of enemy horses.

'The people evinced a tremendous enthusiasm', wrote an eye-witness, Giovita Lazzarini, and indeed they rose to the occasion. In a city where thievery was a way of life, Koelman tells us, everyone suddenly stopped stealing. At night citizens left lamps burning on their window sills, so that work could continue in the streets.

Defensive measures within the walls were thus worked out with considerable ingenuity. But the political leaders, with their limited military knowledge, failed to take a number of steps essential to the city's external defences, such as the reinforcement of the walls, the blocking of gates with earthworks and the demolition of buildings overlooking the walls which might serve the French as bases for attack.

At this point Luciano Manara reached Rome with his eight hundred *bersaglieri*, who had distinguished themselves the year before in Lombardy. They were well equipped and well trained; most of them were Lombards, and most were convinced monarchists with the Cross of Savoy on the buckles of their sword-belts. The *Garibaldini* – who also hastened from Rieti to Rome upon hearing of the French invasion – mockingly called them 'the aristocrats'.

The South Americans were given a rapturous welcome by the Romans. They were less elegant than Manara's *bersaglieri*, but with their experience and their reputation for perseverance in battle they brought with them a welcome sense of military security. They were quartered in the convent of San Silvestro. Here they found quantities of personal linen left behind by the nuns, who had fled; this they used to decorate the façade of the convent. George Thomas of the *Illustrated London News* has left us a vivid pictorial record of the *Garibaldini* at San Silvestro.

The armed forces of the Republic consisted of regular troops and of volunteer corps. The regular troops were made up of line infantry (11,700 men), a Roman Legion (810), a Bolognese Legion (550), the *bersaglieri del Tebro*, otherwise known as *Finanzieri mobili* or frontier guards (750, including horse and foot-soldiers), two Dragoon Regiments (590), *carabinieri*, mounted and on foot (602) and Artillery (700). There were, in addition, 450 engineers of various sorts: sappers, pontooneers, etc., and 256 others belonging to medical corps, technical corps and General Staff.

The volunteer units comprised a University Legion (450 men), the Roman Municipal Guard (1,400), the *battaglione Speranza* (Hope Battalion) of 100 boys known as the *Speranzini*, the Municipal Guard of Umbria (400), Garibaldi's Italian Legion (1,500 men including Masina's 90 Lancers), Antonio Arcioni's legion (300), Manara's *bersaglieri* (600), and the *bersaglieri* of Pietro Pietramellara (475).

Thus regular and volunteer personnel amounted to 21,633 in all. But the picture was not so rosy as the figures might suggest. Of the 21,633 only 13,944 were in or near the capital. The rest were stationed at Bologna, Ancona, Spoleto or Viterbo, or were scattered throughout the countryside fighting the papalist guerrillas known as *Sanfedisti*. And the composition of the regiments looked better on paper than in the flesh. Only one of the Dragoon Regiments was mounted; the other was not even equipped with weapons. Most of the seventy-four guns belonging to the Artillery were old and in poor repair, and of these only about thirty short-range pieces were in Rome. Bells were now melted down for bronze with which to make new guns. Of the various volunteer corps (who were to bear the brunt of the fighting), only the *Garibaldini* and Manara's *bersaglieri* had had much field experience, and only the latter were properly equipped. The rest were undisciplined, and force was often necessary to get them to do tiresome guard duty. Furthermore, ammunition was in very short supply.

Against this motley aggregation four armies were advancing: Spanish, Neapolitan, Austrian and French – the last two among the finest in the world.

The 13,944 fighting men in Rome were

divided into four brigades, under the commands of Garibaldi, Luigi Masi, Cherubino Savini and Bartolomeo Galletti. In overall command was the war minister, General Avezzana.

In 1849 the ancient walls of Rome were – as they are today – more or less intact. Their fortifications consisted of a series of twenty-one bastions, spaced at fairly regular intervals. Between the bastions the walls themselves were fragile, and there were no external defences such as ditches and ramparts. The River Tiber divides the city in two. The centre of town is on the left bank; Trastevere, the quarter on the right bank, was then a sort of working-class suburb. North-west of the city the walls run along the crest of a hill called the Janiculum, which towers above Trastevere. There, the Via Aurelia, the road from Civitavecchia and north-west Italy, enters the city through a gate called Porta San Pancrazio. This gate was defended by the bastion designated as No. 8.

The French, approaching from Civitavecchia, would have to cross the Tiber to reach the centre of the city. There were thus two points where they could be expected to attack. One was the Milvian Bridge, northeast of the Janiculum; the Romans therefore

blew up one span of it as a precaution. The other was Porta San Pancrazio, which gave access to Trastevere and to another bridge, Ponte Sisto.

The First Brigade (Garibaldi's) occupied the zone stretching from Porta Portese, on the right bank of the Tiber, to Porta San Pancrazio; the Second (Masi's), the zone from Porta San Pancrazio to St Peter's; the Third (Savini's), the zone from St Peter's to the Milvian Bridge. The Fourth Brigade (Galletti's) was kept in reserve at Piazza Cesarini, half-way between the Milvian Bridge and Porta San Pancrazio. Other corps were placed strategically about the city: the *carabinieri* and Manara's *bersaglieri* in Via della Lungara (in Trastevere below the Janiculum), and the *Finanzieri* on Monte Mario, a hill outside the walls overlooking St Peter's.

At 9 a.m. on 30 April 1849 the French army was sighted on the Via Aurelia, five miles from the walls of Rome. The bells of the Capitol sounded the alarm, and all the bells in the city rang out in reply. The Roman troops immediately made for the walls, joined by civilians with weapons of their own. Those who had no weapons climbed the Pincio (a hill opposite the Janiculum on the left bank) in order to watch the fighting from that vantage-point. Among the spectators were numerous women, anxious for their loved ones in

Bixio takes the French colonel, Picard, by the hair in the battle of 30 April 1849.

danger amid the clouds of smoke across the river.

At noon the French cannons began to bombard the Vatican, and a fresco in the Cappella Paolina and a coffered ceiling decorated by Michelangelo were destroyed. Oudinot ordered two columns to advance on St Peter's: Mollière's was to attack Porta Pertusa, at the back of the Leonine Walls (the fortifications of the Vatican), while Levaillant's was to make for Porta Angelica, which leads to St Peter's Square.

When the 33rd Regiment – the vanguard of Mollière's column – appeared, it met with such heavy fire from the Romans that Mollière was obliged to change tactics and to attack Porta Cavalleggeri, half-a-mile to his right. At the same time Levaillant's column suffered so many casualties that it was forced to retreat (Captain Fabar was among those killed.)

Mollière arrived at Porta Cavalleggeri and began his attack. But Garibaldi's men were installed on the Janiculum, overlooking this gate, in the gardens of Villa Corsini and Villa Pamphili, and were thus able to subject the French to relentless rifle fire.

Garibaldi was attacked in turn by a thousand men of the French 20th Infantry Regiment, which wrested Villa Corsini from three hundred University Legion volunteers. He was now in danger of being surrounded, so he called in Galletti with the Roman Legion. The ensuing struggle for the position was resolved only when Garibaldi ordered a bayonet charge along the entire front. This was carried out so energetically that the French were routed. In one charge Bixio's men managed to capture three hundred soldiers of the 20th Regiment, including their colonel, Picard, whom Bixio himself seized by the hair.

While the French were being dislodged from the Janiculum, Masi counter-attacked Levaillant outside Porta Angelica. By 5 p.m. the engagement was at an end. The French were in full retreat along the road to Civitavecchia, leaving behind some five hundred dead and wounded and 350 prisoners.

With fresh reinforcements, and without waiting for orders, Garibaldi pursued the French troops and caught up with them at Castel di Guido, a few miles from Rome. Through Ugo Bassi, whom they had taken prisoner at Villa Pamphili, the French then asked for an armistice, which Mazzini granted.

Mazzini was unwilling to inflict humiliation on Oudinot's army, on the grounds that this might provoke such a wave of patriotic outrage in France as to render impossible a negotiated settlement. This, as it turned out, was a grievous error. The expedition was already unpopular in France; it had been fiercely questioned in parliament and there had been street demonstrations against it. A total defeat of Oudinot's forces might quite possibly have resulted in a public outcry for an end to the war. Delighted with the armistice, Oudinot remained at Castel di Guido; the Romans turned their attention to the wounded.

Sixty-nine of the Republican troops had been killed, and some two hundred wounded. The Italian Legion had suffered the heaviest losses, especially among the officers, who had fought in the front lines. Garibaldi himself was wounded in the abdomen, but he implored the doctor who treated him, Ripari (later to become a surgeon with the Garibaldian troops), not to let the fact be known: the legend of his invulnerability was extremely useful psychologically.

Both the French and the Republican wounded were taken to the hospitals which had been set up for the emergency. The French were touched by the kindness with which they were treated, and explained repeatedly that they thought they had come to Italy to fight the Austrians. A committee of women, established on 27 April, was in charge of nursing the wounded (a kind of female *Almanach de Gotha* of the Italian *Risorgimento*). Among its members were Marietta Pisacane (wife of the hero who was to die later while trying to stir up a revolt in the Kingdom of the Two Sicilies), Giulia Bovio Paolucci and Cristina Trivulzio di Belgiojoso, who had previously belonged to the revolutionary *Carbonaro* movement and who, as an exile in Paris and in Switzerland, had kept a salon frequented by Hugo, Thiers, Liszt, George Sand, Chopin and De Musset. Upon her return to Italy Cristina took part in the Milanese revolt of 1848 and organized a volunteer corps at her own expense. Anita Garibaldi was also there: she had come from Nice to be at her husband's side, crossing the French and Austrian lines. Many women of the people also offered their services, and there were actually more nurses than were needed in the hospitals.

But it soon became apparent that there were not enough bandages to go round, and the populace was asked to donate bedsheets or anything else that might be suitable. Giovanni Cadolini, a Garibaldian volunteer and later a senator, tells of a wagon which passed through Via delle Muratte collecting this material. A soldier knocked at a door and called out, 'Linen for our wounded brothers!' At once, from all the houses in the street, there came a shower of sheets, shirts and cloth of every description. So much linen was collected that the surplus was sent to the French camp, together with doctors, camp-beds and medical supplies. These were most welcome, as until now the wounded at Castel di Guido had been stretched out on the ground, their wounds dressed with makeshift bandages.

In the country, meanwhile, the clergy were organizing bands of papalist partisans known as *Sanfedisti*, who were active mainly in the smaller towns. Often at variance with each other, these groups were not powerful enough to represent a serious military threat; but their ferocity sufficed to sow panic among the rural population. The *Sanfedista* oath was certainly uncompromising:

'I swear to remain firm in the defence of the holy cause which I have embraced. I shall not spare a single member of the infamous gang of liberals, whatever their birth, family or wealth; I shall not be moved by the tears of infants or of old men; I shall shed to the last drop the infamous liberal blood, regardless of sex or rank; I swear implacable hatred for all the enemies of our one, true, holy Roman Catholic religion.'

And indeed they were guilty of hair-raising atrocities. Until now, the Roman population

'A Garibaldino Volunteer during the Defence of Rome' by Gerolamo Induno. Induno was one of the major painters of the Italian Risorgimento and as a Garibaldino took part in all the campaigns until 1866, painting both in watercolours and in oils the things he saw.

had continued to treat the clergy with respect. But the crimes of the *Sanfedisti* provoked violent reactions. Three vine-dressers who had the misfortune to be mistaken for Jesuits were murdered at Ponte Sant'Angelo, and six priests were shot in the catacombs of San Callisto, by order of Callimaco Zambianchi – whom Mazzini arrested immediately. On the whole, however, the population remained admirably calm – so much so that the Prussian consul asked the government to remove the armed guard which it had posted in front of the consulate.

The French officers who had been taken prisoner were invited to dinner on 30 April by Colonel Cleter, a Frenchman who lived in Rome and who had embraced the Republican cause. All joined in a toast to the two republics – the Roman and the French – which (with the exception of Switzerland) were at that time the only republics in Europe. Other French residents did their best to convert their captured compatriots. (It was still hoped that the French government might change its policy.) As a token of good will, the French prisoners were released, and the officers had their swords returned to them – with the exception, it seems, of Colonel Picard: a Belgian student by the name of Victor, who had helped capture him, had the sword in his possession and was unwilling to give it up. But the French sent the released prisoners to Corsica and later to North Africa, so that they could not report to the press on what they had seen and heard in Rome. (Oudinot had already released his own version of the facts.) In exchange for the prisoners, the French released the garrison which they had arrested at Civitavecchia.

On 1 May word came that Neapolitan troops had invaded the Republic from the South, with twenty thousand men, thirty-six cannon and a cavalry division. As the French had done, they announced that they were motivated solely by friendship for the Roman people.

On 4 May Garibaldi advanced to meet the Neapolitans with his brigade of 2,700 men and with Manara's *bersaglieri*. He set out at eight in the evening, leaving Rome at Porta del Popolo and heading north on the Via Flaminia – hoping thus to mislead the enemy

spies in the city. During the night he changed his route, and by morning he was at Tivoli, some twenty miles east of Rome. The Neapolitans were encamped at Velletri, further to the south, and knew nothing of this manoeuvre.

Garibaldi was aware that, with the exception of a few veterans, most of his troops were inexperienced. He therefore distributed his Montevideans evenly throughout the various detachments, so that they might provide inspiration and leadership in action. The experiment was a success, and the technique was repeated on future occasions. As many details as possible were left to subordinates, so that Garibaldi himself might be free to circulate among the troops to spur them on during the course of the battle.

On the evening of 8 May the *Garibaldini* encountered a Neapolitan vanguard at Monte Porzio Catone, and forced it to retreat. The next day the Neapolitans, with seven thousand men and eight hundred cavalry, again advanced on Palestrina.

The Neapolitans formed two columns, and tried to encircle the *Garibaldini*. At 4 p.m. they began shelling the legion. The

The attack on the Casino dei Quattro Venti. Garibaldi can be seen on the right.

The Casino dei Quattro Venti photographed just after the fall of Rome. The condition of the building gives a very good idea of the ferocity of the fighting around it.

Garibaldini not only stood fast but returned fire, and then counter-attacked with bayonets. The Neapolitans retreated, and the retreat soon turned into a rout. So precipitate was their flight, in fact, that Garibaldi suspected trickery and forwent pursuit. On 11 May the report drawn up by Garibaldi's Chief of Staff, Francesco Daverio, announcing the victory of Palestrina, reached Rome by the same post as some letters addressed to Neapolitan officers who, evidently, had expected to be in the capital by that date. The Neapolitans were not heard from again, and Garibaldi re-entered Rome on the 12th with three captured cannon.

His presence there was necessitated by dramatic new developments. Nine hundred Spaniards, including four hundred cavalry, had landed in the South and were now marching on Rome, while twenty thousand Austrians, commanded by General Wimpfen,

had invaded the Republic from the North. On 7 May the Austrians had taken Ferrara, and on 8 May they had laid siege to Bologna, which was defended only by the Fourth Infantry Regiment, a detachment of *Finanzieri*, a unit of *carabinieri* and 150 University volunteers led by Colonel Boldrini, who died a hero's death in defence of the city. On the 15 May, after eight days of incessant bombardment, Bologna surrendered. The Austrians then marched on Ancona.

Meanwhile, a number of personages well known for their devotion to liberty were arriving in Rome to offer their services. These included the Polish General Nybinski, the Austrian Colonel Haugg of the famous Viennese Academic Legion, a group of French republican officers including Major Gabriel Laviron, the Englishman Hugh Forbes, and the Swiss Hoffstetter – all of whom were to become officers in Garibaldi's Legion. The Second and Third Infantry Line Regiments appeared, and four batteries of Swiss mounted artillery, who had distinguished themselves the year before in the

Lombard campaign and had now entered the service of the Republic. Medici's Legion arrived with three hundred men, as did the Polish Legion, with two hundred men under the command of Aleksandr Milbitz, who was himself to become a Garibaldian officer. The foreign community in Rome formed a new Legion of 120 men, commanded by Captain Gerard – oddly enough, except for sixteen English and seven Americans, this corps was made up almost exclusively of Frenchmen. Other foreigners preferred to enlist in existing units, including a Swede called Palm who tested his comrades' patience by constantly repeating that he had not forgotten his military training every time he scored a hit.

About five hundred foreigners, all told, participated in the defence of the Roman Republic, which they firmly believed to be the last bastion of liberalism in Europe.

On 14 May General Rosselli was placed in charge of the Republican army, since the double post of War Minister and Army Chief of Staff had proved to be too much for Avezzana. Rosselli was not a bad general, but his approach to war was academic: he could think only in terms of well-ordered groups moving in regular formations upon a battle-field. Furthermore, he was utterly without charismatic appeal – and this was a serious defect in an army made up largely of volunteers. Rosselli, in fact, felt only contempt for volunteers, whereas Garibaldi's special talent lay in knowing how to make the most of their spontaneity and their indifference to danger. Nevertheless, the Triumvirs chose Rosselli over Garibaldi, who, they said, was more like an Indian chief than a general.

Full of optimism, the Romans advanced to meet the Neapolitans, who had once again invaded the territory of the Republic. This time they were led by their king, Ferdinand II, in person. Their force consisted of 16,000 men and 52 cannon. The vanguard of the Republican army – the first brigade, under Garibaldi – made straight for the Neapolitan camp at Velletri. On 19 May Ferdinand II ordered General Casella to lead a sortie from the town with two cavalry squadrons and one infantry battalion.

Masina, with his ninety Lancers, charged the Neapolitan hussars, who were followed by the infantry. But Masina's men were repulsed, and they abandoned the field, leaving their leader behind. (Masina saved himself only by expert swordsmanship.) Garibaldi, accompanied by Bueno and Aguyar, tried to head off the fleeing Lancers, but in the confusion the three of them were thrown from their horses and trampled. Beside himself with rage, Garibaldi cried, 'Lancers – return to your duty, in the name of God!' Before he could recover from his spill, he was charged by a major of the Neapolitan hussars, and would certainly have been killed had not Aguyar seized his lance and brought down the enemy horse with its rider. At this point the fifteen-year-old *Speranzini* counter-attacked with bayonets, permitting the three badly shaken officers to get to their feet. Then, together with the 'South Americans', Daverio and Bixio joined the *Garibaldini* in a charge.

The fighting was intense, but finally the Neapolitans retreated to the safety of Velletri. Then – without even waiting for another, decisive engagement – they withdrew to their own territories. Garibaldi wanted to pursue them, but Rosselli was against taking the risk, and this led to a bitter altercation between the two leaders.

The flight of the Neapolitans was due, in part, to superstitious fear – the notion had spread among the soldiers that the *Garibaldini* were invulnerable: when they were shot down they sprang up again immediately. The legend arose, according to Hoffstetter, because the adolescent *Speranzini,* most of whom were too short to handle their rifles with ease, were in the habit of flinging themselves to the ground to reload, and then of jumping up again to fire.

On 31 May Garibaldi returned to Rome and again dug in on the Janiculum. On that very day, after nearly a month of intensive negotiations, Mazzini and the French envoy De Lesseps (the engineer who was later to construct the Suez Canal) reached a political agreement. But Oudinot refused to confirm it. The long-expected anti-Republican reaction had set in in Paris: the liberal press was muzzled, and Victor Hugo was hampered in his attempts to speak out in the Chamber of Deputies. Oudinot was sent reinforcements and ordered to bring the campaign to a

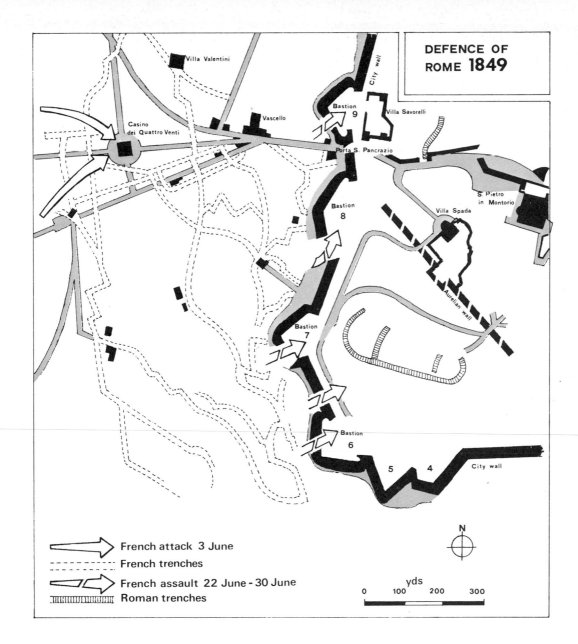

DEFENCE OF
ROME 1849

Villa Valentini

Casino
dei Quattro Venti

Vascello

Bastion
9

Villa Savorelli

Porta S. Pancrazio

S. Pietro
in Montorio

Bastion
8

Villa Spada

Aurelian wall

Bastion
7

City wall

Bastion
6

5   4   City wall

N

French attack 3 June
French trenches
French assault 22 June - 30 June
Roman trenches

yds
0   100   200   300

speedy end. He was aware that General Jean B. P. Vaillant, who had been sent to assist him, had instructions to take command of the troops should Oudinot fail in his assignment. The British diplomatic mission, after a feeble attempt at mediation, abandoned the Republic to its fate.

Oudinot now had thirty thousand infantry, four thousand cavalry, forty pieces of field artillery and forty-eight of heavy-calibre siege artillery, as well as howitzers and mortars.

On the night of 2 June most of the Republican forces were enjoying a furlough in Rome, secure in the knowledge that the armistice was to remain in effect until the 4th. Officers and men were scattered about the city, in private houses and inns; only a few had remained in barracks. Garibaldi himself, suffering from an attack of rheumatism, was reposing in the Hotel Inghilterra. Many of his followers were at the Caffe delle Belle Arti (a favourite haunt of artists and liberals), singing revolutionary and patriotic songs. Koelman remarks that the sound of those young voices singing in unison first *La Marseillaise*, then *God Save the Queen*, then *Wilhelmus van*

Four photographs of the area around Porta San Pancrazio during the defence of Rome. An anonymous photographer immortalized the 360° panorama from Villa Savorelli in 1849, painting in the moving figures on the eleven original plates.

Nassauwen, Was des deutschen Vaterland, and so on, filled hearers with hope for a better Europe.

At three in the morning the French moved on Rome. Outside Porta San Pancrazio there were two villas, Villa Corsini and Villa Pamphili, both surrounded by large parks. Villa Corsini was the closer to the city walls. On this night four hundred men were on guard in Villa Pamphili. Two French columns, led by Mollière and Levaillant, entered the grounds, from the south and from the west respectively. Taken completely by surprise, the Roman soldiers were unable to put up much of a resistance; some of them escaped to the nearby convent of San Pancrazio, while the rest were surrounded and taken prisoner in the garden of the Villa Pamphili.

The French then occupied the convent, Villa Valentini, Casa Torlonia and Villa Corsini. The troops took refuge at Il Vascello, another villa some 250 yards from Porta San Pancrazio. Then Galletti, of Garibaldi's division, ordered Masi's regiment to counter-attack: the objective was the Casino dei Quattro Venti, a building in the park of Villa Corsini which dominated the entire position. They succeeded in taking it, but lost it again after an hour-and-a-half.

Considerable time was needed to rouse the officers scattered about the city. Garibaldi arrived at Porta San Pancrazio at 5.30 a.m. With the few men at his disposal he began a series of daring but foolhardy assaults upon the Casino. That day, in fact, Garibaldi committed the most serious error of his military career – and repeated it a number of times: at an enormous cost in human lives, he sent his men out on frontal attacks without giving them adequate back-up support from his artillery.

The Roman forces now occupied the area between Porta San Pancrazio and Il Vascello. Among the reinforcements arriving on the Janiculum was a military band, which played *La Marseillaise* non-stop: the idea, apparently, was to let the French soldiers know that they

were not fighting against Austrians, but against good republicans like themselves. However, in the din of battle, the music sounded more like a funeral march than a glorious hymn to liberty. Between 9 and 10 a.m. the Romans mounted two more furious attacks on the French positions, particularly on the Casino dei Quattro Venti.

Finally the cannons went into action in support of the infantry. At 10 a.m. Manara's *bersaglieri* charged; then fell back under heavy fire. Manara harangued them: 'Lombards! Your task is to capture the villa – or die in the attempt!' At eleven they charged again; this time they took the building and, stung by Manara's words, refused to retreat despite a fierce French counter-attack. They were leaving themselves open to massacre. The twenty-two-year-old captain Enrico Dandolo was killed in the charge; and his brother Emilio, with twenty *bersaglieri*, led yet another attack on the Casino. He was later to admit that his purpose in doing so was to recover his brother's body – an act of needless heroism that cost fourteen lives. Garibaldi himself had to order the *bersaglieri* to withdraw.

After 1 p.m. Bixio went into action. To reach the Casino dei Quattro Venti from the gate of the villa it was necessary to pass down a narrow lane some two hundred yards long – under French fire all the way. Bixio led a charge down this lane, and his horse was shot out from under him. He obtained a new horse, and charged again. This time he and his men reached the veranda of the Casino; as they were about to storm the interior, a French counter-attack forced them back. Bixio was wounded but, miraculously, the *Garibaldini* managed to carry him to safety.

Later in the afternoon Daverio led a fresh onslaught, took the Casino, but – before he could consolidate his position – was dislodged by yet another French counter-attack. Daverio was killed. Then Masina made the attempt, against Garibaldi's expressed wishes (he had been wounded, and he had already led four attacks that day). Masina charged down the lane with his Lancers, reached the Casino and was about to take it when he was shot down by a violent burst of rifle fire. His crazed horse carried his corpse for seventy yards and there Masina was found, more than

French artillery post at the Casino dei Quattro Venti. In the background, Porta San Pancrazio. Closer to the right is the Vascello.

a month later, with seventy bullet holes in his body.

News of the deaths of Daverio and Masina had a tremendous effect on the Roman troops. Shouting the names of the dead leaders like madmen, they charged the Casino with Laviron at their head. They took it, only to be driven out again. For the rest of the afternoon, one desperate attack after another failed to attain the objective. Garibaldi, clearly recognizable in his poncho, stayed in the midst of the fray. At his side were Manara, who had taken over from the dead Daverio, and the faithful Aguyar, who had recently been made a lieutenant.

By 6 p.m. the battle was over. The French had definitely occupied an excellent position from which they could control the entire right bank of the Tiber. They began at once to fortify the Janiculum, especially the area to the left of Porta San Pancrazio; from there they could concentrate their fire upon bastions 6 and 7. Yet they had not succeeded in entering Rome. Outside the walls, the Romans had kept possession of a few buildings, including Il Vascello. This was held fast by Medici, and

nothing short of an order from Garibaldi could persuade him to abandon it.

On that 3 June Garibaldi's division alone had lost one thousand men, including a hundred officers. The heaviest losses were sustained among the Italian Legion and Manara's *bersaglieri*.

Feats of daring verging upon recklessness had been the order of the day: the charges of Masina and the others down the lane leading to the Casino are good examples. Then there was the unknown *Garibaldino* who leapt with a keg of gunpowder into a hut where some French soldiers had barricaded themselves, blowing them, and himself, to smithereens; and the *bersagliere* Morini who charged the enemy despite a mangled leg, using his musket as a crutch.

The Republican troops were so incensed at the treachery of the French, who had attacked without warning while the armistice was still in force, that some sought to avenge their dead comrades by murdering French prisoners; in several instances the officers had to use force to prevent this sort of killing. The people of Rome were equally enraged. The French had bombed the city indiscriminately all day long, and numerous civilians had been killed. Here again the *Garibaldini* were occasionally obliged to protect their prisoners at bayonet point.

The battle had brought a hero's death to many a young Italian. It also meant the beginning of the end for the Roman Republic. In the evening companies of weeping women circled round the hill, searching for their loved ones.

The French mounted their batteries of siege artillery, dug trenches, and reinforced the positions which they had occupied. Meanwhile, the Romans set up two 32-calibre pieces on Monte Testaccio, across the Tiber from Porta Portese, and three 24-calibre pieces on the Aventine, plus a battery on the Celio. With these inadequate means – they had neither howitzers nor mortars – the Romans, between 5 and 9 June, did what they could to harass the French as they prepared to lay siege to the city. Violent exchanges of artillery fire took place. The batteries on bastions 8 and 9, to the right and left of Porta San Pancrazio, were particularly active. These were commanded by Ludovico Calandrelli and by a Captain Lopez.

The scarcity, and the inferior fire power, of the ordnance at their disposal inspired the

Republican battery on the Janiculum walls. The artillery cross fire was without respite and many civilians and monuments suffered.

Romans to think up some ingenious stratagems. The bastions around the Vatican were furnished with antique culverins dragged out of the museum; fortunately – for the Roman gunners – these were never used. And to reduce the risk of losing precious cannons, whenever one was fired from a particular bastion it was quickly hauled away and remounted on another; so that by the time the French could return fire, the cannon was out of danger. The Swiss mounted artillery units took a leading part in these operations.

On the morning of 3 June the Sauvan Brigade of the Guesviller Division had occupied Monte Mario and attacked the Milvian Bridge. But the bridge had already been partly demolished by the Romans, who were defending it from the left bank; the French were therefore unable to cross the Tiber.

On the 4 June a detachment of voltigeurs succeeded in repairing the bridge, and got across the river. They were promptly repulsed, however, by the University Legion. On the night of the 5th the French attacked again, with the Vincennes chasseurs. This time they not only established a bridgehead but advanced along the left bank, and occupied a strong position at Casa Polverosi, halfway between the Milvian bridge and Porta del Popolo. The University battalion and the

Polish Legion dug in at Villa Poniatowski, about half-a-mile from Porta de Popolo. A Roman battery installed on Monte Parioli, overlooking this zone, did its best to harry the French.

There were no further developments on the front until 11 June; in fact the University battalion asked to be transferred to Porta San Pancrazio, where fighting still went on. But on the morning of the 11th, just as they were setting out for San Pancrazio, they were called back: the French attack had begun. In the afternoon the Polish Legion and the University battalion attacked Casa Polverosi, which was defended by the French 13th Line Regiment under Captain Leclerc. The French were surrounded; they called for reinforcements, and the Romans then found themselves caught between two lines of fire. Colonel Berti-Pichat, with the Bolognese Legion, brought succour: his bayonet counter-attack saved the Poles and the University corps, but failed to drive back the French.

For three days the hostilities continued on Monte Parioli and in the surrounding area, taking the form of small skirmishes of unprecedented savagery. An eye-witness wrote, 'The yells of the fighting-men and the groans of the wounded, the crackle of flames and the thunder of guns – the scene was one of utter horror.'

On 14 June Colonel Milbitz ordered Captain Podulack to charge the enemy with bayonets. Podulack called his attention to the numerical superiority of the French, and expressed serious doubts as to the advisability of the action. Milbitz replied, 'My son, even here the freedom of Poland is at stake.' Podulack and his men charged, but they were soon surrounded and Podulack was wounded. As he lay there a French officer signalled to him to surrender; he responded with a pistol shot, whereupon he was riddled with bullets. His friend Captain Taczanowski had tried to save him, but was himself surrounded and wounded. Pichat's Bolognese then charged with bayonets, failing to rescue Taczanowski, who was taken prisoner by the French, though they did recover Podulack's body.

When they had taken Monte Parioli, the French moved into Villa Borghese. But the Roman battery on the Pincio prevented them from advancing further. On 12 June Oudinot, who had also suffered reverses in the zone near the Milvian bridge, called for a truce and for peace-talks. But the Romans knew that he would insist on their unconditional surrender, and rejected his request. In Paris and Lyons, meanwhile, the people were erecting barricades in protest against the French attack on Rome. These demonstrations were brutally suppressed, but some of the French regiments which had landed at Civitavecchia now refused to march on Rome. On 13 June Oudinot cut several of the aqueducts upon which the city depended for its water supply, and resumed his bombardment. The French bombardment continued, except for brief

Defence of the Vascello. In the background, holding a pistol, Medici can be seen directing the resistance to yet another French attack. His heroic defence of the villa, which he abandoned only upon receiving Garibaldi's specific order to do so, was later to be rewarded by the granting of the title of Marchese del Vascello in the Royalist army.

pauses, for the entire month of June. It was aimed directly at the city, and the damage included the destruction of many priceless works of art. The consulates of foreign governments protested, but Oudinot ignored them.

The hardest hit were the people of Trastevere. Their hatred of the French grew so intense that thickets of bayonets were required to save prisoners from reprisals.

At Porta San Pancrazio the fighting continued day after day, especially in the area of Il Vascello, which was still held by Medici. The building, by this time, was virtually reduced to a pile of rubble. One of the men holed up within described his experience:

'It was horrendous to be inside a house where a bullet might ricochet off any surface at any moment; where if a cannonball didn't get you, you might still be crushed by falling masonry; where the air was full of smoke and dust and the moans of the wounded; where the floor was slippery with blood; and where the entire building shook under the impact of the cannonade.'

But the struggle went on. The Romans never grew dispirited, nor did they cease to jibe at the French. One day a joker from the Italian Legion hoisted a tricolour over Garibaldi's headquarters with 'Good morning, Cardinal Oudinot' written on it – this, together with the expression 'soldier of the Pope', was the worst insult with which one could hope to offend the Frenchmen.

Manara was appointed Chief of Staff of Garibaldi's division. He had magazines constructed in the shelter of the walls, organized ambulance crews and strengthened the fortifications as far as possible.

The ordinary citizens who came flocking to the walls were divided into groups known as the 'Seven Hills Squads'. Their job was to do whatever running about was necessary, so as to keep the movement of troops to a minimum. Even children were assigned to take messages, to carry ammunition and to retrieve shells – the government paid 16 *baiocchi* (about 3p) for every unexploded French projectile, and the boys flung themselves upon live shells like kamikazes, protected only by wet rags or mud.

Many women chose to remain beside their men, and contributed in their own way to the defence of the city. They carried ammunition, loaded rifles, or enlisted as *vivandières*, as sappers, or even as gunners. Colomba Antonietti, a sapper, was killed on the parapet of bastion 13, having fought beside her husband in all the battles of the Roman Republic.

The ceaseless bombardment, and the fire of snipers, began to tell on even the steeliest nerves. Garibaldian officers accused Colonel Amadei of the Engineers of having failed to dig enough trenches for the defence of the more exposed positions; Amadei retorted that the *Garibaldini* had never given him enough fire cover to enable him to do his job properly. General Rosselli accused the volunteer corps of improprieties in their behaviour towards the regular troops – but he never relieved them, so that it was they who had to bear, without interruption, the brunt of the enemy attacks. Garibaldi had an officer arrested for insubordination. Rosselli was openly accused of incompetence, and there were constant mutterings about treason.

The truth was that the French had already won the war, and that the Republicans – who for two months had not even had time to wash the gunpowder off their faces – did not want to admit it. Spies were everywhere. Sleep was next to impossible, thanks to the rockets which continued to explode throughout the night. And the number of troops had decreased alarmingly: even though many of the wounded had returned to the ramparts, the death-toll had been enormous.

The French cannons had made a breach in the wall between bastions 6 and 7. On the night of 21 June an élite detachment of six hundred men, commanded by Colonel Wiel, forced their way through the breach. The Union Regiment, which was supposed to be guarding it, was taken by surprise and offered little resistance. When Garibaldi was ordered to retake the position, he refused; it would have been, he said, a stupendous but futile spectacle.

The city was by now quite demoralized, and Oudinot could have occupied it easily. But instead he chose to intensify the bombardment. He occupied bastions 6 and 7, and on them he erected batteries, trained upon the city. At the same time he increased pressure on Il Vascello – but Medici continued to hold out.

On 28 June the quarrels between Garibaldi and Rosselli came to a head, and Garibaldi resigned his post, though Manara eventually prevailed on him to reconsider.

On the night of 29 June there was a violent storm. Around 2 a.m. all the French batteries began once more to bombard the city; and while the bombs fell indiscriminately, the French took bastion 8.

On the 30th, early in the morning, Garibaldi at last ordered Medici to abandon Il Vascello, where he had been barricaded for twenty-five days, and to join forces with Manara and himself; they were to form a third line of defence, inside the walls. The core of the new defence position was Villa Spada, which was held by Manara's *bersaglieri* and by a Swiss battery. The French attacked the villa and took it, but Manara counter-attacked at once and wrested it away

Villa Spada, one of the last pockets of resistance. Luciano Manara died here. This photograph was taken a few days after the fall of the city.

from them. The French then encircled it. Garibaldi charged, and dispersed them. A series of skirmishes ensued, and for the whole morning the *Garibaldini* and the French fought bitterly, on the Janiculum, just inside the walls. The 'Pino' – the last battery remaining in Roman hands – fired incessantly. With all the attacks and counter-attacks the losses on both sides were so heavy that a truce had to be called so that both armies could gather in their dead. Among those killed were Luciano Manara, the twenty-four-year-old commander of the Lombard *bersaglieri*, and Andrés Aguyar. As his comrades carried away the corpse of the South American lieutenant, a small boy in a red shirt followed the stretcher, weeping disconsolately and crying out, 'Andrés, Andrés!' It was Menotti, Garibaldi's son, who had been tied to Aguyar by a special bond of affection. Manara's body was taken first to the Ospedale della Scala, and then to the church of San Lorenzo; it was attended by the surviving members of his now illustrious corps of *bersaglieri*. That morning, a letter had arrived from his wife, announcing the birth of a daughter.

In the final conflict over five hundred Romans had lost their lives. Acts of heroism

French assault on Bastion 9. This was the last defence to be captured by General Oudinot. Calandrelli was in charge of this key position.

were innumerable, for no one wanted to survive a defeat.

French bombs from Monte Parioli rained on the Pincio, on Via di Ripetta and on Piazza di Spagna. At San Pietro in Montorio and at the 'Pino' the *Garibaldini* were launching their last attacks: 'To the cries of *viva l'Italia* and *vive la France*', writes Vecchi, 'the men hurled themselves upon each other, stabbing, slashing, killing with bayonets and daggers.' When their weapons gave out they fought with their bare hands, or threw stones or anything else that could cause injury. Lieutenant Casini of the Roman artillery abandoned his gun only after his skull was split by ten sabre-strokes and when ten bayonet-thrusts had punctured his leg, according to the *Gazette médical de Paris* of January 1850. Many of the gunners on the bastions were found dead after the last French attack, still clinging to their cannons. Lieutenant Tiburzi withstood seventeen bayonet wounds before he finally fell. A gunner who had broken his sabre defended his post with a cannon-brush; when this was hacked to shreds he fought with his bare hands until, run through by countless bayonets, at last he died. The drummer-boys threw their drums away, seized the weapons of the fallen, and joined the fight. Corporal Parucco of the second company of the Second Grenadiers Regiment fought with his rifle-

stock until he was crucified to a wall by twenty-three bayonets. The stench of corpses drifted down the hillside and into the city. Garibaldi remained in the midst of the mêlée, flailing away with his sabre. The fighting spread down the Janiculum into Trastevere, where the surviving soldiers dug in for the last stand at Ponte Sisto.

Garibaldi was summoned to the Assembly to give his opinion as to the feasibility of further resistance. He arrived oozing blood from several wounds, his sabre twisted and his uniform in shreds; he advised against resisting further. The French, he told the deputies, would not risk a battle in the city streets; they would only continue the bombardment from the surrounding hills.

On 30 June 1849 the Assembly voted to surrender.

The delegation presented itself to Oudinot (who was in full dress), silently placed the document containing the Assembly's resolution before him, and stepped back. The resolution read, 'In the name of God and of the People: the Roman Constitutional Assembly renounces a defence which has become impossible, and remains in its place. The Triumvirs are entrusted with the execution of this decree.'

Oudinot was perplexed by this laconic resolution, and asked under what conditions the Romans expected to capitulate. Enrico Cernuschi, the leader of the delegation, replied, 'You may enter the city and do what you will – Rome has no one left to defend her.' The French did enter the city, but not until 3 July. The population received them with an icy silence, broken only by a few shouted insults to Pius IX and to the foreign invaders. The only individuals who welcomed them – clerics and reactionaries – were knifed on the spot, and the soldiers did nothing to save them.

Garibaldi convened his troops at St Peter's and said to them:

'Fortune, which today has betrayed us, will smile on us tomorrow. I am leaving Rome. Whoever wishes to continue the war against the foreigner, let him come with me. I offer neither pay nor quarters nor provisions; I offer hunger, thirst, forced marches, battles and death.'

Four thousand men followed him. They set out from Porta San Giovanni at 5 p.m. on 2 July 1849. They left behind them 3,500 dead and wounded: that was the cost of a mere month's defence of the Roman Republic.

The army that left Rome included the remnants of the various corps: the *bersaglieri* of Manara and those of Pietramellara, the Union battalion with their brown tunics and the *Speranzini* with their red shirts with green piping. The Italian Legion had gone back to wearing their glorious red shirts on the 27th of the previous month. The University Legion, the Dragoons, and Masina's Lancers were all represented. Anita, who was five months pregnant, had cut her hair short and donned the Legion's uniform – blouse, trousers and boots. She wore the tricolour sash across her breast, and a slouch hat with a plume on her head, and she carried a sabre and pistol. Ugo Bassi also had a red shirt, but he wore a traditional priest's hat and a crucifix round his neck, and he carried a bag with the sacred vessels for Mass.

Garibaldi's goal was Venice, which was still standing up to the Austrian siege. His northward march has been described by experts as a masterpiece of the military art. The troops had to cover more than five hundred miles, mostly through mountainous terrain, with four enemy armies closing in on them: the Austrians were moving south from Ancona, while the French, the Spaniards and the Neapolitans were in pursuit from the south. Garibaldi sought to elude them, first heading east towards the Abruzzi and then north to Terni, where he was joined by Hugh Forbes's column, which had been fighting the *Sanfedisti* in the area. Then he marched through Tuscany, with a series of manoeuvres which thoroughly baffled the pursuing armies. He and his men, faint with hunger and dropping with exhaustion, moved by night as much as possible to conceal their whereabouts. The local populations – who feared reprisals – were often reluctant to help them, and a few towns actually locked their gates. When this occurred at Arezzo, the men were so angry that Garibaldi could scarcely restrain them from storming it.

The hardships of the march, and constant skirmishes with the enemy (especially with the Austrians, the most relentless of Garibaldi's pursuers) further reduced the ranks of the *Garibaldini*. Discipline was by now a thing of the past. There were many desertions, and some of the troops turned highwaymen.

On 31 July the army arrived at San Marino, that tiny, age-old republic in north-central Italy. Fifteen hundred men were left, driven nearly wild by a month's continuous trek through the mountains. San Marino offered its hospitality to the *Garibaldini*, but the Austrians surrounded the little state and demanded that it expel them.

Garibaldi then officially dissolved his force, leaving each man free to decide his own fate. In the night, with 250 of his staunchest followers, he slipped through the Austrian lines and made for Cesenatico, on the Adriatic. He reached this town the next day, seized thirteen fishing-boats, and set sail for Venice. On the night of 2 August they were spotted by the Austrian fleet, which opened fire and captured eight of the boats. Garibaldi, with the other five, managed to get ashore near Magnavacca; he and the survivors then sought refuge in the marshes of Comacchio. He divided the men into two groups, the better to elude the Austrians. But the group led by Ugo Bassi was captured immediately, and all the men were shot on the spot.

With Garibaldi was Anita. The women of San Marino had implored her to remain in the safety of their city, but she had insisted on going on. All she would accept from them was a woman's dress, since her condition no longer permitted her to go about clothed as a man.

Garibaldi's group wandered for two days in the marshes, tortured by thirst and by fear. Anita was by now in a piteous state, her face was livid and her body swollen. Over and over she begged for water. 'Have patience, Anita, have patience', her husband repeated mechanically – there was nothing he could do.

On the afternoon of 4 August, in a farmhouse where they had found shelter, Anita died. 'José, the children', were her last words. With the Austrians in hot pursuit, Garibaldi hadn't even time to bury her. Thus died the hero's wife, the red-shirts' first heroine.

Garibaldi and Major Culiolo then crossed the Apennines again, in the opposite direction. They were helped by a chain of patriots who sheltered them and guided them safely as far as Genoa. Here they were immediately arrested by the Piedmont authorities, but were released again, after an outcry in the press, on condition that they leave Piedmont. Before departing, Garibaldi visited his mother and his three children in Nice. Then he sailed to London, and thence to New York. He was not to return for ten years.

Death of Anita. Exhausted by the long retreat, and without medical assistance, Anita died in a peasant's house in the swamps of the Comacchio.

The *Garibaldini* who were arrested at San Marino or captured at Magnavacca were marched off, escorted by an entire division and under horrifying conditions, to Pietole, near Mantua. No one was allowed to stop for any reason whatever, and for any infraction of the rules the transgressor was thrashed with a cudgel. The Austrian commander had described the *Garibaldini* as 'weeds to be uprooted', and the men took him at his word. Prisoners who were too weak to walk were strapped to the gun-carriages and dragged along by them if they should fall off. Those who survived the march were confined in the terrible prison camp at Pietole; their barracks were half-flooded, and all they had to sleep on were piles of straw, never changed. Infections and disease met little resistance from those bodies, worn out by more than a year of marches and fighting. Whoever rebelled at his treatment was punished by forty blows of the cudgel; few survived. Many prisoners begged to be shot; their wish was granted.

Thus the survivors of the First War of Independence and of the Roman Republic faded away, silently, at Pietole. It is not mere rhetoric to imagine that many of their ghosts kept watch on the quay for the return of their chief, who was to lead a new generation of red-shirts when the time was ripe.

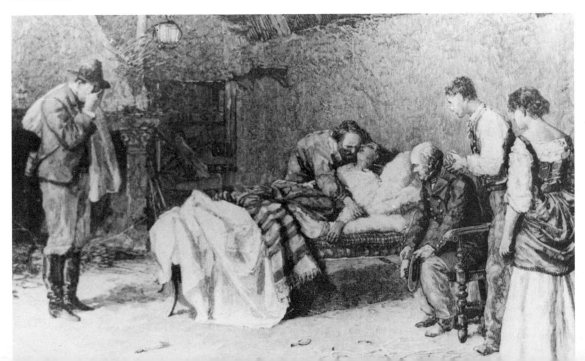

Battle of San Fermo by A. Trezzini. Captain De Cristoforis is killed. An economist, he returned to Italy, after years of exile in London, to enrol with Garibaldi, and fought for the Roman Republic with Manara.

The
Cacciatori delle Alpi

Historians of the *Rinascimento* call the period between 1849 and 1859 – the year when the Second War of Independence broke out – the 'decade of preparation'. An apt designation, for these were the years in which Piedmont, the only state in Italy which had maintained a liberal constitution after the débâcle of 1848–9, steeled itself politically, economically, psychologically and militarily for the war with Austria which it knew to be inevitable.

The artificer of this preparation was the prime minister, Cavour. But two other men had made his work possible for him, by defending the Constitution against all the forces at home and abroad which sought to have it revoked: the King – Victor Emmanuel II – and the Marchese Massimo d'Azeglio.

Charles Albert had abdicated in favour of his son Victor Emmanuel after the defeat at Novara. Piedmont liberals feared that the new King would lean towards reaction, which was now official policy in many other Italian and European states, but Victor Emmanuel promptly issued a proclamation in which he defined his aims as being 'to preserve our national honour, to heal the wounds of public misfortune, and to consolidate our constitutional institutions.' The twenty-nine-year-old King acceded to the throne at a difficult moment: defeat had shaken the country; the state coffers were empty; and the people were disgruntled at the armistice with Austria. At the same time the chancelleries of Europe, as well as local conservatives, were pressing for the abrogation of the much-feared liberal Constitution.

Victor Emmanuel, personally, was no liberal. But he knew that men had died for that Constitution, and he could not take their deaths lightly. As a man of his word he earned the sobriquet 'Gentleman King'. He revered the concept of monarchy, but he would sometimes exclaim to excessively obsequious courtiers, 'Bother "Majesty"; call me *Monsù* Savoia!' His vocabulary and his demeanour were more those of a stable-boy than of a monarch, and he much preferred the barracks to the writing-desk. But no one dared treat him with disrespect, ever-conscious as he was of his descent from a royal house whose origins were lost in the mists of time.

Victor Emanuel II, King of Sardinia and the first King of Italy.

His character was definitively summed up by Queen Victoria, who got to know him well during his visit to England:

'... in spite of every provocation from Austria, to irritate him and make him give up his Constitution, he has remained firm, has kept his word, and is the only King who has remained faithful to the promises given in 1848. ... There is such a total absence of all *humbug*, or playing a part; it is a plain frank nature, wanting in refinement & softness, but liking evidently that one should speak as frankly to him as he does to one.'

The Piedmont Constitution's other defender was, as mentioned, d'Azeglio. This patriot had served as a volunteer in the First War of Independence, and had been badly wounded at the battle of Vicenza. In 1849 Victor Emmanuel II called upon him to head a government. His first task was to supervise the peace talks with Austria. Though d'Azeglio had virtually no political experience, such were his natural abilities that he came through the negotiations more than victorious. The Austrians, whose armies were

Massimo d'Azeglio.

Camillo Benson, Count Cavour

still encamped on Piedmont territory, were demanding the abrogation of the Constitution and an indemnity of 200 million francs. D'Azeglio replied that the Constitution would never be abrogated and that he would pay 75 million and no more. He demanded in turn that the Austrians withdraw their troops from Piedmont, and grant an amnesty to all those Lombard citizens who had been compromised in the revolution.

When well-wishers counselled prudence and, even, a little humility, d'Azeglio replied, 'I may have to give in, because I'm small, but I shall never ask pardon, because I'm right.' But thanks to his tenacity – and also to a revolt in Hungary which posed a serious internal problem for the Austrian Empire – he did not have to give in: the Austrians agreed to all his terms.

Piedmont thus became the exception in a Europe where reaction and repression were now the rule. It soon came to be a place of pilgrimage, not only for those Italians, but for all Europeans who were struggling against conservative regimes; it was, as Palmerston described it, 'the beacon of Europe'.

In 1850 the man who was to be the key figure of the 'decade of preparation' entered d'Azeglio's cabinet: Camillo Benson, Count Cavour.

Cavour was born at Turin in 1810. Culturally, he was more Middle European than Italian. After a brief period of service in the Sardinian navy he had travelled about Europe, observing the technical and commercial aspects of the industrial revolution which was then transforming it. He studied attentively the parliamentary systems of France and England. It was during this period that he developed his passion for politics – not as an end in itself, however, but as a means to one end: the unity of Italy.

In 1848 he was elected deputy to the Piedmont parliament. He was immediately noticed for his special gift – a rare one in Italy – for dealing with problems pragmatically and without empty rhetoric. Cynical by nature, he would side by turns with the Right and with the Left if by so doing he could manipulate the passing of a law he considered useful. He succeeded in planting a spy – the Countess of Castiglione – in Napoleon III's bed. During the war of 1859 he did not hesitate to affix his signature to a bill which actually had not been

73

passed by Parliament, in order to obtain necessary credits. He saw to it that Piedmont kept up with the rest of Europe in industrializing its economy. He was the right man to forge the unity of Italy.

After serving as Minister of Agriculture, of the Navy, and of Finance he became Prime Minister on 4 November 1852, a post he was to hold almost without interruption until his death ten years later. He perceived at once the true reasons for the failure of the First War of Independence: discord between republican and monarchist forces, political isolation, and inferiority to Austria in military strength. He therefore determined to foster a national consensus by reconciling republican circles to the Piedmont monarchy. His foreign policy centred on alliances with England (then the only liberal state in Europe) and with France (which he considered a potential ally in a war with Austria): Austria remained the chief obstacle to any alteration of the *status quo* in Italy.

1854 saw the outbreak of the Crimean War, with England, France and Turkey fighting against Russia. The Allies wanted Austria to join them, but the Austrians were unwilling to commit themselves militarily. Their fear of Russian expansionism in the Balkans was outweighed by their fear that Piedmont (which now had a modern, efficient army once again) might take advantage of the situation by attacking them on the Italian front: they knew that if Piedmont moved against them, all Italy would rise in revolt. The Allies, however, could do nothing without Austrian support; so they presented Piedmont with what amounted to an ultimatum: it was to send an expeditionary corps to the Crimea.

At Turin, where foreign interference was always bitterly resented, all hell broke loose. But Cavour cleverly sent the ball back into the Allied court: yes, Piedmont would send an expeditionary force of 15,000 men, not as mercenaries (as the British and the French would have preferred), but at state expense and as an integral part of the Allied forces. His only condition was that when the time for peace negotiations should come, the Italian question would be among the topics discussed. It was a great political victory for Cavour, thus to obtain for his tiny country a

place among the great European powers.

The war came virtually to an end with the fall of Sebastopol in September 1855; the peace conference opened in Paris on 25 February 1856. A special session was devoted to the Italian question, and Cavour managed to obtain strong support, not only from the British and the French, but also – by appealing to their bitterness towards Austria – from the Russians.

The British minister, Clarendon, pronounced a savage diatribe against the Pope and the Bourbons of Naples, seriously embarrassing their protectors the Austrians. And Napoleon III fell right into Piedmont's trap. He was eager to re-establish his nation's diplomatic hegemony in Europe, so Cavour artfully insinuated that France might one day supplant Austria as the dominant force in Italy. From now on, despite momentary perplexities and hesitations, the Emperor was to remain Piedmont's ally.

On 24 January 1859, France and Piedmont signed a military treaty: in the event of an Austrian 'attack' on Piedmont, France would fight on the Piedmont side to liberate the Lombardo-Veneto.

Cavour saw to the *casus belli*. Opening Parliament on 10 January, Victor Emmanuel II had uttered a fateful phrase: '. . . we are not deaf to the cries of pain which reach our ears from every part of Italy.' The words made the rounds of the peninsula, and immediately volunteers began to set out for Piedmont. Twenty thousand had arrived there before 20 March, and by the end of June the number had grown to over forty thousand; they were incorporated into the Sardinian Army. The chancelleries of Europe proposed all sorts of solutions in the hope of avoiding war, but on 23 April Austria issued an ultimatum: Piedmont was to disarm, and to disband the volunteers, within three days. Cavour danced for joy. He refused the ultimatum, and war was declared.

On 26 April the Austrians advanced on Piedmont with five army corps: 120,000 men and 400 cannon. Inexplicably, however, they moved very slowly, and by so doing they lost their chance for a major victory, for the Piedmontese, until the arrival of the French, had only 60,000 men against them. Not until

Uniforms worn by the Garibaldini in 1859. Left, an unknown Mounted Guide in red dolman trimmed in black. Centre, a captain of the Cacciatori delle Alpi, Giuseppe Setti, who had distinguished himself in Rome defending the Vascello. Right, the commander of the Genoese Carabinieri, Antonio Mosto, in the pale grey-blue uniform piped in black of the corps.

29 April did General Gyulai, commander of the Austrian army on the Italian front, give the order to cross the Ticino, the river which separates Piedmont from Lombardy. The Piedmontese obstructed the enemy's operations by flooding the Lomellina plain as well as the lowlands around Novara.

While the Sardinian army remained on the defensive, the man who had now become the 'Hero of Two Worlds' launched an attack on the Austrians with his legion, the *Cacciatori delle Alpi*. The first engagements took place near Casale.

After his exile from Italy in 1849 Garibaldi, like so many of his comrades-in-arms, had attempted to start life over again as a civilian. He arrived in the United States on 30 July 1850. The city of New York offered him public honours and a stipend, but he refused; instead he found a job as a manual labourer in a candle factory owned by an Italian called Meucci. But he could not lead so unadventurous a life and, after obtaining American citizenship, he went back to being a seaman. Between 1851 and 1854 he voyaged

between China, Australia and South America. In February 1854, in London, he became engaged to an English gentlewoman called Emma Roberts. But the engagement did not last: Garibaldi thought Emma too frivolous, deploring her habit of staying up until late at night.

This was certainly one of the grimmest periods of Garibaldi's life. He had already fallen out with Mazzini in Rome; in London the rupture became irreparable. His family was scattered: Menotti was at military school at Nice, Ricciotti at school in England, and Teresita boarded with friends. His own friends seemed more interested in the Garibaldi myth than with the man he now was.

The Italian question itself now seemed remote, though he longed to return home and bring his family together again. He asked the Piedmont government for permission to re-enter Italy, and this was granted, on condition that he cause no trouble. His reputation was such that a word from him could sow panic among the European powers, and this would be incompatible with the subtleties of Cavour's diplomacy.

He returned to Nice in May 1854. The following November, with his savings and with a small legacy from a dead brother, he bought half of the island of Caprera, off the northern tip of Sardinia; in 1865 English friends were to make him a gift of the other half. He settled there, after another stay in London, in January 1857, and built a house of the South American type: one floor and a flat roof. He constructed it with his own hands, with an ex-priest called Gusmaroli to advise him. Gusmaroli treated him with some disdain, as his talents as a bricklayer were rather limited. He passed his time fishing, looking after his animals and tending the vegetables which, with characteristic stubbornness, he had succeeded in growing on that mass of granite, more suitable for goats than for gardens.

Caprera became a kind of Grand Hotel. Politicians from all nations were constantly arriving, as were exiles and adventurers with the most improbable schemes in their heads. He received tons of letters from a variety of female admirers, including Emma Roberts (still hopeful, perhaps) and Jessie White, another Englishwoman who was later to marry the Red-shirt Alberto Mario, serve as a nurse and write Garibaldian history. The Countess Maria Espérance von Schwartz wrote to him, in a desperate bid to obtain his memoirs for publication. His other correspondents included the Duchess of Sutherland, Mrs Seely, and the celebrated Florence Nightingale.

From Caprera Garibaldi once again established contact with the liberal movement, and especially with the so-called 'Genoa Group'. This consisted largely of ex-*Garibaldini* who had given up their republicanism and adhered to the programme of the National Society, an association which envisaged a unitarian struggle with a monarchy at its head. The Marchese Giorgio Pallavicino Trivulzio, one of the founders of the National Society, had been explicit: 'Arms are what we need, not Mazzinian chit-chat. Piedmont has soldiers and cannon; therefore I am a Piedmontese. Piedmont today is monarchist, by ancient custom, by genius, and in duty; therefore I am no republican.' The logic of his argument seemed impeccable, and Garibaldi joined the National Society. When that happened, even the last of Italy's republican zealots were converted to the monarchist principle.

Throughout 1858 Garibaldi met with Cavour in secret. In February 1859 he was summoned to Turin and appointed Major

General. He did not realize – or perhaps he only pretended not to realize – that he did not owe this appointment to his military abilities. It was merely a way of co-opting a popular hero, whose name alone would now suffice to bring swarms of volunteers to enlist in the regular army. (Napoleon III had vetoed the use of irregular troops.)

Garibaldi was placed in charge of the *Cacciatori delle Alpi* (Alpine chasseurs), a corps created on the spot. According to the politicians' designs, it was not to consist of more than three thousand men, nor was it to include cavalry, artillery or support and service troops. To it were assigned only the volunteers who were not wanted elsewhere: those who were too young or too old, or physically unfit, although the majority of the whole volunteer intake had come to Piedmont with the express intention of fighting under Garibaldi. Nor was this the only humiliation that the *Garibaldini* had to put up with. General La Marmora, the war minister, refused to recognize the corps' officers, so Cavour placed it under the Ministry of the Interior, personally signing the patents. Many of the officers and n.c.o.s, furthermore, had to accept lower ranks than those they had earned on the field of battle in 1848–9. Worst of all, the red shirt was banned; they all had to wear Piedmontese uniform. Garibaldi was even obliged to wear a cap with embroidery, though once outside the city he replaced it with his famous slouch hat.

The uniforms arrived in bits and pieces, and hardly anyone's was complete, but still the men had to observe the Piedmontese army's rigid regulations. All of them, including Garibaldi, had to shave off their beards and cut their hair short. The officers were not even issued horses, so Garibaldi set off for the campaign mounted on his Zani, a little black horse better suited to a lady than to a soldier.

The soldiers were issued mid-blue overcoats with green lapels, mid-blue jackets without lapels, and trousers of various colours: dark blue, mid-blue and the drab of Piedmontese fatigues. The cap was dark blue with a green band. The officers wore dark blue cloth tunics with green lapels, caps of the same colour and mid-blue trousers with green stripes. So as to distinguish them from the 'gentlemen-officers' of the regular army, their insignia of rank were worn on their sleeves, in the form of gold badges, rather than on their shoulder-straps. This distinction was imposed on them in 1859, but it was one that Garibaldian officers would maintain with pride in the future. Incidentally, the officers' uniforms also arrived late, and those who could not afford to have their own made to order set out on the campaign wearing plain soldiers' overcoats.

Garibaldi's treatment at the hands of the authorities, then, left much to be desired. But he could at least count on the support of men whose experience he valued, for among those who joined him were Medici, Sacchi, the surgeon Bertani, Bixio, Cadolini and Guglielmo Cenni – all of them veterans of the 1848 campaign and of the Roman Republic, and the first two were 'South Americans'.

They were joined by a new recruit, Enrico Cosenz, who was to distinguish himself for his technical and military abilities. Cosenz was born at Gaeta in 1820. He had served in the Neapolitan army; then, in 1848, he went over to the republican side and became one of the key figures in the defence of Venice. He was one of the most extraordinary of Garibaldi's generals. Though a southerner he was taciturn and phlegmatic. He lacked the authority of a Medici and the sanguine will-power of a Bixio. For him, war was an exact science which admitted no compromise, and it was said that he would have preferred a well-planned defeat to a chance victory. It is odd, then, that he found himself among the *Garibaldini*, who owed all their successes to their genius for turning total chaos to their advantage.

As usual all social classes were represented among the Garibaldian volunteers: labourers, peasants and many professionals, especially men of law. Once Medici had a difficulty in choosing a corporal, as the four candidates for the post were all lawyers. Doctors and surgeons were plentiful, so that the medical corps was first-rate. There were also architects, painters, poets and actors; during the pauses, one might hear one volunteer declaiming verses composed by another, or see still others drawing ground-plans or sketching landscapes.

The five Cairoli brothers – Benedetto, Ernesto, Enrico, Giovanni and Luigi – stood out among the volunteers. Their Milanese mother, Adelaide, had instilled into them from childhood a deep love of their country. So great was her desire that they participate in the struggle for national independence that she personally accompanied them when they went to enlist in 1848 and again, as *Cacciatori delle Alpi*, in 1859. From this moment on they were to remain *Garibaldini*. Only Benedetto was to survive the Wars of Independence – and went on to become Prime Minister of Italy. Ernesto was killed at Varese in 1859, Luigi during the expedition of the Thousand, and Enrico and Giovanni at Villa Glori during the ill-fated campaign of 1867.

The three thousand men were divided into a General Staff and three regiments of two battalions each, commanded by Cosenz, Medici and Arduino. Once the offensive

Adelaide Cairoli photographed with her surviving sons shortly after the expedition of the Thousand. From the left: Benedetto, Giovanni (wearing cadet uniform of the military academy), and Enrico. The last two were to die in 1867 trying to deliver arms to the Roman revolutionaries.

The Cacciatori delle Alpi *land at Sesto Calende, depicted by E. Pagliano.*

began, they were joined by about fifty mounted Guides, who provided their own uniforms and horses. For the rest of the Garibaldian campaigns, these guides were to remain the classic Red-shirt cavalry, even though they were gradually complemented by hussars and other types of specialized light cavalry.

The Guides included a few men who were to make their mark in Garibaldian history. Their creator was Francesco Simonetta, who was to prove the bravest and most energetic officer of the 1859 campaign. He would soon leave the corps for assignments of even greater responsibility, and we shall encounter him commanding a brigade during the expedition of the Thousand. His place would then be taken by Giuseppe Missori Torriani, who had fought in the 1848 war, aged sixteen, and who would remain in command of the Guides until his retirement in 1867.

Fifty-six Genoese self-styled *carabinieri* under the command of Antonio Mosto also presented themselves: they were members of a target-practice society, and had trained for years with 1851-model Federal Swiss carbines. They could perform miracles with this weapon, and were by far the best trained and best equipped marksmen in either army. The Genoese *carabinieri* were to have a special rôle in all the Garibaldian campaigns from now on; at times they were also called *bersaglieri*, though they are not to be confused with the Piedmontese *bersaglieri*.

The influx of volunteers continued long after the campaign began; two more regiments were created, and in time each regiment was composed of four battalions. The following groups were to join the five regiments during the course of the campaign: three companies of *bersaglieri*, one battalion of *bersaglieri valtellinesi* (i.e., from the Valtellina, an Alpine valley in Lombardy), one youth battalion, one battery of artillery and one company of Engineers. The left flank of the Franco-Piedmontese offensive was assigned to the *Garibaldini* as their theatre of operations.

On 16 May 1859, they were taken by train to Biella. Here Garibaldi (who had been told to follow his own judgment) instructed his men to leave behind everything which might slow them down on the march, such as their haversacks, the officers' boxes, tents and camp equipment: he wanted them absolutely mobile, always ready for one of the surprise moves with which he liked to outwit the enemy.

On 21 May they crossed the Ticino and on the 23rd they entered Varese. A furious storm was raging (bad weather was to plague them throughout the campaign). The townspeople opened their doors to the soldiers and helped them get dry, but no-one had a thought for Garibaldi himself, who would have been given not so much as a cup of hot broth had not a poor priest by the name of Della Valle eventually taken him in.

On the morning of 24 May, word came that the Austrian Lieutenant Marshal Urban, who had been assigned the same theatre of operations as Garibaldi, was marching on Varese with six thousand infantry, two hundred cavalry and eight cannon. The *Garibaldini* immediately began to prepare for the defence of the city by erecting barricades, opening loopholes in the walls and fortifying positions in the neighbourhood.

At 2 a.m. on 26 May three enemy rockets streaked through the sky. It was the signal for the battle to begin. The Austrians tried to seize the emplacement at Biuno Inferiore, south of the city, but were driven back by a bayonet charge led by Captain Suzini. Not long afterwards they tried again; now Sacchi came to Suzini's aid and, after a violent struggle, the Austrians were once again repulsed.

After firing on the emplacement from two cannons and opening a large breach, they attacked for the third time. Medici, who had arrived on the scene meanwhile, ordered his troops to lie flat and not to return fire. Cosenz also appeared with his regiment and took up a position to the right of the Austrian line of attack. When the Austrians saw that their fire was not returned, they thought that the emplacement had been abandoned, and made to occupy it. They were then caught in cross-fire from Medici and Cosenz, and were forced to fall back once more.

Garibaldi had meanwhile come out from the city with four companies and had made a wheeling movement around the enemy's left flank. He now attacked with zest, and obliged the enemy to fall back as far as the heights of Belforte, a mile from the outskirts of the town. Garibaldi, Cosenz and Medici then joined forces and attacked again. The Austrians abandoned their position, and tried to dig in again at Malnate, but Garibaldi continued charging them, and finally put them to flight. By noon everything was over. Urban had withdrawn completely, and the *Garibaldini* re-entered Varese.

On the morning of 27 May, they set out for Como. But in order to reach that town they had to get past an Austrian emplacement at San Fermo. San Fermo is a village on the side of a steep hill, from which it dominates the road into Como. The Austrians had six thousand men there, and a reserve force of seven thousand in Como itself. They had foreseen an attack, and had opened numerous loopholes in the village walls and stationed sharpshooters on the church tower. They had also placed troops in a semicircle at the bottom of the hill, blocking the road.

At 5 p.m. Garibaldi ordered Captain De Cristoforis to attack San Fermo from the road with Company 3 of the Second Regiment. De Cristoforis obeyed, but his men were greeted by such a dense volley of fire that eleven soldiers and all the officers were killed. Urban felt secure, and understandably so: he had control of the road and the surrounding hills were an insurmountable obstacle to any Italian advance. He was unaware that Garibaldi was attempting the impossible. In fact, while De Cristoforis' company was making its suicidal charge, the greater part of the *Garibaldini* were climbing up the hillside like goats to reach the opposite side of the village. The Austrians were taken by surprise, and their rear guard took refuge inside the walls. At first the fighting was from house to house, with the *Garibaldini* under fire from crack Tyrolese marksmen; then, gradually, the Austrians were dislodged and pursued down the hillside. At 7-o-clock a blast of the trum-

pets gave the signal for a final attack, led by Garibaldi, Medici and Cosenz. The Austrians fell back to Borgo Vico, a hamlet near Como.

In marching order once again, and now preceded by the 'Genoese *carabinieri*' (who had been exchanging fire earlier with the Tyrolese marksmen), the *Cacciatori delle Alpi* moved on to Borgo Vico, prepared for another encounter with the Austrians. But the Austrians had gone; they had even abandoned Como. The Italians entered the town at 9 p.m. and were received as enthusiastically as they had been at Varese.

The war as Garibaldi and Urban conducted it was a manoeuvring contest which did not require the permanent occupation of cities. History has not yet done justice to the valorous but unlucky Austrian general, undoubtedly the ablest adversary Garibaldi ever had. Urban understood Garibaldi's psychology and even adopted his tactics. Unfortunately he lacked one crucial element on which Garibaldi could count: the support of the population.

Though it was not necessary for the *Garibaldini* to hold on to the positions they conquered, they nevertheless had to guard against attacks from the rear. The enemy forts at Laveno were in this respect a threat. Laveno is a small town on Lake Maggiore, near the Swiss border. The Austrian installation there consisted of three forts – Forte Nord, Forte Cerro and Forte Castello – defended by sixteen cannon and a sturdy system of ramparts, ditches and trenches, plus a number of small gunboats on the lake.

On the night of 30 May, in driving rain, Simonetta and Bixio attempted to capture the boats, while Captains Landi and Bronzetti, with two companies of the First Regiment, moved on Forte Castello, the keystone of Laveno's defences. But the Austrians spotted them and drove them back with their rifle-fire. At 4 a.m. Landi attacked again. Bronzetti was meant to attack simultaneously from the opposite direction, but he had lost his way in the woods. Landi's company succeeded in taking the cannons surrounding the fort, and now prepared to assault the armoured entrance-way. But Bixio and Simonetta had failed in their mission, and the Austrian boats peppered Landi's men with grape-shot until

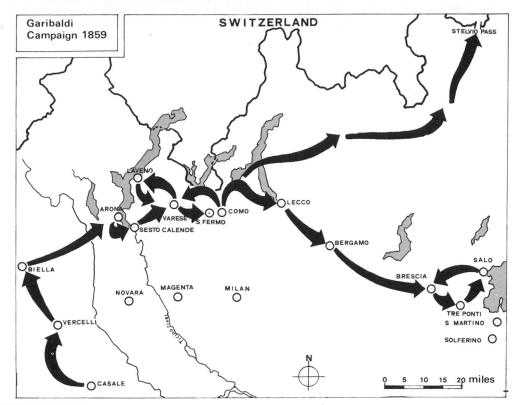

SWITZERLAND

STELVIO PASS

LAVENO

ARONA

VARESE S FERMO

SESTO CALENDE

COMO

LECCO

BERGAMO

SALO

BRESCIA

TRE PONTI
S. MARTINO

SOLFERINO

BIELLA

NOVARA

MAGENTA

MILAN

VERCELLI

CASALE

N

0   5   10   15   20 miles

they were forced to retreat.

Urban, who had meanwhile reorganized his own forces – he now had fourteen thousand under him – marched on Varese, and occupied it on the afternoon of 31 May. The *Garibaldini*, who had failed to occupy Laveno, now fell back towards Como rather than risk getting caught between Varese and the forts.

Meanwhile the Fourth Piedmontese Division, under General Cialdini, had been victorious over the Austrians at Palestro and Vinzaglio. On 1 June the Franco-Piedmont army took Novara from the Austrians and crossed the Ticino. Urban ought to have covered his army's right wing, but he feared an attack from the rear by Garibaldi and stayed holed up in Varese. Now that the Franco-Piedmont army had crossed the Ticino, however, he was in danger of being crushed between them and the *Cacciatori delle Alpi*; he had no choice but to retreat.

Garibaldi hounded him relentlessly. On 6 June the *Cacciatori* took Lecco and on the 8th they arrived at Bergamo, only to find that the Austrians had fled. Just then, a message from the Austrian command at Verona came over the telegraph: 'Do not abandon position.'

Garibaldi replied: 'Garibaldi's arrival imminent send reinforcements.' The Austrians, unaware that Bergamo had already fallen, wired, 'Sending reinforcements immediately.' Only 1,500 troops were sent, but when they arrived at the station of Seriate the *Cacciatori delle Alpi* were there waiting for them.

All this time the Garibaldian ranks had been swelling rather alarmingly. Officially they were now ten thousand but this figure is certainly too low. Not even the perspicacious Cosenz was able to determine how many the new recruits were, or where they came from. Besides the genuine patriots, there were now criminals and ex-collaborationists among the volunteers. Many of them took it upon themselves to requisition lodgings, victuals, clothing and horses, for which they signed false receipts. Others took to thievery – even Garibaldi's monogramed pistols were stolen – and the officers had to resort to violent methods to put a stop to these abuses. In the chaos, heroes mixed with blackguards and idealists with profiteers.

Among the new arrivals were a select group of officers of the Hungarian Legion, led by three colonels: István Türr, Lajos Tüköry and

Sándor Tèleki. Upon entering the service of the Piedmontese they were assigned to the General Staff of the *Cacciatori delle Alpi*. These men had been leaders of the Hungarian liberation movement; from now on they were to remain attached to the Garibaldian cause. Tèleki was to become a cavalry brigadier; Türr and Tüköry would take part in the expedition of the Thousand; Türr, in fact, was to become General of Division and the chief logistics officer of the Thousand and, later, of the Southern Army. He would tarnish his reputation at Caiazzo by ordering a senseless attack which almost brought the entire expedition to a disastrous end.

Garibaldi took Brescia on 13 June. Now the Piedmontese generals ordered him to attack Tre Ponti, which was held by 200,000 Austrians. Without knowing quite what he was getting into, on 15 June he attacked; the *Garibaldini* took a severe beating. Garibaldi was furious over the senseless orders he had received, and exclaimed, 'They wanted to make fools of us, but they have gone to tragic extremes!' What the generals really wanted was to make sure that the 1859 campaign would not be an uninterrupted series of victories for the *Garibaldini*.

The battle went as follows. Approaching the Austrian position, the First Regiment came under heavy fire from the enemy vanguard. The encounter which followed was a muddled one. Cosenz arrived on the scene, realized that he was up against Urban's entire division and made a desperate attempt to disengage himself. He would certainly have been annihilated had not Garibaldi covered his retreat. The day was marked by magnificent, though unavailing, feats of bravery. Türr, for example, led a charge across the bridge called Ponte San Giacomo and was wounded in the arm (which was threatened with amputation). Captain Bronzetti's arm was shot to pieces by enemy bullets, but he continued to urge his men on until a final shot killed him.

The victory at Tre Ponti was the only one Urban was to know – and he failed to take advantage of even this one by pursuing the *Garibaldini*. He permitted them to outflank him, and to capture the city of Salò to his rear.

After Tre Ponti, the *Cacciatori delle Alpi* were ordered to guard the Passo dello Stelvio, an Alpine pass through which, it was feared, the Austrians might send reinforcements. Nothing happened; the tedium of their long period of inaction in the mountains was broken only by news of the Franco-Piedmontese victories at San Martino and Solferino (24 June 1859) and of the peace of Villafranca (11 July). Those two fierce battles had been fought simultaneously and only a few miles from each other. The Piedmontese carried the day at San Martino and the French at Solferino. Afterwards, Napoleon III demanded that the Austrians agree to an armistice. An armistice was signed, later converted into a permanent peace.

Some thought that it was the horrid spectacle of the two battles (22,000 Austrian dead and 17,000 Franco-Piedmontese) which caused Napoleon to end the war. But his true motives were military and political: the Austrians were now barricaded within the Quadrilateral, and to dislodge them would be difficult and costly; England looked with favour upon the Italian cause, but not upon excessive French expansion on the continent; Prussia was still hesitant, but as a member of the German Confederation it could be expected sooner or later to join the war on the Austrian side.

In France Catholic forces were opposed to the Austrians being chased out of Italy as this would weaken the temporal power of the Pope; they were actively conspiring against the war. The French people were proud of their army's victories, but they were beginning to wonder what France had to gain by fighting for Italian independence – and matters in Italy were not progressing as Napoleon III had hoped.

According to the secret agreement between Cavour and the Emperor, once the Austrians were expelled from the Lombardo-Veneto this region would be annexed by Piedmont. France, in return for its aid, was to receive the city of Nice and the province of Savoy, and the Central Italian states were to be amalgamated into a single monarchy under a Bonaparte ruler.

But when the Central Italian states deposed their own monarchs they requested annexation by Piedmont, leaving Napoleon to make the best of a bad job. As a gesture, he was given Nice and Savoy, though by agreeing to the terms of the Peace of Villafranca – which Piedmont had no choice but to sign as well – he failed to keep up his end of the bargain: the Veneto remained in Austrian hands. In parliament Garibaldi delivered a tirade over the cession of his native city to France; but it was a *fait accompli*. Garibaldi resigned his seat in the Piedmont parliament in protest.

The *Cacciatori delle Alpi* were dissolved when the peace was signed. Garibaldi was now needed in Central Italy, where the old rulers had been deposed, and many of the veterans went with him. Those who remained in the Piedmont army were regrouped to form the 'Alpi' Brigade: to this day, its members wear a red cravat in memory of its founders.

It was by popular demand that Garibaldi was called to Central Italy, to take charge of the armies until the fusion with Piedmont might be arranged. The faithful followers who went with him hoped to take up arms against Austria once again, for the liberation of those territories still under her control. But the politicians, anxious as ever as to what he might get up to, placed him under the com-mand of General Fanti. Fanti was a good general from a liberal background, but the two men were incompatible.

In Florence, in fact, Garibaldi at once began sending off proclamations to regions still dominated by Austria or by the Papacy, such as the Veneto, the Marches and Umbria. And he opened a subscription to raise funds for 'a million rifles', to the consternation of the chancelleries of Europe, which already had their hands full thanks to recent developments in Italy.

Cavour, fearful lest some rash gesture of Garibaldi's endanger his precarious diplomacy in Italy, implored the King (who was the only Piedmontese Garibaldi would listen to) to ask him to resign his command and hold his peace. Garibaldi sized up the situation, and resigned.

The diplomats of Italy were highly satisfied with the results of the Second War of Independence, which had in fact surpassed their expectations. But the *Garibaldini* were less satisfied. Waiting for the right moment to present itself, they began making plans for an expedition which, when it came, was to be nothing short of a miracle. ↵

Genoese Carabinieri.

The Battle of Calatafimi

The Thousand

When it became clear early in 1859 that war between Piedmont and Austria was imminent, the Sicilian members of the National Society did what little they could to bring the South of Italy into the conflict. But this did not enter into Cavour's design, and the Peace of Villafranca made no mention of the South. The Sicilians now pinned their hopes on Garibaldi, and sought to convince him to invade the island at the head of a volunteer corps.

This was not a new idea. Garibaldi himself had entertained the notion of a campaign in Sicily since the time of his return from South America; but he had always decided against it. Even now he hesitated. When a group of young Sicilians appealed to him for aid in September 1859, he replied, 'If you have a reasonable chance of success, revolt. If not, work on.' And on 15 March 1860, he wrote to the Sicilian liberal Rosolino Pilo, 'I never recoil from an undertaking, no matter how hazardous it may be. But I do not believe that the time is now ripe for a revolution in any part of Italy.' But the Sicilians would not give up so easily, and while they waited for Garibaldi to change his mind they went on plotting a rebellion. Francesco Crispi toured the entire island, surveying its revolutionary possibilities.

Crispi had been an exile, first in Malta and then in London, ever since the fall of the Sicilian provisional government in 1849. In London he had married Rosalie Montmasson de Saint-Jorioz, a Savoyard lady who was of great assistance to him in his work. An obstinate, persevering man (who would go on to become prime minister of Italy), Crispi was the real artificer of the expedition of the Thousand: he it was who succeeded in persuading the reluctant Garibaldi.

There were two reasons for the General's hesitations: he had grave doubts as to the outcome of a rebellion in Sicily, and his own government had asked him not to make trouble. Medici and Bixio had gone to Cavour to get his approval for a possible intervention in Sicily, and the Prime Minister had repeated his request that the *Garibaldini* should not take any action which might interfere with his diplomatic schemes. Medici was inclined to co-operate with Cavour, but Bixio, Agostino

Francesco Crispi at the time of the expedition.

Bertani and Türr, together with Crispi and Pilo, decided to contrive a *casus belli* which would force Garibaldi's hand.

It was decided that the insurrection should begin on 4 April 1860. Crispi's wife went to Sicily to prepare the local Revolutionary Committees for the event. Rosolino Pilo and Giovanni Corrao, another Sicilian patriot, also set sail, with a view to taking charge of the operations, but the sloop which was carrying them ran into difficulties and they arrived five days too late.

On 4 April the revolt broke out as planned at Palermo and, later, at Messina and Catania. But the Neapolitan royalist troops put it down before it could get underway. When Pilo arrived, all that was left for him and Corrao to do was to round up the surviving rebels and flee with them to the mountains.

Rosolino Pilo was a realist and a calculator. He knew that the liberation of Sicily was unthinkable without Garibaldi. In order to stir the General to action, therefore, he sent off a series of dispatches to the committee at Genoa in which he gave a completely false account of the insurrection: it was meeting with success, he wrote, and he himself was about to enter Catania at the head of a multitude of patriots. In actual fact, he and poor Corrao were being tracked by the Neapolitan police from one end of the island to the other. As they fled, however, they ignited the flame of revolt among the local populations by spreading the word, 'Garibaldi is coming! Garibaldi is coming!' Pilo – the 'precursor' as Garibaldi called him – was to die in combat with the Neapolitans on 21 May a few miles from his native Palermo.

The first report of the revolt at Palermo, a dispatch from the Stefani news agency, reached Genoa, where the National Society had its headquarters, on the evening of 6 April. An 'Aid Committee' was formed at once. Bixio and Crispi went to Turin, where Garibaldi was still inveighing against the government over the cession of Nice to France, and begged him to take command of an armed expedition. He was not easily convinced; only after a long discussion did he agree to act, and then only on condition that the revolt had widespread support.

Crispi, with a letter from Garibaldi in his pocket, left immediately for Milan, to obtain arms and raise money for the 'Million Rifles Fund'. Bixio returned to Genoa to confer with the Garibaldian General Staff there and to set about procuring ships.

Hoping that the government might be induced to help, Garibaldi went to the King and asked that the Reggio Brigade (the 45th and 46th Regiments), in which many former officers and soldiers of the *Cacciatori delle Alpi* were now serving, be placed at his disposal. Victor Emmanuel consulted with Cavour, and turned down Garibaldi's request. Bixio and Medici then went to Cavour in a last effort to change his mind, but in vain. Cavour, in fact, urged them to abandon the whole undertaking, and showed them the dispatch he had received from the Piedmontese consul in Sicily: 'Rebels surrounded and outnumbered. Have laid down arms. Catania, Messina, Palermo besieged. General disarmament.'

The *Garibaldini*, naturally, were not so easily dissuaded. On 12 April Medici, Bixio, Bertani and Giuseppe Finzi decided to begin recruiting troops, and the National Society notified its provincial branches that Garibaldi needed men. On 15 April Garibaldi took up residence at Villa Spinola, in a suburb of Genoa called Quarto.

Preparations were now well underway, but still Garibaldi hesitated, partly because of continuing pressure from the government and partly because of the contradictory reports which kept coming in from Sicily. There were stormy meetings of the General Staff. Bixio, Türr, Crispi and Medici were in favour of the expedition; Gaspare Trecchi and Sacchi against it. Crispi frequently lost his temper with his adversaries, and when Garibaldi asked him why, he said, 'I am convinced that this cause is in my country's interest and in yours; my only fear is of the sea.' Garibaldi was piqued: 'At sea you can count on me', he said. 'And on land you can count on me!', replied Crispi – meaning that the revolt in Sicily was in fact a reality.

Thus the expedition was made ready amidst quarrels, worries and doubts.

On the evening of 27 April a telegram came from Nicola Fabrizi, one of the organizers of the campaign together with Crispi, who was now in Malta. It confirmed the failure of the insurrection at Palermo; many liberals had fled to Malta aboard British ships. There was yet another stormy meeting at Villa Spinola. In the end Bixio left the room in a rage, slamming the door, and announced to the sympathizers who were waiting apprehensively outside that they were not going. Garibaldi had decided to cancel the expedition and go back to Caprera.

But not long afterwards another telegram arrived: 'Palermo fallen to rebels, revolt spreading provinces.' It was a forgery: Bixio and Crispi had sent it in a last-ditch effort to save the expedition, and now they themselves waved it under the General's nose. Garibaldi gave in, and preparations were resumed.

A thousand rifles had already arrived, the American colonel Samuel Colt had sent a hundred of his famous pistols, and negotiations for the ships were in their final stages. On 9 April Garibaldi had written to Giovan Battista Fauché, a veteran of the Venetian rebellion of 1849 who was now a director of the Rubattino steamship company in Genoa. The General explained that he only had 100,000 francs at his disposal for the entire expedition, and that he could not spend them all on the voyage alone. Then Bertani went to discuss matters in person, and Fauché told him that Garibaldi could have the *Piemonte* for nothing, but that he would have to arrange to 'steal' it: the company could not be compromised in this affair, because the State was a shareholder. But it soon became apparent that one ship would not suffice to transport all the volunteers. Garibaldi asked Fauché to call on him, and received him in Bixio's presence, sitting on his bed with a map of Sicily open on his knees. 'Well, Fauché', he said, 'do you think we'll bring off this expedition?' 'Yes, General.' 'Well, then', said Garibaldi sweetly, 'what if I needed two ships instead of one?' Fauché offered him the *Lombardo* in addition to the *Piemonte*. That very evening the details of the 'theft' of the two steamers were worked out between Bertani, Bixio and Fauché.

The *Lombardo* had been built at Leghorn in 1849. She was 157 ft long and 24 ft wide, with a tonnage of 238 and a 220-horsepower engine. Her value was estimated at £15,000. The *Piemonte*, built at Glasgow in 1851, was 164 ft long and 23 ft wide, with a tonnage of 180, a 160-horsepower engine, and an estimated value of £11,600.

Time was running short. The European governments were putting pressure on Piedmont, and though Cavour would not of his own initiative take such an unpopular step as to prohibit the expedition, there might soon come a time when he would be forced to. He had already interfered by seizing a portion of the weapons which were being shipped from Milan. Volunteers were roaming the streets of Genoa and it was feared that they might disturb the peace; feeding and lodging them was becoming a problem. And so it was decided to sail on 5 May without waiting for further recruits.

The last few days were hectic ones. Bertani was ill, but he continued to direct operations from his bed. Everything had to be bought on credit, because the funds which had been pledged had not yet arrived. They were not to arrive, in fact, until the very night of departure, and when they did, they came in the form of drafts on the Bank of Genoa, which could not be used in Sicily. (Bertani, fortunately, was able to change them into metallic currency despite the late hour.) Ninety thousand lire were brought from Milan by Filippo Migliavacca, 30,000 had been raised by Enrico Besana, and 35,000 came from various other sources: 155,000 lire in all – an absurdly low figure.

On the night of 4 May Nino Bixio, Benedetto Castiglione and thirty men, weapons in hand, assaulted the two ships in the port of Genoa. The seamen, roused from sleep, put up no fight; in fact, when they learned where the ships were bound for, they enlisted on the spot. The *Piemonte*, commanded by Bixio, got underway at once; the *Lombardo*, however, could not do so until finally Bixio took it in tow and got it out of the port (following instructions which Fauché had given him).

Giovan Battista Fauché was to pay dearly for his aid to the *Garibaldini*. He was immediately dismissed by the steamship company, whereupon he joined Garibaldi in Sicily and saw to the organization of the fleet there. After the unification of Italy he was given a job with the National Seaports Administration, but his role in the expedition of the Thousand was never acknowledged; and the company later took all the credit for providing the ships. Fauché was a Socialist, and during the strikes of 1883 he sided with the workers and lost his job again. He died impoverished in a public hospital in Venice.

While Bixio and Castiglione were carrying out their act of piracy, on the rocky shore at Quarto the *Garibaldini* were getting ready to board the fishing boats which would carry them out to sea. The scene has been described by many eye-witnesses. The volunteers assembled in front of Villa Spinola, where they were issued with weapons; then they proceeded to the shore in an orderly fashion. Under a brightly shining moon, volunteers and spectators alike kept silent; the only sound to be heard, now and again, was the weeping of a wife or mother. Sympathizers who were staying behind moved from one group to the next, exchanging simple handshakes with the volunteers. There was no singing, no shouting, no bluster. The correspondent from the *Daily News* asked, 'What can have happened to these Italians? They are no longer the frivolous and insouciant beings we all once knew.'

Towards midnight Garibaldi went down to the beach in his picturesque red shirt, poncho and sabre. With him were 1,049 men. (Around 30 were already aboard the steamers; 78 volunteers from Leghorn, under Andrea Sgarallino, were to come aboard near Piombino, and another 60 at Talamone, bringing the total number to 1,217.) As they went aboard, Garibaldi asked, 'How many are we?' and was amazed to hear that, counting the sailors, there were more than a thousand.

The cream of the European revolutionary movement took part in the expedition, including many veterans of Garibaldi's earlier campaigns. Besides Bixio, there was Hugh Forbes, the Englishman who had fought for the Roman Republic; Türr and Tüköry, who had taken part in the war of the previous year; Milbitz, another Roman veteran; Girolamo Ulloa and György Klapka; Giorgio Manin,

the son of Daniele Manin, who had been president of the Venetian Republic in 1848–9; the Cairoli brothers; Ippolito Nievo and Cesare Abba, two promising young authors; the painter Gerolamo Induno, who had served at Rome and in 1859; Rosalie Montmasson, Crispi's wife; and a new face – Giuseppe Sirtori, who was to play a conspicuous part in the expedition. The Genoese *Carabinieri* were present, under Mosto's command, as were the Guides (not at the time mounted) under Simonetta, Missori, Stadella and Francesco Nullo. There were also ordinary civilians who had stayed at their work until the last minute, such as the stockbroker Davide Uziel.

A survey published in 1910 informs us that the largest proportion, some 50 per cent, of the volunteers were students, followed by landowners, business-men, clerks, shopkeepers, doctors, lawyers and engineers. Nor was there any shortage of bakers, porters, innkeepers, waiters, mechanics, greengrocers or farmers. The average age was 20: of the 1,087 who were to disembark at Marsala, 92 were 20 years old and 76 were 21. The youngest was Giuseppe Marchetti, aged 11, but there were also five men in their sixties. The Thousand also included fifteen foreigners: four Hungarians, three Austrians, three Swiss, three Frenchmen, one Englishman and one Greek from Corfu.

For the most part they wore civilian dress,

The departure of the Thousand from the rock of Quarto by Van Elven, probably a spectator since this picture is closest to the description given by eye witnesses. The only contradictory note is the presence of Bixio at Garibaldi's side lighting up a cigar, when he was supposedly already aboard one of the ships.

though a few had a red shirt or the remains of a *Cacciatore delle Alpi* uniform in their haversacks. Crispi wore a frock-coat, as though he were on his way to an official reception; Sirtori had a red and white chequered shirt beneath his impeccable black overcoat. The only one wearing his red shirt was Garibaldi, and the only one in full uniform was Lieutenant Costantino Pagani of the Piedmont infantry, otherwise known as De Angelis: he had deserted his regiment to join Garibaldi and was destined to die at Calatafimi.

Cosenz, Medici and Bertani remained in Genoa to organize the expeditions which were to follow.

As dawn broke the steamships finally appeared off Quarto. The boarding operation was managed quickly. Garibaldi took command of the *Piemonte* and Bixio of the *Lombardo*. They had barely gone a mile when it was noticed that, while they had about a thousand rifles, they had no ammunition at all. The ammunition, in fact, with the rest of the rifles, was to have been rowed out to the *Piemonte* and the *Lombardo* in two big boats. But the pilot who was lighting the way, a certain Sella, suddenly disappeared into the night with his skiff, leaving the boats helpless. They made it back to shore in the morning, and Bertani sent the arms to Sicily with the second expedition.

There was no time to turn back. Garibaldi decided to head for Orbetello on the Tuscan coast, and try to acquire some ammunition there. When they arrived, Türr introduced himself as Garibaldi's *aide-de-camp* to Colonel Giorgini, the commander of the local garrison. With an artfully fabricated story – the invasion had the full approval of the King, who could not, however, support it openly for diplomatic reasons – he convinced Giorgini not only to supply him with ammunition and provisions but to turn over to him an artillery piece as well. Giorgini was court-martialled for his gullibility but, fortunately for him, by the time the case came to trial Garibaldi's expedition had won the support of the authorities, and he was acquitted.

On 9 May the two ships set sail once again. They left behind a detachment of 130 volunteers commanded by Callimaco Zambianchi (the rabid anticlerical who had ordered the execution of the six priests during the days of the Roman Republic), who were assigned the task of creating a diversion in the Papal States. The details of the plan were known only to Garibaldi and Zambianchi: theoretically, the detachment was meant to touch off a revolt in the Papal States and then proceed to invade the Kingdom of the Two Sicilies from the north.

The Red-shirts were known for their reckless enterprises; it is nevertheless difficult to understand how Garibaldi could have expected Zambianchi – in whom he had never had much confidence – to carry out such an arduous mission with only 130 men. It was later claimed that Garibaldi's only purpose was to give the false impression that his expedition was directed against Rome rather than Sicily, but the small size of the detachment and the equivocal character of its leader make this explanation sound equally unlikely. In any event, Zambianchi's column entered the Papal States on 19 May, encountered a squadron of pontifical gendarmes at Grotte di Castro and put them to flight. But then, inexplicably and despite the opposition of his men, Zambianchi ordered a retreat and crossed back into Tuscany, where they were all arrested by order of the Piedmont government and taken to Orbetello. They were later released, and, a few at a time, they joined Garibaldi in Sicily – except for Zambianchi who, by threatening to reveal the truth behind the whole obscure manoeuvre, obtained from Bertani, with Cavour's approval, 20,000 lire and a passport for America. (He did not enjoy the fruits of his blackmail, however, for he died during the voyage.)

The Kingdom of the Two Sicilies, whose territory the *Garibaldini* were now invading, was the most backward state of the Italian peninsula. After the war of 1848–9 it had completely isolated itself, and it remained unaffected by the industrial revolution which was rapidly transforming the rest of Europe. Socially and culturally, it had changed little since the Middle Ages. The land belonged to the nobility and the clergy and was undercultivated, in some places not cultivated at all. The rural population was illiterate and destitute; the few industries which existed were state-protected, and were so inefficient that they were destined to fail, in the face of competition, after the unification of Italy. Communications were extremely difficult: 1,500 of the Kingdom's 1,800 municipalities were without roads. This, it is true, was the first Italian state to construct a railway – but the railway was only sixty miles long, and was virtually reserved for the King's private pleasure.

Most of the budget went for the support of the Army; thanks to his army Ferdinand II had been able to put down liberal uprisings without help from the Austrians, but such independence was costly, as uprisings were extremely frequent, especially in rural areas. The police were efficient enough to keep liberal ideas from circulating easily. So repressive was the regime, in fact, that Gladstone – in an open letter which stirred consciences all over Europe – denounced it as 'the negation of God'.

Between 1849 and the Liberation there were various attempts at revolt in the Kingdom of the Two Sicilies, some popular in origin and others fomented by middle-class liberals. The two most important were led by the Bandiera brothers and by Carlo Pisacane. But they, like the others, were put down by Neapolitan bayonets.

The intransigent Ferdinand II died in 1859 and was succeeded by his son Francis II. Francis was a less successful tyrant than his father, and soon political parties – which the old King had completely suffocated – began to reappear on the scene. The most subversive of these were the Sicilian separatists, and the *Murattisti*, who wanted to call to the throne a descendant of Napoleon I's brother-in-law Joachim Murat, who had reigned in Naples from 1808 to 1815. The *Murattisti* had the support of Napoleon III, eager as he always was for a return to French hegemony in Italy.

Cavour was so disturbed by this political ferment that he wrote to the Piedmont ambassador in Naples on 30 March 1860:

'In the event of an insurrection, which party would have the upper hand? Have the *Murattisti* many supporters in the army and among the bourgeoisie? Is there any chance of

Francis II, King of Naples.

an annexationist movement such as we saw in Tuscany? Are the republicans still numerous and influential in Calabria? You know that I do not desire in the least to hasten the Neapolitan question towards a premature solution. On the contrary I believe it to be in our interest that the *status quo* be maintained for a few years more. But I have it from a good source that England has already despaired of the *status quo*; certainly it is with a view to coming changes that she has stationed her fleet in Neapolitan waters. I think, then, that we shall have to make a plan of our own, though I would have preferred more time in which to mature it.'

After the Second War of Independence, the Piedmontese had repeatedly sought to enter into an alliance with the Kingdom of the Two Sicilies; in this they were encouraged by their European allies, who were anxious to avoid another war in Italy. Some of the Neapolitan Bourbons, such as the King's uncle the Count of Syracuse, were in favour of an alliance with Piedmont, but the dominant faction at court, headed by the Queen Mother, would hear of no such thing. By the time the Bourbons were beginning to think favourably of the idea, it was too late: the *Garibaldini* had already conquered Sicily, and it was no longer to Cavour's advantage to negotiate. It was also too late for mediation by foreign powers. The last-minute Constitution proclaimed by the monarchy came much too late – only the army took any notice of it, and they protested against it.

The voyage to Sicily was relatively uneventful. The volunteers had to endure cramped quarters, and one of Bixio's men fell overboard, but was rescued. However, on another occasion tragedy nearly struck. The night of 10 May was foggy, and the ships had just entered Neapolitan waters when smoke was glimpsed in the distance. It was feared that this might indicate the proximity of the enemy fleet, so lights were extinguished. Shortly before midnight the *Piemonte*, as was her custom, slowed down so that the much slower *Lombardo* might catch up. Bixio, at the helm of the *Lombardo*, saw a shape looming before him, which he took to be a Neapolitan ship, and he tried to ram it. Fortunately, Garibaldi was more aware of what was happening, and he shouted, 'Bixio, do you really want to sink us?' Bixio recognized the voice, and barely managed to avoid the collision.

Garibaldi divided the Thousand into eight companies: the First was under the command of Bixio, the Second under Giuseppe Dezza, the Third under Francesco Stocco, the Fourth under Giuseppe La Masa, the Fifth under Francesco Anfossi, the Sixth under Giacinto Carini, the Seventh under Benedetto Cairoli, and the Eighth under Edoardo Bassini. Mosto's Genoese *carabinieri* remained an autonomous corps. Sirtori was made Chief of Staff, with Crispi and Manin next in command; István Türr and Lajos Tüköry became the General's *aides-de-camp*. Giovanni Acerbi was placed in charge of the Commissariat, Filippo Minutilli of the Engineers, Vincenzo Orsini of the Artillery, and Pietro Ripari of the Medical Corps. Garibaldi selected these officers on the basis of their performances in previous campaigns, and he allowed them to choose their own junior officers on the same principle.

On 11 May the two steamers arrived at Marsala. The choice of this port was not due to strategic considerations; it was determined by the fact that smoke had been sighted in the night, and was now drawing closer. It came, in fact, from the *Stromboli*, a steamship of the Royal Neapolitan Navy, which was accompanied by another steamship and by a frigate under sail.

When they entered the port at 2 p.m., they saw two warships anchored there. There was a moment of panic, but the vessels turned out to be British – the *Argus* and the *Intrepid* – which had arrived that morning to protect the interests of the British community at Marsala. The role played by these British ships was afterwards much discussed in the European press, and it is still a matter of conjecture whether or not they actually aided the *Garibaldini*. It would seem that they did not do so directly, but it is clear from the British officers' letters to *The Times* that they sympathized with these Italians 'of fine aspect, well equipped, and with medals from the Crimean War.'

Piemonte hauled alongside the pier without difficulty, but the *Lombardo* ran aground some hundred yards off. While all the small

The landing of the Thousand at Marsala. (Left)

István Türr. He suffered from severe bleeding during the expedition, and Nandór Eber often took his place. (Above right)

Fra Pantaleo. This colourful character served with the Garibaldini both as a priest not above fighting and years later, having abandoned the cloth, as a trooper in the French campaign. (Below right)

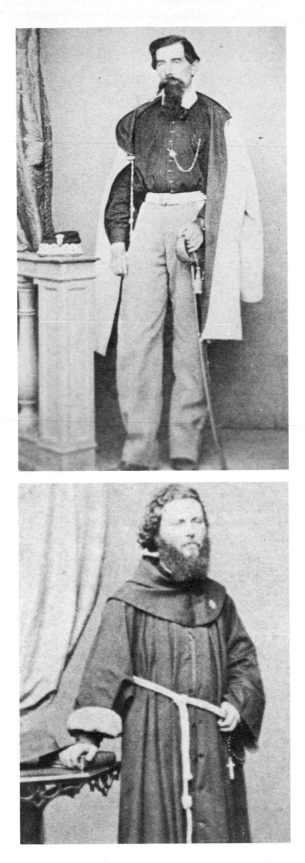

boats in the port raced to get the men ashore, the Neapolitan ships opened fire. Then suddenly they stopped again, and the *Garibaldini* were able to complete their disembarkation by four o'clock. The commander of the *Intrepid*, Captain Marryat, had requested the commander of the *Stromboli*, Ferdinando Acton (a member of an Irish family which had been in the service of the Bourbons for generations), to respect the Union Jack, which was flying over the houses of the British residents, and had informed him that a number of British officers had gone ashore. Acton evidently considered it more important to avoid a diplomatic incident than to defeat the *Garibaldini*, and to everyone's astonishment he called off the shelling. Perhaps he decided that 'discretion was the better part of valour', as one British officer stated; more likely, though, as Marryat put it, he was simply 'unnerved, confused, and irresolute'. (Later he made the quite absurd request that he be allowed to demand Garibaldi's surrender from a launch flying the British flag.) At 6.30 p.m. Acton gave the order to assault Garibaldi's ships, which were now empty, and to open fire upon the town, where he succeeded only in sowing panic among the population.

By way of excusing his bungling of the incident, Acton later accused the British of having deliberately placed their ships in his line of fire. This was followed by a diplomatic note. Lord Russell explained to the British House of Commons that Acton had ceased fire as an act of courtesy, so that the English sailors could re-board their ships. He also pointed out that Captain Marryat and Captain Winnington-Ingram of the *Argus* had advised that British merchant vessels be removed from the port so as not to get in the way of the Neapolitan operations.

The *Piemonte* was captured by the Neapolitans and towed away; the stranded *Lombardo* was removed some weeks later. The two ships came to rather inglorious ends, considering their role in the expedition of the Thousand. With the unification of Italy the *Lombardo* became part of the merchant fleet, and she sank on the night of 12 March 1864, off the Tremiti Islands, while carrying troops. The *Piemonte* ended her days moving mud in the harbour of Bari.

After the landing the *Garibaldini*, in groups of four, occupied Marsala without incident. Garibaldi sent messengers to the Revolutionary Committees in the nearby villages, while Türr quickly took over all the means of communication and cut the telegraph lines.

The invasion stirred up a hornets' nest in Europe: the fear was widespread that one power or another might intervene, and that the intervention might touch off a general war. The French foreign minister, Thouvenel, sent a sharp note of protest to the Piedmont government, casting doubts upon its loyalty to the terms of the alliance. (This was understandable, since only a few days previously Cavour had assured him that there would be no Garibaldian expedition.) Austria also blamed Piedmont for the whole affair, Prussia proposed a political and military alliance against 'the unbridled ambition of the King of Sardinia', and Russia threatened an armed intervention on the side of the Bourbons of Naples. Cavour, we may be certain, called down all the curses imaginable upon the heads of the Red-shirts. But he turned the diplomatic tables with his usual dexterity: 'By what right', he wrote to the British ambassador at Turin, 'may Sardinia be held responsible for the landing of a bold adventurer in Sicily when the entire Neapolitan navy was unable to prevent it?' He went on to confess that the Piedmont government was powerless to deal with Garibaldi, whose popularity exceeded that of the King himself.

On the morning of 12 May the *Garibaldini* left Marsala and headed towards Salemi. The General Staff did not have a detailed map of the area, so they had to rely upon a small-scale survey map and on information gathered along the way. The column was led by Missori's Guides (who were still trying to obtain mounts), followed by the Genoese *carabinieri* and the companies in numerical order. Then came Orsini's men, trundling their four cannon along on decrepit carriages; then the seamen from the *Piemonte* and the *Lombardo*, who had now been placed in charge of the ammunition waggons. To the rear came Ripari with four doctors and Rosalie Montmasson, Acerbi with four commissaries, and Minutilli with the officers who were meant to be heading the Engineers but who for the moment had not so much as a shovel. Garibaldi rode up and down, followed by Sirtori (still in his black overcoat), by Türr, and by Cenni, one of his tireless adjutants from the Roman campaign.

The General remarked to Türr, 'In a few days every company will be a battalion, and later on a regiment.' In fact, 150 more volunteers had enlisted at Marsala, and they now numbered 1,237. But the enemy numbered 140,000 of whom 25,000 men were in Sicily.

The Neapolitan army was well armed and well outfitted, and it had excellent special units, such as the *Cacciatori a Piedi* (*Chasseurs à Pied*) and the Cavalry. It was unmatched when it came to religious ceremonies, parades and elegant uniforms. But its flaws were to become manifest on the occasion of its first clash with the *Garibaldini*.

The weakness of the Neapolitan army lay not so much with the troops – who, as Garibaldi himself recognized, were combative and courageous – as with the officers, who were cowards. It soon became apparent that they were more prone to adapt to changing circumstances than to fight, and on several occasions they were shot by their own men for suspected treason. Naples had a fine military academy, the 'Nunziatella', but the best among the officers had resigned their commissions, had been transferred to remote provinces, or – suspected of liberal instincts – had been obliged to flee. This was the case with former Neapolitan officers like Pisacane, Mezzocapo, Cosenz, Ulloa and Orsini. The Neapolitan generals were elderly, for the most part, and their experience dated to the Napoleonic Wars or to the repression of the 1849 revolution in Sicily. The few competent leaders among them – Bosco, Clary, Polizzy, Von Mechel and Pianell – were insufficient compensation for the mediocrity of the command as a whole.

The only dependable units of the army had been the Swiss regiments; but these had been dissolved the previous year and replaced by 'foreign regiments' (made up of Bavarians, Austrians and Swiss) which tended to desert, or defect to Garibaldi as soon as they had the chance.

Garibaldi arrived at Salemi on 13 May and there, the following day, he was proclaimed Dictator of Sicily in the name of Victor Emmanuel II.

At Salemi the *Garibaldini* acquired two more cannon. A priest called Gaspare Salvo had buried them in 1849, and now he dug them up again. Though they were old bronze wrecks they could still be fired. The volunteers increased in number as well: they were now joined by the Baron Sant'Anna and his men from Alcamo (a cross between liberals and *mafiosi*), by a squad from Santa Ninfa, by a mounted unit from Monte San Giuliano under Giuseppe Coppola, and by another squad from Vita armed with pikes and blunderbusses. But the most important of the new arrivals was Fra Pantaleo. Brother Giovanni Pantaleo of Castelvetrano was a strange sort of Capuchin, more soldier than priest. He took part in the campaign of the Thousand and continued to serve as the Red-shirts' chaplain

right up to the time of the campaign in the Vosges.

Garibaldi was not at all sure what he should do next. Three days had passed since the landing, and the Neapolitan royalist forces had not made a move; he feared a trap. In fact, the failure of the Neapolitans to take the initiative was merely a colossal error on their part, and one which not only allowed Garibaldi to consolidate his position at Salemi but also gave La Masa a chance to proselytize the interior of the island. The royalists had indeed ordered the Bonanno Brigade to break up the rebel column; but the brigade could not bring itself to attack, and eventually it was recalled to Palermo.

The *Garibaldini* had to decide whether to attack Palermo at once or to proceed first to the interior of the island with a view to building up their forces. The latter strategy involved a number of unknown factors – the reliability of the Sicilian volunteer squads, for instance, had not yet been demonstrated. The conquest of the island's capital, of course, would be an immense psychological victory; it was decided, therefore, to march directly on Palermo – Bixio, in fact, had already begun shouting 'To Palermo or to Hell!'

But to get to Palermo it was necessary to pass Calatafimi, a town held by General

The uniforms of the Expedition of the Thousand. Although no real uniform as such existed, and all the Garibaldini *wore their own clothes, there was a prevalent trend. From the left: Francesco Simonetta in the Red Shirt; an unknown trooper probably from Medici's Division; Malachia Di Cristoforis (brother of the Di Cristoforis killed at the battle of San Fermo) who was to become an authority in the field of medicine, specializing in women's ailments.*

Landi. Until now Landi had been inactive, but when he received the order to return to Palermo for a meeting of the commanders of all the mobile columns, he decided not to leave the road to the capital undefended. He sent out a few detachments in the direction of Salemi, and sat in wait with the bulk of his troops near Calatafimi. He was not eager for a confrontation with the Red-shirts; his main objective was to intimidate the local population and prevent them from abetting Garibaldi.

Very probably, the Neapolitan command as a whole wished to avoid a premature showdown. Both sides were aware that the first engagement, no matter on how small a scale, would influence the amount of popular support which Garibaldi could count on. This is the only rational explanation of the fact that 25,000 men remained immobile while their adversaries desperately sought a confrontation.

The conflict, when it came, was provoked by the *Garibaldini*. They had set out from Salemi on 15 May, heading for Alcamo, at 5.30 a.m. Not many miles along the road Missori and his Guides arrived at a village called Vita, where they found the six companies which constituted the Neapolitan vanguard on a nearby hill. After an exchange of shots, Missori and his men turned back to inform the General of the enemy's whereabouts. The *Garibaldini* continued their march as far as Calatafimi, where they occupied the hill of Pietralunga. On the hill opposite, called Pianto di Romano, was the Eighth Battalion of the Neapolitan *Cacciatori a Piedi*, under the command of Major Sforza.

Sforza had been ordered to avoid combat. But so sure was he that the 'beggars' would disperse at the first glimpse of his own troops, that he disregarded the order. First, however, he tried to impress his adversaries by putting his men through a series of manoeuvres. (The Red-shirts cheered the impeccable performance.)

Türr disposed the *Garibaldini* in a semi-circle on the summit of Pietralunga. In the centre were the Fifth, Sixth and Seventh Companies with the flag, on which Italy was represented in the form of a beautiful woman flanked by gold and silver trophies (on the

other side was the inscription, 'To Giuseppe Garibaldi, from the Italian Residents of Valparaiso': it had been donated by them in 1855). Behind these were Bixio's company in the centre, the Ninth Company to the left and the Eighth to the right. The Sicilian volunteers, 200 in all, were placed to either end of the formation. Dezza's company was held in reserve; Orsini's artillery was still en route from Salemi. Anfossi's assignment was to guard the artillery and to cover the rear of the entire operation.

Garibaldi sat on a rock and calmly smoked a cigar. But his calm was only apparent; he knew well that the success of the entire expedition was at stake. The Sicilian volunteers had not performed well so far, and now, on the sidelines, they were more inclined to observe than to fight.

For hours the armies stared at each other across the low valley which separates the two hills. Each was satisfied with its own position and was therefore reluctant to attack first. It was a sultry, airless day. At noon, the silence was broken by Neapolitan bugles. In reply, Garibaldi had his bugler blow the only call he knew: *reveille*. The enemy charged down the slope of Pianto di Romano and up Pietralunga, shouting insults.

Garibaldi was with the Genoese *carabinieri*, and gave his customary order that they should not fire until the enemy were right on top of them. But some of his men, unable to wait, counter-charged nevertheless. Chaos ensued. Türr, on horseback, led the attack; behind him were Bixio, Sirtori and Carini.

The *Garibaldini* turned the Neapolitans back, and pursued them down into the valley, across it, and up the slope of the other hill. Pianto di Romano is neither high nor steep. Much of it was given over to gardens, which were laid out on walled terraces two or three feet high. The *Garibaldini* took it one terrace at a time, taking shelter behind the walls between charges. So ferocious was the counter-attack that the Neapolitans called for reinforcements from the village. They were soon joined by five line infantry companies, a few cavalry units and two cannon. They now numbered 2,300. The cannon began to pepper the *Garibaldini* with grape-shot.

The *Garibaldini* occupied the lowermost

The Battle of Calatafimi. Fra Pantaleo can be seen behind the cannon inciting the men.

terrace, and the Neapolitans, instead of counter-attacking at once, gave them a chance to catch their breath in the shelter of the wall. For a moment it seemed that the first charge had completely exhausted them. Bixio ran up and down, cursing and swearing, trying to rekindle their ardour. Sirtori, whose coat was now in shreds, did what he could to reorganize their ranks. Then they moved to take the second terrace. This time they relied almost exclusively on their preferred weapon the bayonet; their smooth-barrelled rifles were not very accurate. The Genoese *carabinieri* supported them with their renowned Swiss carbines.

Garibaldi was now fighting out in the open, in the front line, where his red shirt made an excellent target for the Neapolitans. The men begged him not to expose himself, and one volunteer threw a dark cloak around him, while Manin, Sirtori, Stocco and Nullo took turns at placing themselves between him and the enemy.

The battle was not going well. Bixio sug-

gested a retreat, but Garibaldi replied, 'Here we make Italy or die trying!' Then he went back to the front line. He suspected that Bixio was right, but he was determined to gamble all. He was about to call in the reserves under Dezza, when Dezza appeared: 'the Engineer', as Garibaldi always called him, had seen the gravity of the situation and, without waiting for orders, had brought up his troops from the rear. And at the same moment Orsini succeeded in getting his cannons within range of the battlefield: they were not of much use in practice, but their psychological value was considerable.

At 3 p.m. Garibaldi raised his sabre as a signal to attack the last of the terraces; he himself led the charge. Once again, confusion reigned. When the Neapolitans had run out of ammunition and broken their daggers they continued to fight, hurling stones and wielding their rifles like clubs. Menotti Garibaldi, Augusto Elia and Simone Schiaffino, known as the Three Musketeers, fought side by side in defence of the flag which had been entrusted to them. The Neapolitans now attempted to capture it. Schiaffino was shot dead; Menotti took charge of it, but was himself wounded; Elia tried to save it, but in vain. The Neapolitans seized the flag, though Damiani, one of the Guides, managed to tear the ribbons off it. The *Garibaldini* were left holding the pole. Shortly afterwards Elia, who was shielding Garibaldi, got a bullet in the mouth. When Bixio heard of this he said, in his usual manner, 'Tell him to spit it out.'

By 5-o-clock the battle was over. The exhausted Neapolitans had no choice but to retreat, leaving the town of Calatafimi and one cannon in Garibaldi's hands. The *Garibaldini* were now looked after by the admirable Rosalie Montmasson, who had spent the whole day on the battlefield, nursing the wounded.

The Neapolitans had suffered 150 casualties, including the dead and the wounded; the *Garibaldini* suffered 210. Among those wounded were Nullo, Missori, Elia and Sirtori. But the road to Palermo now lay open, and the support of those Sicilians who had been waiting to see what happened was now assured.

The victory at Calatafimi was of more importance psychologically than militarily. As Garibaldi wrote in his memoirs, it 'demoralized the enemy who, with their fervid southern imagination, attributed prodigies to the Thousand.' In other words, it added to the popular belief that the *Garibaldini* were unbeatable.

General Landi's retreat was discomfited by revolts in the towns he passed through along the way, and by the growth of the Sicilian Action Squads. A relatively minor shock was bringing the profound weaknesses of the Royalist regime out into the open. The Neapolitan General Staff kept ordering its troops to withdraw rather than to attack, even when they were winning. The King, in whom resided the ultimate decision-making authority, was mainly preoccupied with the problem of what uniforms his troops should wear if they should be forced to leave the island. No one, in short, knew which way to turn.

The only Neapolitan who showed some common sense was Colonel Bosco, the commander of the Ninth Regiment of *Cacciatori*. He saw that his army's defensive tactics were only aiding the rebellion, and he proposed that a corps of six thousand men be formed immediately, for the purpose of driving the *Garibaldini* back into the interior of the island, where they could easily be defeated. Bosco's plan was perfect, from a psychological as well as from a military point of view – but nobody paid any attention. Bosco wrote to a friend, 'It is disgraceful that all our energy be wasted in actions so misguided that they call down the malediction of Heaven!'

After Calatafimi the advance of the *Garibaldini* was a triumph; they were greeted ecstatically every step of the way. The only sour note was the incident at Partinico. The rebellion of that town had provoked the reaction of the troops; this in turn had kindled the ire of the populace, which degenerated, after the army had withdrawn, into an anarchistic orgy. 'The town was half burnt', wrote Abba, 'and Garibaldi had to pull his hat down over his eyes to avoid the sight of a group of women dancing in a circle round some Neapolitan corpses.' The scene was so horrendous that the troops preferred to bivouac in the rain rather than stay in this town 'that God had abandoned'.

Garibaldi ordered Pilo and La Masa to advance as far as Monreale with the Sicilian squads and to occupy the heights surrounding Palermo. The Sicilians fought in the neighbourhood of Palermo for four days, without respite. They plagued the columns of Von Mechel and Bosco, which were pursuing them, with attacks, feints and ambushes. On several occasions they were temporarily dispersed, but they never lost control of their positions. Luck was on their side.

At one point Von Mechel and Bosco, having got the better of them, started to pursue the rebels towards Piana dei Greci. They were met by the Neapolitan General Colonna, who ordered them to turn back: operations were to be limited to the district of Palermo.

The Sicilian volunteer squads – about three thousand men in all – acquired invaluable military experience in those four days, but they remained, for the present, a disorganized, ill-equipped rabble. After the conquest of Palermo Garibaldi would organize them in two regiments, and they were later to take part in operations on the continent. Two of these squads were to stand out with particular distinction: that which Corrao took command of after Pilo's death – it was to become a fine regiment – and the *Cacciatori* of Mount Aetna, made up of Albanians from Piana dei Greci, an ethnic group which had settled in Sicily centuries earlier and which to this day maintains its language and traditions.

On 22 May the Thousand arrived at Parco; from there, guided by the Sicilian squads, they moved on to Piana dei Greci.

The citizens of Palermo, meanwhile, were living in trepidation, despite their rulers' attempts to reassure them. Offices and shops were closed; many families fled to Naples by sea, while foreign warships entered the port to protect their governments' consulates. General Lanza was sent from Naples to take over as Governor of the island from the Prince of Castelcigala. Lanza proclaimed an amnesty for all insurgents who would lay down their arms, and announced that a prince of the royal blood would soon be arriving to satisfy 'the just expectations of the Sicilian people'. But it was too late; no one was listening.

Though the Sicilian squads had held on to their positions around Palermo, the operation was by no means concluded. The city was defended by twenty thousand men, a fortress and the Neapolitan warships. While the Royalist forces remained vigilant, it would be nearly impossible to overcome them; Bosco's and Von Mechel's columns, moreover, were still a threat. So a manoeuvre was planned, one which military historians were later to christen 'the diversion of Corleone'. The idea was to lure a significant portion of the Neapolitan army away from the city and its defences, by creating the impression that the *Garibaldini* were withdrawing to the interior of the island.

Orsini was placed in charge of the operation. With his broken-down cannons, forty gunners, some of the wounded, and 110 Sicilians of the Corleone Squad, he began his march south, 'raising as much dust as possible'. Orsini was a native of Palermo, and had been educated at the Neapolitan military academy. In 1848 he had taken part in the

Nino Bixio: one of the most courageous of Garibaldi's generals.

Sicilian insurrection as an artillery officer, and had afterwards gone into exile in Turkey. As soon as he had got wind of the proposed invasion he had joined Garibaldi at Genoa. Now, as he filed past the General with his men, Crispi remarked, shaking his head, 'Poor Orsini – he's on his way to be sacrificed.' Poor Orsini was in fact the guinea-pig. Only thanks to his extraordinarily good luck did he survive the coming engagement with the loss of only seven gunners.

Von Mechel and Bosco set out in pursuit of Orsini, as they had been expected to do. When they discovered the ruse, it was too late: the *Garibaldini* had entered Palermo.

On the night of 24 May, while Orsini was on his way south, Garibaldi marched on Gibilrossa. La Masa was already there, trying to deal with the impressionable Sicilians, who had believed the report that Garibaldi was fleeing southward. The arrival of the General put an end to the discussion.

Garibaldi reorganized the Sicilian volunteers, dividing them into squads of ten men, each led by a corporal who could be recognized by his tricolour armband. He now had 3,750 men, while the garrison at Palermo, even in its present reduced state, consisted of 15,000 men and 30 artillery pieces. But the

most competent of the Neapolitan officers were in hot pursuit of Orsini's cloud of dust.

On the evening of the 25th, at Gibilrossa, Garibaldi was called upon by three British naval officers and *Times* correspondent Nandór Eber. Eber was born in Hungary in 1825. Exiled in Turkey for his role in a Hungarian revolt, he had become a knowledgeable orientalist. In 1851 he moved to London, where he studied the art of war. He followed the Crimean War as correspondent for *The Times*, but he also took an active part in the combat: he rose to the rank of colonel in the Turkish Army. In 1859 *The Times* sent him to Italy. The Hungarian revolutionary committee in Piedmont recognized his rank, and he fought in the battles of Magenta and Solferino. When he heard of Garibaldi's landing in Sicily, Eber rushed to Palermo – and then to Gibilrossa, bringing with him detailed information about the capital's defences. He fought with the *Garibaldini* throughout the campaign and eventually became a brigadier, though he continued all the while to send his articles to *The Times*.

Eber was not the only journalist to join the *Garibaldini*. First-hand reports of the campaign are to be found in many newspapers of the time. In England, these included, in addi-

The skirmish at Ponte dell'Ammiraglio.

Entering Palermo.

tion to *The Times*, the *Daily News*, the *Morning Post* and *The Observer*; the *Illustrated London News* featured the dispatches of Barx Tucket (who was to be killed at Capua on 19 October) and the drawings of George Thomas and Frank Vizetelly. In France, the campaign was covered by *Le Siècle*, with illustrations by Hugues de Montalant, and by *L'Opinion Nationale*, with the correspondence of Emile Louis Maison, who fought with Rüstow's sharpshooters in Medici's division. America was represented by the *World*, the *Herald* and the *Daily Tribune* – whose correspondent was no less a personage than Karl Marx. Other papers which sent correspondents were the German *Kladderadatsch*; *Etoile Belge* and the *Journal de Bruxelles* of Belgium; the *Neue Zürcher Zeitung* and the *Revue de Genève* of Switzerland; and the *Corriere Mercantile, Il Diritto, La Gazzetta del Popolo, Il Mondo Illustrato* and *L'Opinione* of Italy.

Garibaldi decided, on the basis of what Eber had told him, to centre his attack on Palermo at Porta Termini. This would not be easy as it would involve crossing a narrow bridge, called Ponte dell'Ammiraglio, over a canal. But Porta Termini was the only city-gate without artillery to defend it.

What ammunition was left was distributed among the troops: four cartridges each. There were always bayonets – though many of the Sicilians had brought hunting-rifles to which bayonets could not be fixed. La Masa, who had been placed in charge of the Sicilian volunteers, told them, 'Use whatever arms you have, and God will protect you.' The arms they had ranged from sawn-off shotguns to halberds, pikes and pitchforks.

On the night of 26 May they began their descent from the mountains. At the head of the column was Missori with a select vanguard of thirty men. Next came La Masa with the Sicilians. And then Garibaldi, with his men divided into two battalions led by Bixio and Carini, and the Genoese *carabinieri* in between. Sant'Anna's squad formed the rear guard. All the troops had been exhorted to stay calm and to keep silent, but the descent grew increasingly chaotic until, at two in the morning, Garibaldi ordered a halt. Only Tüköry was to go on ahead with a small party of scouts, backed up by La Masa's Sicilians. But order collapsed when the first houses on the outskirts of town came into sight. Shouting, 'Palermo! Palermo!' the Sicilians

attempted to get ahead of Tüköry's scouts. Fra Pantaleo, La Masa and Bixio managed to persuade them to hold back and calm down, but the damage was done: the troops guarding Ponte dell'Ammiraglio had woken up, and the surprise-attack had failed.

Though it had no artillery, the Ponte dell'Ammiraglio was well defended. Tüköry and his scouts hurled themselves forward, hoping to make a breakthrough, but they were driven back by dense rifle-fire. La Masa's boys, after their premature display of enthusiasm, now panicked and dispersed.

At that moment Garibaldi appeared with the Genoese *carabinieri* and Bixio's battalion. 'Set an example; attack!', Garibaldi shouted to Nullo, and Nullo charged on horseback, as he had done years earlier when he was with Masina's lancers. He broke through the Neapolitan lines, and was followed immediately by Tüköry and Bixio. Tüköry fell, wounded; a few days later he died of gangrene. Bixio was also wounded, in the chest, but he extracted the bullet himself and carried on fighting.

The conflict lasted half an hour. Led by Bixio the *Garibaldini* now entered Palermo through Porta Termini. Inside the city, however, scattered fighting continued for days. All the bells rang the tocsin, and the people left their houses to give the liberators a helping hand. Barricades sprang up everywhere. Garibaldi set up headquarters in Palazzo Pretorio, and ordered Sirtori to occupy the port and cut the Neapolitans off from the sea. Crispi, meanwhile, met the Revolutionary Committee to organize a provisional government.

A few pockets of Neapolitan resistance, such as the Sant'Antonio Barracks, were easily overcome, but at Porta Maqueda, where the Royalist forces had two cannon at their disposal, the struggle was a bitter one. Vittore

The barricades erected in Palermo during the fighting:

Royalist cannons in a Palermo square. (Top left)

Barricades at Correria Vecchia. (Centre left)

Barricades at Mercato Nuovo. The cannons are very old and unusuable, placed there by Türr simply to trick the enemy. (Bottom left)

Fighting in the ruins of Palermo. The continuous fighting was often in narrow streets strewn with corpses and among the ruins of the city under constant bombardment from the Neapolitan artillery. (Right)

Tasca's company, from Bergamo, and Luigi La Porta's Sicilian squad eventually took the enemy position, but only at the cost of many lives. Sirtori occupied the port and left it in Giovanni Corrao's charge. He then turned his attention to the district of Porta Montalto, but here the Neapolitans were so firmly entrenched that, despite repeated attacks, it took him until late that night merely to occupy the Convent of the Annunziata.

As they fought their way through the alley-ways of Palermo the *Garibaldini* frequently came up against formidable opposition. They then resorted to an old ruse, according to an eye-witness, G. Romano of Catania. Gesticulating towards imaginary comrades outside the range of the enemy's vision, they would shout fictitious orders, such as 'First Company – bayonets!' or 'First Battalion – charge!' As often as not the ruse worked and the Royalists, believing themselves to be out-numbered, fled.

Towards midday the Neapolitans began to fall back on the Royal Palace, where they barricaded themselves in. Bixio, who had continued fighting all morning though he had lost a great deal of blood, turned up at Garibaldi's headquarters, brandishing the

stump of a sabre. He was enraged because someone had had the impertinence to advise him to get medical aid. 'Come on', he shouted, 'I need twenty men of good will. We'll all be dead in half-an-hour anyway. To the Palace!' Garibaldi cut him short with an order to go and rest, and courageous, indomitable Bixio obeyed him without question.

The attack had taken General Lanza by surprise, and he could think of no other response than to order the fort which dominated the city and the ships at anchor in the harbour to shell Palermo indiscriminately. In three days, three hundred of the population were killed and five hundred wounded. Corpses piled up in the streets; homeless families wandered about looking for shelter – at their peril because the Neapolitan troops were shooting all the civilians they saw on the grounds that they might be revolutionaries. The soldiers turned to looting, and numerous women were raped, murdered with bayonets and left in the streets to rot.

The shells also fell on churches and convents, which had for the most part been converted into hospitals or shelters. The church of Sant'Anna and the convent of the Scalzi were completely destroyed, and doctors, nurses and patients were buried in the rubble. Stefano Canzio, Benedetto Cairoli and Giorgio Manin, who were among the wounded, were rescued only with great difficulty.

But the bombardment did not have the desired effect. The people of Palermo sided with the *Garibaldini*, served as guides through the city's maze of alleys, erected barricades and took part in the fighting.

In the afternoon the Neapolitans attempted a counter-attack. Their objective was to recover the positions they had lost at Porta di Castro and around the port, but they were everywhere repulsed. By evening all they had left was the Royal Palace, the Finance Office, the fort of Castellamare and a few isolated pockets of resistance. Even after nightfall the fighting went on in the blaze of burning buildings; as the Romans had done in 1849, the people of Palermo placed lights in their windows for the benefit of the combatants in the streets.

At dawn the Neapolitans resumed their

Garibaldi shakes hands with Admiral Mundy.

shelling and their attacks in the streets. It was a ferocious struggle. Not even religious edifices were spared: many were set fire to, such as the convent of the Badia Nuova and the monastery of the Seven Angels (where the *Garibaldini* managed to rescue the nuns from the flames). This action gave rise to a legend which helped to improve Garibaldi's reputation among the Sicilians. The nuns invented the story that the General was a direct descendant of the Sinibaldi family of Palermo, to which Saint Rosalie, the protectress of the island, had belonged. Garibaldi, it was claimed, had now been sent by the Saint to save Palermo from fire. Fra Pantaleo, who knew his fellow Sicilians well, confirmed the story in all its details.

The Neapolitans gradually had to give up their pockets of resistance, and by the evening of 28 May they had only one position left. On the 29th the shelling began later than usual, around 10 a.m. Garibaldi had given orders to complete the occupation of the area around Porta Montalto, and after four hours of inhu-

manly savage assaults Sirtori, with the help of the Sixth and Seventh Companies, had succeeded. Abba wrote, 'There were so many Royalist corpses lying about, that I still fail to understand who can have killed them all.'

While the fighting raged at Porta Montalto, Neapolitan troops came out from the Royal Palace to attack the barricades in Via Bonello, Via Papireto and, especially, Via Toledo. These were defended by the citizens with the help of the Sicilian Volunteers. Garibaldi turned up with two companies, and after an hour the Neapolitans were obliged to retreat.

Neapolitan officers and men who deserted to join the Garibaldian side brought the information that their former comrades could not hold out much longer. And in fact on 29 May the Royalists – through the British Admiral Mundy – asked for a truce. That afternoon Garibaldi, wearing the uniform of a Piedmont general and accompanied by Crispi, went aboard HMS *Hannibal* to confer with the Neapolitan General Letizia. The talks got off to a poor start. Letizia did not want the captains of the foreign ships to be present, and he refused to recognize Garibaldi's title of Dictator. In the end he gave in, and read the draft of an agreement, which had been dictated by Lanza. But Garibaldi rejected a few of the clauses, and the meeting broke up without concrete results. The following morning, however, Lanza called for an armistice.

Bosco, Von Mechel and Polizzy begged, with an insistence verging on insubordination, to be allowed to attack the *Garibaldini*. But in vain: the armistice was signed, and it was agreed that on 6 June the Neapolitans – who had suffered 816 casualties – would clear out of Palermo. Lanza was to suffer the consequence of this surrender, though the fault was not his alone. He was the victim of a system which did not allow him to exercise fully his command. Signing the armistice was no doubt a grievous error, since many of the troops were still capable of fighting. But it was the King who had decided to surrender.

Political considerations aside, though, there can be no doubt that from a military point of view the Neapolitan conduct of the campaign was inexcusable. The *Garibaldini* had succeeded in pulverizing an army of 25,000 well-armed men who had fortresses at their disposal and who could bring in reinforcements by sea. The troops were never used in a mass offensive. The Neapolitans had not tried to stop Garibaldi directly after the landing at Marsala, and at Calatafimi they had failed to send Sforza reinforcements until it was too late. Landi's retreat to Palermo, by order of Castelcigala, had been an error, as the troops could easily have dug in at Alcamo. And at Palermo, finally, only those troops who happened to come into direct contact with the *Garibaldini* took part in the action. True, Garibaldi had gained a psychological advantage at the very beginning – he was a master at this form of combat – but the Neapolitans never seriously attempted to resist him.

Garibaldi himself best summed up the spirit of the occasion: 'It truly seemed a portent when twenty thousand soldiers of tyranny capitulated to a handful of citizens pledged to sacrifice and martyrdom.'

With the fall of Palermo the expedition of the Thousand, as such, came to an end. When the Italian government, years later, assigned a pension to all those who had taken part in the conquest of the Kingdom of the Two Sicilies, it made a special distinction between the troops who had landed at Marsala and those who came later. Two commissions, presided over by Medici, Bixio and Türr, established the names of the participants, and a certain Pavia collected their portraits in a photograph album in 1882.

While the citizens of Palermo recovered the bodies of their dead from the rubble, the *Garibaldini* put on their red shirts once again and began to work out a new political structure for the city. Garibaldi had won many campaigns, but he had never ruled a single province. His only experience in government had been as a member of the 'defence triad' at Montevideo, but there he had been occupied exclusively with military problems.

Contrary to what many people expected, Garibaldi's statesmanship was, if not outstanding, at least perfectly competent. Though he kept the title of Dictator, he wisely allowed Crispi, his Secretary of State, to manage the details of government. Crispi knew how to defend Garibaldi's interests against the political intriguers who still hoped to block the expedition or at least limit its scope. And he had an intimate knowledge of the Sicilian people, who even now were beginning to reveal the true reasons for the support they had given in the struggle against the Bourbons.

When the Sicilian volunteers enlisted, in fact, they were motivated not so much by the ideal of national unity as by the hope that the defeat of the Neapolitans might lead to the realization of their social aims – land reform, equal rights, a more humane treatment of workers and so on. In many villages the cry of 'Long live Garibaldi!' was now mixed with that of 'Death to the aristocracy!' In some instances, the wrath of a people humiliated by centuries of exploitation gave rise to sanguinary excesses. But the *Garibaldini* (most of whose mentalities were rooted in entirely different historical traditions) had no sympathy for such excesses, and they themselves resorted to violence in order to put a stop to them. At Bronte, where the population had assassinated the local notables and looted their houses, Bixio intervened with his troops and hanged seventeen of the villagers, as a warning to the rest of the island.

The injustices of which the rural masses in Sicily and the rest of southern Italy were victims were not eliminated by the *Garibaldini* or, later, by the government of unified Italy. The incomprehension of the liberators was so complete that many of the Sicilian peasants who had joined Garibaldi in hopes of a better world now turned to banditry. The ensuing repression only widened the gulf between the 'two Italies', the baleful effects of which may be noted to this very day.

Back at Genoa, meanwhile, the indefatigable Bertani was organizing other expeditionary forces. On 7 June Carmelo Agnetta arrived in Palermo with sixty men and a thousand rifles. Fabrizi sent 1,500 rifles from Malta. On the 8th Clemente Corte set sail with nine hundred men on the American clipper *Charles and Jane*. Though it was flying a United States flag, this vessel was seized by Neapolitan ships, the *Fulminante* and the *Fieramosca*, and brought to Gaeta. The American government intervened and on 30 June Corte and his men were freed and allowed to continue their voyage.

Bertani had been one of Garibaldi's most faithful followers since the time of the Roman Republic. He was an able physician, and served as a medical officer in all the campaigns of the Italian *Risorgimento*. He directed the organizational and financial side of the expedition of the Thousand, and served as liaison between the General and the various 'Garibaldi Funds' which had sprung up all over the world. As a passionate republican, he was bitterly opposed to the idea of laying all of southern Italy at the feet of Piedmont's King. This fact created numerous problems for Garibaldi, though the two never ceased to collaborate and they remained good friends. Under Mazzini's influence Bertani attempted to use against the Papal States some of the reinforcements meant for Garibaldi in Sicily. This would have aroused the strong opposition of the Piedmont government and would no doubt have led to the armed intervention of France. Fortunately men like Medici, Cosenz and von Rüstow were able to resist the temptation to take part in such a project, which would certainly have detracted from the positive results obtained so far.

Medici and Cosenz found it more difficult

Agostino Bertani. The man who served as a surgeon with the Garibaldini was one of the finest medical men of the period. He openly neglected his career to dedicate his life to the liberation of Italy.

than did Garibaldi to oppose Bertani's designs, as they were more closely bound to him in friendship. But they found an ally in Cavour who, after the success of Garibaldi's adventure, had changed his mind about the Sicilian campaign: he was now willing to support it, so as to be able to condition its outcome. He vetoed an attack on Rome – the recurrent dream of the *Garibaldini* – but in return he provided them with diplomatic coverage. Thus they were able to purchase a significant quantity of Enfield rifles, and to organize the new expeditions quite openly.

The purchase of three ships at Marseilles, with 752,000 lire provided by the Garibaldi Fund in Paris, was somewhat more complicated. The French authorities were opposed to Garibaldi's expedition, and it was necessary to pretend that the money was for a shipment of sugar, burlap and other merchandise. The three ships were bought officially by the American commodore William De Rohan (later to become a Rear Admiral in

Giacomo Medici.

Enrico Cosenz.

Garibaldi's navy), who re-christened them the *Washington*, the *Franklin* and the *Oregon*.

Franklin headed for Leghorn to pick up Colonel Malenchini's Tuscan volunteers, while Medici's 2,500 men boarded the other two ships at Genoa on 10 June. Flying the American flag, the three then came together off the Ligurian coast and sailed to Cagliari, where the volunteers were issued a very non-Garibaldian uniform: blue cap with red piping and a black leather peak, coffee-coloured blouse with a broad red band down the front and red breast pockets, drab linen trousers, a haversack, a flask and a military blanket to be slung over the shoulder. The officers' uniform was identical, but for rank badges on the sleeves and cap.

Medici landed at Castellamare in Sicily on the night of 17 June. On 9 July Cosenz and 1,500 additional troops arrived aboard the *Washington* and another, recently-acquired, steamer the *Wellington*.

These Italian volunteers were joined by conspicuous numbers of foreigners, attracted by Garibaldi's championship of the cause of liberty. It is not within our present scope to give account of single individuals; here we can only indicate the more important legions and other groups.

A number of Hungarians had found their way to Palermo, and on 16 July they obtained Garibaldi's permission to constitute a legion under Major Adolf Mogyoródy. This Hungarian Legion started out with 51 men, but it grew rapidly until it comprised 504 in all. In addition there were numerous Hungarian officers and private soldiers who did not join this Legion but chose to serve in various other Garibaldian units. On 27 July the First Squadron of Hungarian Hussars was constituted, commanded by Major Fülöp Figyelmesy; later a Second Squadron, under Major Scheiter, was formed. The two together accounted for some 215 horse.

The Legion and the Hussars joined the Eber and Milan Brigades of Türr's division. Among the best known of the Hungarians, besides Türr, Tüköry and Eber, were Sándor Téléki (who had fought with Garibaldi the previous year), Lieutenant-Colonels Kiss and Csudaffy, Konrad Eberhardt (who was to lead a brigade in Bixio's division and would later

join the Italian army and fight against Garibaldi at Aspromonte), and Gusztav Frigyesy, one of the leading figures of the international Garibaldian movement. Frigyesy was a veteran of the 1859 war. He was to take part in the entire campaign of 1860, and later in those of 1861, 1866 and 1867. (He was to die in 1878 at Milan, penniless and insane.)

Towards the middle of June the Englishman John William Dunne, with forty compatriots, set up an English Battalion at Palermo. As time went by other Englishmen and a number of Sicilians joined it, and it eventually grew into a regiment of 1,500 men and, later, a brigade. Dunne remained in command. He was one of the great protagonists of the European liberal movement: after acquiring his military experience in India and the Crimea he went on to fight for national independence in Italy, Poland and Denmark.

A month after its constitution the battalion won high praises from Garibaldi for its performance at the battle of Milazzo. Thereupon Hugh Forbes, the English *Garibaldino* from Rome, proposed the formation of a British Legion. The idea was received with enthusiasm by John Peard, Edward and Alfred Styles, Percy Windham, Peter Cunningham (the former sailor who was the first to scale the walls of Milazzo), Lieutenant Blakeney and other English Red-shirts. Dunne, who was the most serious soldier of them all, agreed on condition that he be allowed to vet all of the troops personally. The plan was put into action, but it turned out disastrously.

The British Legion did not effectively enter Garibaldi's service until 15 October, when he was already at Naples. Its chronic indiscipline created all sorts of problems for the Southern Army, to the point that Garibaldi considered disbanding it. The Legion was perfectly capable of fighting valiantly on the battlefield – as it proved at Capua on 19 October – but it was dogged by ill luck and was burdened with a

Colonel John Peard, commander of the British Legion. Peard had already served with Garibaldi in the Cacciatori delle Alpi *as a volunteer. (Above left)*
John Dunne, Brigadier General, photographed shortly after the expedition when he served for a while in the regular Italian army with the rank he had received from the Garibaldini. Like the others who joined the Italian army, he had to shave off his thick beard, which was against regulations. (Below left)

English volunteers enter Naples.

thoroughly unsuitable commander.

Things began promisingly enough. Alfred Styles went to London to look for recruits, and the number of volunteers exceeded all expectations. But he left the work of organizing the legion to a certain Captain Boyle Minchin, who assigned the various commands to officers of the Volunteer Rifles Corps rather than to soldiers who had proved their mettle in India and the Crimea. (The experience of the Volunteer Rifles was limited to target practice and to colourful parades in Hyde Park.) Boyle Minchin's methods offended numerous veterans, who either withdrew their offer of service altogether or enlisted privately in Dunne's brigade or in other divisions. Other defections were due to the gross mismanagement of the local Garibaldi Fund, which kept the volunteers waiting for weeks without sustenance in the streets of London.

But the worst error was committed by Garibaldi himself when he made John Peard commander of the legion. Peard was forty-nine; he had fought the previous year with the *Cacciatori delle Alpi* as an ordinary volunteer. He was, undeniably, a brave man, but he had none of the other requirements for commanding a volunteer corps. Years later, seeking to lay the blame on others, he wrote, 'Many of the officers were undisciplined and some were worse than that. I thank God that the legion no longer exists.' But he himself was chiefly responsible for the bad reputation of the British Legion.

The performance of the legion was more than compensated for, however, by other Englishmen in Garibaldi's service. In addition to Dunne's brigade, there were the sailors of the *Agamemnon* and of the *Renown* who deserted to join the *Garibaldini* and who, under the command of Lieutenant Cooper, manned a battery valiantly at the battle of the Volturno; there were also Wyndham's zouaves (infantry) and Hugh Forbes' battalion. Other prestigious names among the English were Charles Stuart Forbes, who was then thirty and who was to end his career as commodore in the British fleet, D. Dowling, a former artillery captain who joined Garibaldi with a battery of Whitworth cannon and who was to become inspector-general of the

Garibaldian artillery, and Edward F. Jarvis and R. L. Weeks, who resigned from the Royal Navy to serve under the General.

But most outstanding of all was Jessie White Mario. She was a lively and intelligent woman, a former medical student who had married one of Garibaldi's close associates, Alberto Mario, and joined the General with the second expedition under Medici. She worked with Ripari in setting up and running the hospital service, enlisting the aid of the Ladies' Garibaldi Benevolent Association, which was headed by the Countess of Shaftesbury. One of her letters, published by all the English papers, brought in an avalanche of medical materials, including a number of artificial arms and legs. She was, in short, the Red-shirts' Florence Nightingale. After 1860 she joined in the social conflicts with which the *Garibaldini* were to become increasingly involved, though her interest was more humanitarian than political.

It was relatively easy for an Englishman to join Garibaldi, but it was much less so for a Frenchman, since Napoleon III's government was bitterly opposed to the Garibaldian cause. Garibaldi had fought the French in 1849, but he had nevertheless many sympathizers in France, especially among the republicans. During the days of the Roman Republic the Emperor had had to resort to force to put down the demonstrations in favour of Garibaldi in the streets of Paris and Lyons. *Le Siècle* and *L'Opinion* opened a subscription to raise funds for the *Garibaldini*, but they were hindered in this operation by the police. The Garibaldi Fund of Paris was forced to place a notice in the papers to the effect that it could offer no assistance to volunteers who sought to join the General. When it managed to elude police surveillance, however, the Fund did send money, and men; its greatest *coup* was the surreptitious sale of the three ships to De Rohan.

Unlike the other volunteers, who were motivated by liberal ideals or by hatred of the 'Octopus of Reaction', the French were true 'eighty-niners', inflamed by the spirit of the glorious French Revolution. In fact when Paul de Flotte, the undisputed head of the French Legion, hurled himself at the fortress of Torre Cavallo in order to provoke the

Jessie White Mario. As long as she was able, she followed all the Garibaldini *campaigns, both military and political. She then wrote biographies of the men and their times.*

Neapolitans, he did not cry 'Long live Italy!' or 'Long live Garibaldi!' as did the other volunteers, but rather 'Long live the Republic!' For the French Red-shirts, Garibaldi was essentially a leader of the international republican movement.

The first French volunteers arrived at Palermo with the expedition led by Cosenz. They were sixty-four in all, led by Paul de Flotte and Philippe Bourdon. De Flotte was a lieutenant in the French navy who resigned his commission in 1849 when the reactionary aims of Louis Napoleon became manifest. Garibaldi made him a major. (He was to die in Calabria after the landing there.) Bourdon, who was thirty-nine, had fought with the French army in the Crimea and in Italy. Under Garibaldi he became chief of the Engineers. He was to take part in all Garibaldian campaigns until, in 1870, he became Chief of Staff of the Army of the Vosges. Like many other *Garibaldini*, he was destined to die in poverty.

The French Legion (which after the death

of its leader was to take the name De Flotte Legion) grew rapidly until, by the end of July, it numbered five hundred men. Grouped in the division led first by Cosenz and then by Milbitz, it distinguished itself at Milazzo and at the Volturno.

It is difficult to establish the identities of the French volunteers because most of them used assumed names to avoid being registered by Napoleon III's police. Of those known to us, the most important are: Maxim du Camp, an officer of Türr's General Staff, who was to write a fine book about the expedition; Ulrique de Fonvielle; Jules Abric Baillot, an artillery captain in the Second Regiment of Cosenz's division; Kolbi, one of Bixio's ordnance officers; Rouet, a cavalry captain; Delacroix, a lieutenant who had served in Algeria; Colonel Galopain; Franqueville d'Orthal; and Colonel Gustave Paul Cluseret, a thirty-seven-year-old Parisian who had fought in Algeria in the 1848 revolution, and in the Crimean War, and who was to take over the command of the Legion after De Flotte's death.

But the most celebrated of the Frenchmen who joined Garibaldi was Alexandre Dumas *père*, the novelist and playwright. He stood out from the start, thanks to his extravagant behaviour – and thanks as well to his companion, a beautiful girl called Emma who liked to dress up as an admiral. Dumas was later to write a rather romanticized biography of the General and a history of the expedition of the Thousand in which he himself figures heroically (whereas in truth he followed the campaign from the comfort of his yacht). He did – or rather, Emma did – provide a welcome touch of colour, however.

On 19 June the Foreign Legion was formed. It consisted of about a hundred men, mostly Swiss and Germans who had fought for the Neapolitans at Calatafimi in the Eighth Battalion of *Cacciatori* and the *Carabinieri* Battalion, and who had now changed sides. They were received with misgivings by the *Garibaldini*, who could not understand how they could be trusted to fight their former comrades-in-arms. But their performance soon won the respect and admiration of their new comrades, and they were granted permission to call themselves the 'Foreign *Cacciatori* Company'.

They got off to a rather bad start – marked by indiscipline and a few cases of theft – but their commander, Adolf Wolff, undertook a relentless purge of the cadres, and succeeded in turning the Legion into a small but extremely effective military instrument which was to distinguish itself throughout the campaign as part of Eber's Brigade in Türr's Division. Wolff was a Bavarian disciple of Mazzini who had learned the art of war in the Crimea. After 1860 he fought again with the *Garibaldini* in 1866 and took part in various abortive attempts at a republican revolution. Only after the fall of the Second Empire in 1870 did the world discover that for more than twenty years Wolff had been a secret agent, responsible directly to Napoleon III at a salary of 12,000 francs per year.

At first the troops of the Foreign Legion continued to wear their Neapolitan uniforms, with a different cap and a red handkerchief round the neck. After Wolff's reorganization they wore red shirts.

The German contribution was not limited to the Foreign Legion; the Garibaldian army included quite a few German-born officers and men. The most prestigious name is that of Friedrich Wilhelm von Rüstow, a Brandenburger and an expert on military science. He eventually became Garibaldi's Chief of Staff, and wrote valuable studies of the *Garibaldini* and their campaigns.

There was, of course, no lack of Polish volunteers: the Poles had been among the first foreigners to fight under Garibaldi. This time the Polish contingent was smaller than it had been in 1849, but it was perhaps qualitatively superior. Among the outstanding officers who served in the 1860 campaign were Marian Langiewicz, Garibaldi's *aide-de-camp*, Konstantin Ordon, Eduard Lange (who was to become a Garibaldian general), General Ludwig Mierolawski, who had been in charge of the defence of Sicily during the revolution of 1849, and General Aleksander Milbitz. Milbitz had commanded the Polish Legion of the Roman Republic. Soon he was to become a General of Division (in command of the Sixteenth), and he would later lead his troops with great distinction at the battle of the Volturno.

Active support also came from the United States, where many Italian political exiles – including General Avezzana, war minister of the Roman Republic – had made their homes. Fund-raising for the Italian cause had begun in 1859, when a draft for £784 on the Rothschild bank had been sent over from San Francisco.

News of Garibaldi's success in Sicily now stimulated a huge increase in the contributions. The city of New York alone came up with $100,000, while California sent $3,000 and a contingent of German volunteers. Small contributions came from such sources as the German community in Newark, the Peru Union of Lexington and the Rifle Club of Worcester, Massachusetts.

Funds for the liberation of Italy continued to be raised in the United States even after the end of the campaign. On 3 April 1862, L'Opinione of Turin announced that thirty-four 16-calibre rifled cannon had been constructed with American contributions, and that four of them (numbered 1, 12, 13 and 27) bore the inscription 'To Italy, from her sons in California.'

America sent volunteers as well as economic aid, though they did not come in vast numbers and never formed a legion of their own. Here we may recall Colonel C. C. Hicks, who became a member of Garibaldi's staff, Captain Van Benthuysen of Louisiana, Lieutenant Frank Maury of Tennessee, Lieutenant Spencer, son of the United States consul in Paris, Baughman of Virginia, Alexander Moore of New York, General Wheat and – most important of all – William de Rohan, who became Rear Admiral in Garibaldi's navy.

Sándor Téléki, ex-officer of the Austrian army, joined Garibaldi together with Türr and Tüköry, and became a general during the expedition of the Thousand. (Above)

Adolf Wolff. (Below)

General Aledsander Milbitz, commander of the (Garibaldino) 15th Division at the battle of the Volturno. He had already fought with Garibaldi for the Roman Republic. (Above right)

Nandór Eber, a Hungarian Brigadier General who, after fighting for the liberation of Hungary, fought in the Crimean War and in the second Italian War of Independence in 1859, continuing to send dispatches as a special correspondent of The Times. He joined Garibaldi at Gibilrossa. (Below right)

When these new forces had assembled, Garibaldi could resume his campaign against the Royalists. The Thousand were restructured to form four divisions, which were numbered as though they were additions to the fourteen existing divisions of the regular Italian army: the Fifteenth under Türr, the Sixteenth under Cosenz and later under Milbitz, the Seventeenth under Medici and the Eighteenth under Bixio. They were now designated the Southern Army, with Türr named as its Inspector-General. But the *Garibaldini* preferred to go on calling their divisions 'brigades', and they continued to refer to each regiment by the name of its commanding officer.

Their next strategic aim was the invasion of continental Italy; but first it would be necessary to gain possession of all the fortresses which protected the Strait of Messina, particularly the fortress of Milazzo. Medici's division therefore set out along the coast in the direction of Milazzo, while Türr's and Bixio's headed for the interior, where they hoped to rouse the population against the remaining Neapolitan garrisons. The army was to reassemble at Punta del Faro on the Strait of Messina.

On 14 July the Neapolitan commander at Messina, General Clary, ordered Colonel Bosco to move to the defence of Milazzo with four battalions, one cavalry squadron and one battery. Medici, who had occupied the nearby town of Barcellona, sent Lieutenant Colonel Simonetta with 250 *Garibaldini* to a crossroads hamlet called Archi, which lay on the route from Messina to Milazzo. Bosco had already passed by the time Simonetta arrived, but he had left Major Maring to guard the crossroads with the Eighth Battalion of *Cacciatori*, a cavalry platoon and two howitzers. A skirmish ensued, and the Neapolitans trounced the *Garibaldini*, who were forced to retreat.

Fearing, however, that they would return in force, Maring failed to consolidate his position, and withdrew to Milazzo. Bosco was furious, and had him placed under arrest, ordering the column to return to Archi. But the soldiers remained loyal to their commander, and refused to budge, so that Bosco had to send six other companies, led by Lieutenant

Colonel Marra. During the confusion the position had been occupied by Colonel Interdonato's Sicilian volunteers, and the frustrated Bosco had to recall his troops definitively to Milazzo. All the roads leading to Milazzo were now in Medici's hands. There was nothing for Bosco to do but await the attack.

Medici had 2,500 men. On 19 July Cosenz's division turned up with 1,500 troops. Garibaldi, who had arrived on 18 July, now had a force of four hundred at his disposal. Bosco's troops, on the other hand, together with those of the Milazzo garrison under the command of Colonel Pironti, numbered 120 officers and 4,500 soldiers. They were deployed across the neck of the promontory on which the town and the fortress of Milazzo stand.

The *Garibaldini* began their attack on the morning of 20 July 1860. The first to advance was Medici, with two columns led by Simonetta and Malenchini; each consisted of four battalions. Nicola Fabrizi was sent down the main road to Messina to head off Neapolitan reinforcements. But he never had

Türr's General Staff.

to fight: the reinforcements turned back to Messina when they learned that Milazzo was already cut off by the *Garibaldini*. Cosenz stayed at Meri with a reserve force.

When Malenchini reached the village of San Pietro he was greeted by a dense round of artillery fire, his troops were dispersed, and it appeared that the whole attack was getting off to a very bad start. When Garibaldi realized what was happening he sent Cosenz to head off an enemy counter-attack. Simonetta's column was also halted by Royalist gunfire, and the situation stagnated until about noon. The Genoese *carabinieri* were the hardest hit; they left half their men on the battlefield.

Then Garibaldi, who had dismounted and gone too close to the enemy lines, was surrounded by a detachment of Neapolitan cavalry led by Captain Giuliani. He was saved by Missori, who successfully charged Giuliani, and put the Neapolitans to flight. Shortly afterwards, from the roof of a house where he had gone to observe Neapolitan movements, Garibaldi spied the steamer *Tüköry* off the coast. This was one of the first Garibaldian warships, and it was now arriving from Palermo with a battalion of reinforce-

Colonel Bosco. Together with Von Mechel, Bosco was, without a doubt, Garibaldi's most tenacious adversary and the most intuitive of the Garibaldini's *weaknesses.*

ments. Garibaldi rushed to meet it, and ordered it to proceed full speed towards the beach of San Papino. There, out of the range of the cannons of the fortress of Milazzo, the *Tüköry* calmly began to shell the right flank of the Neapolitan force. The bombardment broke up the Royalist lines, and the troops retreated.

Medici then ordered his men to attack. Dunne's brigade broke through the Neapolitan lines and entered the city, obliging the enemy to take shelter inside the fortress. Meanwhile the *Tüköry* entered the port – under sail: its engines were out of order.

Garibaldi notified Bosco of his terms: unconditional surrender – except for the officers, who would be free to return to Naples. Bosco refused; he declared that he could capitulate only under honourable conditions and with the consent of his government. Meanwhile, he intended to defend himself with honour. 'If

Garibaldi chose to mine the fortress', he added, 'he himself would sit right over the tunnel, smoking his cigar, and as he was blown up he would cry, "Long live the King!".'

Talks were suspended. Then four Neapolitan frigates appeared off Milazzo. For a moment it was feared that they carried reinforcements. But then General Anzani came ashore: he had been entrusted with negotiating the capitulation.

It was agreed that the Neapolitans would leave the fort with full military honours, while the fort would be turned over to Garibaldi with all the matériel and livestock it contained. The Royalist troops were sent back to Naples on the frigates; Bosco set off for Messina.

Garibaldi's casualties came to 750 dead and wounded. Among those wounded was Cosenz, but, like Bixio, he immediately threw himself back into the fray. Neapolitan casualties were 132.

On 25 July Messina opened its gates to Medici's troops, though the Neapolitans kept control of the Citadel. On 1 August Syracuse and Augusta fell. All Sicily was now in Garibaldi's hands, except for the Citadel of Messina, which was to hold out until 12 March 1861, when at last – after heavy shelling by the Piedmont general Cialdini – it surrendered.

The *Garibaldini* now prepared to begin their invasion of the continent. But once again Piedmont diplomacy tried to stop them. The King, still the only Piedmontese Garibaldi would listen to, wrote a letter entreating him not to go on. The letter of course emanated from Cavour, concerned, as ever, about the possible repercussions of Garibaldi's actions. But Garibaldi decided to go ahead. He concentrated his forces in the vicinity of Messina, the base of his operation being the small port at Punta del Faro, at the northern extremity of the Strait. Orsini, who was now Commander General of the Artillery, set up thirty-five guns of various calibres which had been captured from the Neapolitans.

On 8 August De Flotte requisitioned two hundred boats and got them ready to ferry the troops across the Strait.

As the *Garibaldini* were converging on

Punta del Faro, a fourth expeditionary force was being organized at Genoa. It was commanded by Colonel Pianciani, a dedicated republican; von Rüstow was his Chief of Staff. The troops consisted of 6,000 men, divided into four brigades under Colonels Eberhard, Tarrena, Gandini and Puppi. A fifth brigade was formed in Tuscany and Romagna by Giovanni Nicotera. (According to an unofficial plan concocted by the irrepressible Bertani, these men were not to go to Sicily. They were, rather, to invade the Papal States, liberate Rome, join forces with Garibaldi, and then march on Venice to settle the Italian question once and for all.)

The Piedmont government was vehemently opposed to the project. Cavour ordered Admiral Persano to prevent any landing of volunteers in Papal territory, and the army was ordered to guard the frontiers. The astute Cavour had deliberately allowed Pianciani to assemble this expeditionary force seething with republicans. He intended that the project should become public knowledge, and that news of it should reach the court of Napoleon III, so that he could appeal to the Emperor for support against a republican threat in Italy. It was by no means certain, in any case, that if the republican faction should gain the upper hand Garibaldi would maintain his promise to deliver the south of Italy to Victor Emmanuel II. Furthermore, it was quite possible that, after taking Naples, the *Garibaldini* would march on Rome. If the Pope was to be saved, Garibaldi would have to be stopped. But if the Piedmontese were to stop him, they would have to march south through the Papal States, and the Pope feared (with good reason) that such an operation would lead to the annexation of a large part of his territory by Piedmont. But Napoleon III, who was perhaps tiring of the burden of defending the Pope's temporal power, gave his consent.

But now that things were going their way, the Piedmontese were in no hurry. It took them a month and two days to arrive at the Volturno; they defeated the Papal army at Castelfidardo and then calmly headed south, leaving only Lazio (the province around Rome) under the Pope's control.

Garibaldi himself was opposed to Bertani's plan, as he feared it might compromise the entire expedition, and he informed Pianciani that his presence would be more desirable in Sicily. Pianciani obeyed orders, and landed his troops in Palermo on 14 and 16 August. Immediately afterwards, together with Tarrena, he resigned his commission.

Tarrena's brigade was assigned to Major Spinazzi. Von Rüstow took command of three brigades (3,500 men) and moved on to Milazzo, while Eberhard's brigade was joined to Bixio's division, which was now stationed at Taormina.

The Thousand who had landed at Marsala had increased in number, until now – 20 August 1860 – there were approximately 20,000 Garibaldian volunteers in Sicily. The two Neapolitan divisions defending Calabria consisted of 17,000 men with thirty-two cannon. They were commanded by General Vial, and were divided into four brigades under Generals Ghio, Melendez, Briganti and Caldarelli. Additional support came from the garrison at Reggio, and the batteries at Alta Fiumara, Villa San Giovanni, Punta del Faro, Torre Cvallo and Castello di Scilla.

The Strait was defended by about ten ships under the command of Admiral Salazar; but they did not constitute much of an obstacle. Persano, at anchor in Palermo, had written to Cavour on 31 July, 'The presence of a few of our ships at Punta del Faro would suffice to neutralize the Neapolitan fleet. If they fight at all, it will only be a gesture; they will retire at the first sign of difficulty. Such, at least, is our agreement with certain of their officers.' On 16 August Persano wrote again, 'We can now count on the majority of the officers of the Neapolitan navy.' The Royalist fleet, in fact, was content to fire a few shots at the batteries at Punta del Faro; when Garibaldi landed on the Calabrian coast, General Melendez wrote, 'The navy did nothing whatsoever to stop him.'

Though the navy were not doing anything, however, the forts on the Calabrian shore were in an advantageous position for keeping an eye on the movements of vessels in the waters of the Strait. On the night of 8 August a little fleet of twelve boats, with four hundred *Garibaldini* aboard, crossed the Strait of Messina in absolute silence. But they were sighted nevertheless, a few hundred yards off shore, and fired upon by the Neapolitan cannons. Only 150 men managed to come ashore; they were too few to establish a bridgehead, and they had to hide out on Aspromonte (the mountain range above Reggio) to wait for the reinforcements which, according to the plan, were on their way from Taormina.

Naples, meanwhile, was preparing for her own defence, as a landing on the coast near Salerno was now feared. Garibaldi learned of this, and sought to aggravate the apprehension of the Royalists by an ostentatious build-up of activities at Punta del Faro. Then he hastened to Taormina to join Bixio, who was putting his division aboard the steamers *Torino* and *Franklin*. On the 19th, they crossed the water, landed at Melito and began their march on Reggio Calabria.

The city was defended by the Fourteenth Line Regiment under Colonel Dusmet. Dusmet was a brave soldier, and when he heard of the landing at Melito he set out from Reggio to confront the *Garibaldini*, leaving

The Battle of Milazzo by C. Bossoli. The episode depicted here is when Garibaldi was surrounded by Captain Giuliani's Neapolitans.

the city in charge of one battalion of *cacciatori* and a field battery commanded by General Gallotti. The conflict began at noon on 20 August. The Royalists fell back at first, then rallied to the cry of 'Long live the King', and regained the offensive. But this time they were definitively repulsed, and retreated to the Cathedral Square of Reggio.

In the evening the *Garibaldini* attacked the city. The Neapolitan troops fought superbly under the leadership of their colonel, but when Dusmet was mortally wounded in the abdomen – he died in the arms of his son, an n.c.o. in the same Regiment – they dispersed and then surrendered.

Neapolitan casualties had been negligible. The volunteers, on the other hand, had lost 147 men, counting both dead and wounded (the indomitable Bixio among the wounded). But they had conquered a city, a castle, thirty position-cannon, eight field pieces and almost two thousand rifles.

Without wasting time, Garibaldi marched on Villa San Giovanni with the bulk of his forces. He wanted to reach the plain of Maida as quickly as possible. On the night of 21

August Cosenz landed at Favazzana with De Flotte's legion and Assanti's brigade. He attacked the village of Solano, which was so admirably defended by a unit of *cacciatori* that he had to order a bayonet charge. During the course of this, De Flotte was killed.

After occupying Solano, Cosenz moved south to join up with Garibaldi at Villa San Giovanni. Caught between the two advancing columns were the Royalist troops of General Briganti. The *Garibaldini* numbered about five thousand, while the Neapolitans were slightly more numerous. General Briganti was aware of the danger. But the Royalist commanders had by now succumbed to fatalism, and he did nothing. He allowed himself to be attacked, lost two hundred men and retreated to Gallico.

This was virtually the only armed conflict of the whole Calabrian campaign. Melendez with seven thousand men and twelve cannon was surrounded and surrendered without a fight. The other pockets of resistance did likewise. General Ghio, it is true, made an attempt at defence, rounding up about ten thousand dispersed Neapolitan soldiers in the plain of Maida. But when Eber's brigade and Cosenz's division appeared, he too surrendered, handing over ten thousand rifles, twelve cannon and three hundred horses.

The Neapolitan army had virtually abdicated. Very often, and without quite knowing how, it had found itself surrounded: the capable Türr had been using the Garibaldian fleet (as he would continue to do throughout the campaign) to send troops ashore behind the Neapolitan lines. The Royalist fleet never intervened: after the landing in Calabria, in fact, the fleet set sail for Naples, circumnavigating Sicily so as to avoid all possibility of a conflict.

Their officers' propensity to surrender aroused the indignation of the Neapolitan troops, who sometimes went so far as to shoot their superiors. General Briganti was killed by his own men, but the King's only response was to court-martial the soldiers, blaming them for the whole disaster. Similarly, the crew of a warship were punished for having locked the officers in their cabins; the officers, who had done nothing to oppose the *Garibaldini*, were acquitted.

The landing of the Red-shirts on the continent touched off a revolt in a number of cities in Calabria, Apulia and Lucania. Armed bands were organized, especially in Calabria; they called themselves a National Guard. But the support of the masses was less fervent than it had been in Sicily: much of the population remained loyal to the Bourbons, particularly in the region of Naples itself.

With the army of Calabria destroyed, the road to Naples now lay virtually open before Garibaldi. A state of siege had been proclaimed in the capital on 14 August, but this did not prevent two committees of liberals which had been formed with Cavour's encouragement, known as 'Order' and 'Action', from operating more or less openly. Revolution was in the air, but it failed to materialize, partly because of the presence of the King and partly because the stand which the army would take remained an unknown factor.

But the court at Naples had to do something. The Piedmontese were on their way from the North, and the *Garibaldini* from the South. Some, such as the prime minister, Liborio Romano, and the King's uncle the Count of Syracuse (a convert to the cause of Italian unity), were already calling for the abdication of the sovereign. But Francis II could neither accept this solution nor come up with another. The only thing to do was to defeat the *Garibaldini*; this, in turn, would stop the Piedmontese.

The King concentrated all his troops in the zone between Eboli, Salerno and Avellino, and he himself went to join them. It seemed to everyone that he would at last lead his army in a decisive encounter with the invader. But when he learned that Avellino had risen in revolt and that Türr's division had landed at Sapri (on 2 September) and was joining the rest of Garibaldi's forces, he decided, against the advice of his own generals Pianell and Bosco, to withdraw his troops north of Naples, concentrating them along the river Volturno and relying on the fortresses of Gaeta and Capua.

On the evening of 6 September King Francis II left Naples. He was never to see it again.

The uncertain loyalties of the Neapolitans,

Garibaldi at the time of the expedition of the Thousand.

would have been ready for him with his entire army concentrated at Sapri.

When Garibaldi learned that Salerno had been abandoned by the Royalists he ordered von Rüstow to take Spinazzi's and Puppi's brigades and the Milan brigade and occupy the town. He himself entered on the 6th with his entire General Staff and was welcomed ecstatically by the population.

Here he received a letter from Liborio Romano, who had taken over the reins of government after the departure of the King. It said that 'Naples awaited the Redeemer of Italy, that she might place her destiny in his hands.' Clearly, the Prime Minister was quite ready to change allegiance.

The next morning a deputation from Naples arrived. They confirmed Liborio's message and begged Garibaldi to set out immediately for the capital, where he was ardently awaited. And no doubt he was – in the absence of any sort of authority, the situation could easily get out of hand.

His General Staff, however, was of the opinion that the General should not go to Naples until a sizeable number of *Garibaldini* had occupied the city. Gandini was sent from Eboli to Vietri, a town on the railway to the capital; there he requisitioned all the railway carriages he could find, crammed them with troops, and set out.

Garibaldi, however, was too impatient to wait for Gandini's brigade to arrive. He left on the same day, in a special train, accompanied by an escort of seven men.

On the afternoon of 7 September, in an open carriage, he entered Naples amidst manifestations of popular joy. He went directly to the Royal Palace and there, from a balcony, he thanked the Neapolitan people 'in the name of all Italy which, thanks to their co-operation, had at last become a nation.' This was complete falsehood: the Neapolitan people had done nothing at all to co-operate. (Evidently the politician in Garibaldi was getting the upper hand of the soldier.)

The ships in the harbour fired salutes and raised the tricolour with the arms of the House of Savoy; the Royalist garrison, ten thousand men commanded by General Cataldo, stood silently by.

A few incidents, however, demonstrated

and the definitive retreat of the King, could only facilitate Garibaldi's advance. He was already moving north at a rapid pace, thanks to the genius of Türr, who was moving the various units by sea and landing them at key points along the coast. As he continued to advance, therefore, Garibaldi constantly found fresh troops at his disposal. If Francis II had really intended to attack along the road between Salerno and Sapri, the General

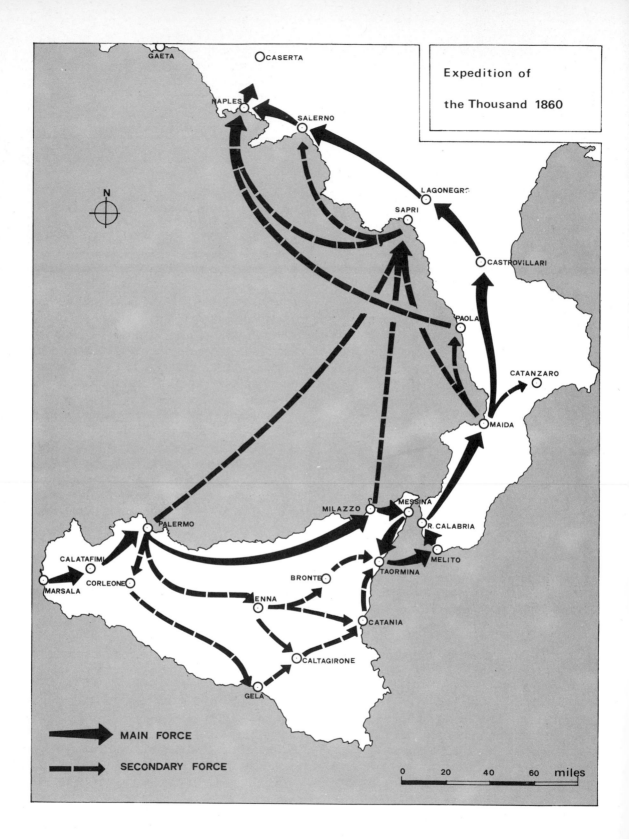

Expedition of
the Thousand 1860

GAETA
CASERTA
NAPLES
SALERNO
LAGONEGRO
SAPRI
CASTROVILLARI
PAOLA
CATANZARO
MAIDA
MILAZZO
MESSINA
R.CALABRIA
PALERMO
MELITO
CALATAFIMI
CORLEONE
BRONTE
TAORMINA
MARSALA
ENNA
CATANIA
CALTAGIRONE
GELA

N

→ MAIN FORCE

→ SECONDARY FORCE

0   20   40   60   miles

that the Neapolitan troops were not wholly lacking in loyalty and honour, and that they could still defend a lost cause with dignity. A group of cadets from the military academy fled to join the King at Gaeta; they were immediately promoted to the rank of Standard-bearer. Colonel de Liguori marched the Ninth Line Regiment through the streets of Naples, flag flying and band playing, bound for Capua. He was followed by eight companies of the Sixth Line Regiment under Lieutenant Colonel Perrone, and by the First Line Regiment, which had been routed at Villa San Giovanni and which was to redeem itself by fighting valiantly during the defence of Gaeta. The Marine Infantry Regiment mutinied, and many officers and soldiers joined the King. The elderly Major Livrea, with his 145 men, resisted every attempt to persuade him to surrender the fort at Baia.

The General tried to curb these 'desertions' by issuing a proclamation:

'If you will not disdain Garibaldi as comrade-in-arms, his only desire is to fight the enemies of the Fatherland side by side with you.'

But it was to no avail. Though loyalty to the crown had vacillated until now, it revived with a vengeance as the tragedy of the House of Bourbon drew to a close. Garibaldi assumed the Dictatorship of Naples and formed a new government, with Cosenz as war minister and Sirtori as Pro-Dictator of Naples' continental territories. Türr was entrusted with the military command of Naples. The Neapolitan navy and merchant marine were incorporated into the Garibaldian fleet, and the former officers of the Kingdom of the Two Sicilies swore allegiance to the new regime.

The ranks of the Southern Army were now swollen by some twenty thousand new recruits. Most of these, however, were National Guardsmen, who remained in their own towns and villages to assure public order. The actual fighting force did not exceed twenty-four thousand.

In the region around Naples many of Francis II's former subjects remained faithful to the Bourbon cause. Together with dispersed troops from the defeated army, they began to organize an anti-Garibaldian resist-ance. This movement was especially strong at Isernia; from here it spread to Ariano, where the local bishop, with the support of Generals Flores and Bonanno, fomented a revolt. It might have become dangerous if Türr had not moved in quickly with the Milan brigade. At the same time the National Guard defeated and dispersed a band of Royalists at Dentecane.

At Naples, meanwhile, Garibaldi was at the centre of a political storm. His intention was to defeat Francis II once and for all, and then continue the war until Rome and Venice should be liberated. In order to carry out this plan, he hoped to exploit the authority he enjoyed as Dictator of the Two Sicilies. But Cavour feared that allowing him to continue in this office would give the republican faction an advantage over the monarchists: he therefore wanted the immediate annexation by Piedmont of the territories conquered by the *Garibaldini*, and the resignation of the General as Dictator.

The struggle was between revolutionary Italy and the Italy of the Establishment. The moderates tried to exert pressure on Garibaldi by inciting against him the same mob that had applauded him only a few days before, while Bertani and Mazzini rushed to Naples in the hope of winning him back to the republican cause.

Cavour saw where the danger lay, and instead of negotiating with the General he deprived him of his principal advantage: the King's support. Garibaldi's own intransigence, in fact, facilitated the Prime Minister's manoeuvre.

At one point it looked as though the political struggle would result in civil war. Cavour wrote to an agent of his at the French court, 'The National Guard of Turin would take up arms against him, and Fanti and Cialdini [the Piedmontese generals who had occupied Umbria and the Marches] would like nothing better than a chance to rid the country of the Red-shirts. The King has resolved to put an end to the matter, and I myself would not hesitate.' This may have been an exaggeration designed to tranquillize Napoleon III, but there must have been some truth to it if the King, always an admirer of Garibaldi, could say to the General's envoy, 'Tell him to proclaim the annexation at once, or else resign.'

Garibaldi had not much political sense. But he realized that he would have little chance of success in a civil war in which his adversaries would have the support of France and Austria. Not only would he fail to win Rome and Venice; in all probability his entire achievement would be undone. He gave in, therefore, and invited Victor Emmanuel to come to Naples to take possession of it.

But he had not yet seen the last of the Neapolitan army. Francis II was not only unwilling to give up; he expressed his intention of retaking the capital and recovering his former authority. His marshal Giosuè Ritucci concentrated his troops along the Volturno, while Gaeta and Capua prepared to hold out at any cost.

Garibaldi returned to Palermo, where the annexationists had begun their agitations, while Türr, with 7,000 men, headed towards the Volturno to make a reconnaissance of the enemy's positions and intentions. The base of his operations was Caserta.

On 14 September the *Garibaldini* began to concentrate along the Volturno line. The first to move were Spangaro's, La Masa's, Sacchi's, Puppi's and the Milan brigades, and La Porta's and Corrao's regiments (the latter being known as the Sicilian *Cacciatori*). On the 15th, the Royalists attacked the town of Santa Maria, but were repulsed by Eber's brigade. Next day they tried to take San Leucio, and this time Puppi's brigade beat them back.

Türr deduced that the Royalists were planning a general offensive, and that these thrusts were meant to sound out the *Garibaldini's* positions and test their strength. So he decided to confound his adversary by being the first to attack, even though Medici's brigade had not yet arrived at the front. This was an error.

On 19 September 1860 he ordered La Masa's, Spangaro's and the Milan brigades, commanded by von Rüstow (whom he had appointed his Chief of Staff on the 16th), to advance on Capua; Eber's brigade was to move on Sant'Angelo. But things went badly from the very beginning.

Von Rüstow pursued the Neapolitan in-

fantry as far as the walls of Capua, but there he suffered heavy damage from the enemy cannon. Puppi's brigade came to the rescue, fighting valiantly, but the Neapolitan artillery halved its forces; Puppi himself was killed. The situation was critical, and von Rüstow ordered a retreat. The Royalists tried to follow up their advantage by pursuing them, but the swift intervention of La Masa's brigade drove them back.

The Neapolitans destroyed a Garibaldian battery at a place called La Fornace, while Sacchi just managed to hold out at La Scafa della Formicola.

At 11 a.m. Türr ordered a retreat all along the line. This gave the Neapolitans a chance to attack Santa Maria, but von Rüstow stopped them with a counter-attack.

While all this was going on, Major Cattabene and his Bolognese *Cacciatori* crossed the Volturno, occupied Caiazzo despite the two Neapolitan brigades which were defending it, and dug in until reinforcements could be sent. But none of the troops in the area could be spared. Colonel Vacchieri's regiment in Naples was sent for; it moved as fast as it could, but it arrived too late. Two Neapolitan columns under Von Mechel and Colonna had counter-attacked at Caiazzo, Cattabene was surrounded, and the local population – who were loyal to the Bourbons – began sniping at his men. Cattabene was badly wounded; he ordered a retreat, but many of his men were drowned trying to get back across the Volturno. When Vacchieri arrived on 21 September the Neapolitans were once more firmly entrenched at Caiazzo.

This was the only defeat suffered by the *Garibaldini* in the entire campaign. Of the 1,200 or so men in Cattabene's and Vacchieri's regiments, only 450 returned to Caserta. In addition to the casualties, two hundred of them were taken prisoner, including Cattabene himself.

Vacchieri went to the Garibaldian camp at Maddaloni and protested strenuously that he and Cattabene had not been given adequate backing in this arduous and difficult enterprise. The main object of his criticism was General Türr, who was in charge of the operations and who, as Garibaldi wrote, 'supposed that no undertaking was beyond the powers of our bold volunteers'. Years later Missori as well was to express a highly negative opinion of Türr's leadership at Caiazzo. When this happened Türr made a special trip to Rome to plead his case before Ricciotti Garibaldi (the General's son, now the recognized leader of the *Garibaldini*): he had been spitting blood during the whole campaign, he said, and this had seriously weakened him; Medici should have relieved him, but had arrived too late. Controversies of this sort are inevitable after a defeat, and Türr remains one of the most admirable figures of the Garibaldian epic. The attack at Caiazzo, furthermore, disastrous though it was, served to delay the decisive battle by ten days, giving Garibaldi a chance to bring all his troops up along the Volturno.

In any case, Medici now took command of the reconnaissance corps on the Volturno, with von Rüstow staying on as his Chief of Staff; Milbitz took over the line troops.

The next few days along the line were marked only by minor skirmishes. On 30 September, for example, the Neapolitans made a show of strength at Santa Maria and tried to cross the river at Triflisco, only to be repulsed by Spangaro's brigade. The Royalist forces were getting nervous: they were beginning to feel the hot breath of the Piedmont army, which was approaching from the North. They decided, therefore, to launch a decisive attack on 1 October.

According to the plan, the divisions led by General Afan de Rivera and Brigadier Tabacchi were to attack Santa Maria and Sant'Angelo directly, then break through Garibaldi's lines, and head for Caserta. Von Mechel's columns under General Ruiz and Colonel Perrone were to set out from Ducenta and Limatola, occupy the heights above Maddaloni and Caserta Vecchia, and cut off communications between Caserta and Naples. General Sergardi, with two Lancer regiments, was to attack San Tammaro and occupy it. General Colonna, with the Third Division, was to back up these operations by shelling the *Garibaldini* from the right bank of the Volturno.

The total Royalist forces at Gaeta, at Capua and on the Volturno between Triflisco and Caiazzo – 50,000 men and 42 cannon – were twice as numerous as Garibaldi's, but they only sent half their troops into the battle of the Volturno. These were organized in two infantry divisions and one cavalry division. The total force was commanded by Marshal Ritucci.

1st Division (Gen. Afan de Rivera): 10,000 men

1st Brigade (Brig. Polizzy):
4 regiments of *cacciatori* (7th, 8th, 9th and 10th)
8 pieces of artillery

2nd Brigade (Brig. Barbalonga):
2 regiments of *cacciatori* (2nd and 14th)
1 battalion *tiragliatori* (sharpshooters)
8 pieces of artillery
2 cavalry squadrons

2nd Division (Brig. Tabacchi): 7,000 men

1st Brigade (Col. D'Orgemont):
3rd Infantry Guards Regiment
1 battalion *tiragliatori* (sharpshooters)
4 pieces of artillery

2nd Brigade (Col. Marulli):
1st and 2nd Infantry Guards Regiments
9th Line Battalion
1 position battery (Col. Negri)

Cavalry Division (Brig. Ruggero):
21 squadrons and 9 artillery pieces

The triumphant entry into Naples. Garibaldi, on foot, is visible in the background.

2nd Hussar Regiment
1st and 2nd Lancers Regiments
1st and 2nd Dragoons Regiments

In addition to these troops, there were Von Mechel's brigade (three foreign battalions and three batteries) and those under Ruiz and Perrone. Reserve forces consisted of three cavalry regiments and General Colonna's Third Division, which was to supply reinforcements for the men attacking Sant'Angelo.

The *Garibaldini* were spread out between San Tammaro, Santa Maria, Sant'Angelo, San Leucio and Valle. They seem to have numbered 25,600; the figure is not entirely accurate because there are no records for some of the units. Others had been drastically altered by the fighting on 19 and 21 September: Puppi's brigade had suffered such severe losses, for example, that it was now reconstituted as a regiment, commanded by Lieutenant Colonel Bossi. And it must be kept in mind that while other units still called themselves regiments, they were in fact hardly more numerous than an average battalion.

In deploying his troops along the Volturno, Sirtori altered the internal structure of the divisions. This is how they were composed on the morning of 1 October:

15th Division (Türr): 9,327 men (in reserve at Caserta, except for Sacchi's brigade stationed between Castel Morone and San Leucio; a constant source of reinforcements for Medici and Milbitz)

Sacchi's Brigade:
3 regiments (Lt. Col. Isnardi, Pellegrini, and Lt. Col. Bossi)
1 battalion of *bersaglieri* (Maj. Bronzetti)
1 regiment of Engineers (Col. Brocchi)

Assanti's Brigade:
3 regiments (Lt. Cols. Fazioli, Borghesi, Albuzzi)
1 battalion of *bersaglieri* (Maj. Sgarallino)

Eber's Brigade:
2 regiments (Lt. Cols. Bassini, Cossovich)
1 battalion of *bersaglieri* (Lt. Col. Tanara)
Foreign Legion (Wolff)
Hungarian Legion (Lt. Col. Magiarody)
1st squadron Hungarian Hussars (Lt. Col. Figyelmesy)

Corte's Brigade:
2 regiments (Lt. Cols. Cararà, Graziotti)

Milan Brigade (De Georgis):
3 battalions
Lombard *bersaglieri*
2nd squadron Hungarian Hussars (Maj. Scheiter)

Artillery:
2 batteries (12 cannon)

16th Division (Milbitz): 5,089 men (between Santa Maria, San Tammaro and San Prisco)

La Masa's Brigade:
2 regiments (Lt. Cols. La Porta, Corrao)

Malenchini's Brigade:
Malenchini's regiment
6 battalions (Palizzolo, Pace, Laugè, Sprovieri, Fardella, Bentivoglia)
Mountaineers of Vesuvius (Lt. Col. Casalta d'Ornano)
French Legion (Col. Cluseret)

Artillery:
1 battery of 2 pieces

17th Division (Medici): 4,585 men (at Sant'Angelo)

Spangaro's Brigade:
4 battalions
1 battalion of *bersaglieri* (Farinelli)

Simonetta's Brigade:
2 regiments (Lt. Col. Cadolini, Col. Vacchieri)

Dunne's Brigade:
(not subdivided into regiments)

Genoese carabinieri
(Maj. Mosto)

Artillery:
1 battery of 6 cannon
1 battery of 3 howitzers

18th Division (Bixio): 6,087 men (between Valle and Monte Caro)

Spinazzi's Brigade:
2 battalions of *bersaglieri* (Majs. Menotti Garibaldi, Boldrini)

Dezza's Brigade:
8 battalions

Fabrizi's Brigade:
6 battalions

Eberhardt's Brigade:
2 regiments (Col. Penzo, Maj. Dunyow)

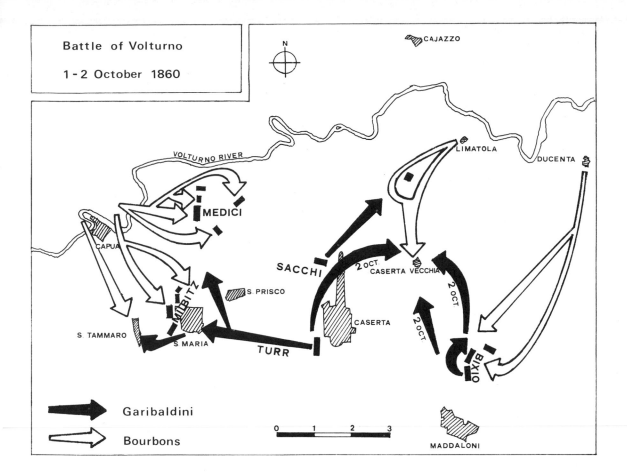

Battle of Volturno

1 - 2 October 1860

Garibaldini

Bourbons

Artillery:
1 battery of 2 cannon

An additional 452 gunners spread out among the line forces, and 60 Lancers, known as 'Garibaldi's Lancers', assigned to various commands as guides and messengers.

At dawn on 1 October 1860, the Neapolitan 10th Regiment (Lieutenant Colonel Capecelatro, Polizzy's brigade) opened fire. It charged the Garibaldian outposts near Sant'Angelo, forcing the troops to retreat. The *Garibaldini* countercharged and regained lost ground. Barbalonga's brigade then intervened, and occupied the houses on the outskirts of Sant'Angelo; it held them until the afternoon.

At the same time, Tabacchi's division attacked Santa Maria and broke up La Masa's outposts, while Sergardi and his Lancers had the upper hand of Fardella's volunteers at San Tammaro. Meanwhile, Francis II himself appeared at the front with his brothers the Count of Trapani and the Count of Caserta. His presence, as well as the initial advantages which they had gained, inspired his troops with confidence.

But the Neapolitan attack soon lost its impetus. Laugè's and Sprovieri's battalions, supported by Corrao and La Porta, put up a determined resistance, and routed the Neapolitan brigade led by Colonel D'Orgemont (Tabacchi's division). Marulli's brigade came to its rescue, while Colonel Negri bombarded Garibaldi's lines from his eight-piece battery.

Brigadier Tabacchi reorganized his ranks and sent out a few detachments to encircle Santa Maria and cut off communications with Sant'Angelo. This operation was almost successful, but Assanti's brigade, with the 2nd battalion (Gioacchino Bonnet's *bersaglieri*) and two regiments (Borghesi's and Fazioli's), arrived on the scene in time to thwart it.

Meanwhile Afan de Rivera's division, backed up by heavy cannon fire, attacked Medici at Sant'Angelo. Medici counter-

Battle of the Volturno. With Türr's reinforcements, the Gari-baldini were able to break through the Neapolitan lines and win a total victory.

attacked, but Polizzy managed to reach the outskirts of the village and to drive the *Garibaldini* back towards Monte Sant'Iorio. Medici knew that to lose Sant'Angelo would be tantamount to losing the battle: the positions at Santa Maria would immediately be encircled, and there would be nothing to stop the Neapolitans from occupying Caserta and, afterwards, Naples. Relying on Lieutenant Cooper's battery and Spangaro's brigade (both part of Medici's division), he put up a resistance quite equal in ferocity to the Neapolitan attack. Still, however, it looked as though they would outmanoeuvre him.

Then Garibaldi left Santa Maria for Sant'Angelo, accompanied by Missori, Arrigo Basso, Giovanni Arrivabene and some of the Guides. When they arrived at the outskirts of the village, they found themselves in the midst of the Neapolitans, who were trying to get at Medici from the rear. In a flash they were surrounded. The Neapolitans fired on the General's carriage, one of his horses was killed, and Arrivabene was wounded and taken prisoner.

At that moment Captain Pratelli's 7th Company (of Spangaro's brigade) appeared. The newcomers cut their way through the Neapolitans with their bayonets, and freed Garibaldi, who hastened to join Medici on Monte Sant'Iorio. Here he assembled the troops that were available (the Genoese *carabinieri*, Farinelli's and Morici's battalions) and, backed up by two cannon, hurled himself upon the Neapolitans, who were completing the encirclement. Medici counter-attacked as well, and retook Sant'Angelo, while Dunne's brigade managed to win back the batteries it had lost earlier in the day.

Meanwhile the situation at Santa Maria was becoming critical. General Milbitz was wounded and carried away from the front. Major Angherà's battery, which had performed admirably all day, was showing signs of fatigue. And the French Legion, which had been under attack for hours at the edge of the town, was beginning to weaken. Garibaldi went to Santa Maria and ordered Türr to join him there with Eber's and the Milan brigades, the only units which were still being held in reserve: they moved by railway, and arrived at the front in no time. With Türr came Sirtori.

As soon as the Milan brigade arrived, Garibaldi took charge of it and set forth from the town. Eber's brigade was divided into smaller units and sent where the troops were most needed. The Hungarian Hussars, the *bersaglieri* and the 1st Regiment headed for San Tammaro, while the Hungarian Legion, the Foreign Legion and the 2nd Regiment moved into the area between Sant'Angelo and Capua.

Thanks to these actions – and thanks especially to the relentless charges of Major Scheiter's Hungarian Hussars – Medici was able to regain control of the situation. With Simonetta's and Dunne's brigades he convincingly forced Afan de Rivera's division back towards the walls of Capua.

Meanwhile at Santa Maria, a combined attack by Lieutenant Colonel Bassini, La Porta and Corrao on the convent of the Capuchins, the last pocket of resistance, concluded the day's action in that sector. Tabacchi's division also withdrew towards Capua. By 6 p.m. the line from Santa Maria to Sant'Angelo was safely in Garibaldi's hands once again. While these engagements had been going on, two others had been taking place, on the line between Monte Tifata and Monte Viro, and on the road to Maddaloni, which was defended by Sacchi's brigade and by Bixio's division.

On the morning of 1 October the Royalist column of two thousand men led by Colonel Perrone set out from Limatola and attacked the positions at Grottole and Sant' Annunziata. Ferracini's battalion fell back to San Leucio where Sacchi was. Sacchi quickly got the battalion back in order, reinforced it with Bossi's regiment, and sent it off to the heights of Castel Morone, where Pilade Bronzetti with a force of only 250 *bersaglieri* was having difficulty holding out.

But help came too late. Bronzetti was short of ammunition and outnumbered. He fought as best he could, but when he was killed by the rifle fire his few surviving troops had no choice but to surrender. Bronzetti's brother had been killed the previous year with the *Cacciatori delle Alpi*.

Another scene of the Battle of the Volturno. The Neapolitans pull back from Santa Maria.

When Bossi arrived at Castel Morone he too found himself in trouble. So as not to be surrounded, he had to fall back to the dairy farm of San Silvestro, where he succeeded in stopping the Neapolitans. They, however, after an unsuccessful assault, moved off into the surrounding hills and then advanced, unopposed, on Caserta Vecchia.

Bixio, meanwhile, was confronting Von Mechel's column of seven thousand men and three batteries, which had descended upon him between Monte Caro and Valle on the road to Maddaloni.

On the night of 30 September Von Mechel had crossed the Volturno and occupied Ducenta. From here, at dawn on the 1st, with the aid of the artillery, he attacked the outposts of Bixio's division. Eberhardt's and

Spinazzi's brigades were overwhelmed; they abandoned their positions and retreated in disorder.

As a result of this setback, Bixio had to retreat in order to protect the road to Caserta at Villa Gualtieri. Then he ordered Fabrizi's brigade to station itself between Maddaloni and the San Leucio Aqueduct so as to prevent Von Mechel and Perrone from joining up. Colonel Dezza was ordered to retake Monte Caro.

Dezza joined forces with Menotti's *bersaglieri* and, flanked by Taddei, moved to attack. Monte Caro was held by the Neapolitans' Foreign Battalions, with line units, one cavalry squadron, and a strong artillery force. Dezza and Menotti resolutely led a frontal attack, one charge bloodier than the other. Von Mechel defended himself with intelligence, threatening his assailants with an attack on one flank. But Dezza countered this move by sending in troops which he had been keeping in reserve. The Neapolitans were driven from Monte Caro, retreated to Ducenta, and then abandoned this village as well.

Bixio lost 221 men that day, and the Neapolitans 125: once again the enemy suffered lighter casualties but was put to flight.

On the evening of 1 October General Sirtori wired Cosenz at Naples: 'We have been successful along the whole front. One isolated Royalist column is near Caserta.' Perrone's column, in fact, unaware of the outcome of the day's fighting, was marching on Caserta Vecchia that night, without establishing contact with Von Mechel. Perrone had added the Sixth Line Regiment to his own unit, and he now commanded three thousand troops. It was not a huge number, but it was enough to represent a threat to Garibaldi's rear.

But the General's men had fought for twelve hours without respite, and now they were exhausted. Many of them were sleeping on the very positions which they had so laboriously reconquered. Sirtori, therefore, assembled an attack force at Caserta, using those troops who had seen the least action: one regiment from Corte's brigade, one from Assanti's, a few companies from Spangaro's brigade and the Genoese *carabinieri*. The last

were quite worn out, but their support was necessary.

Bixio was ordered to head for Monte Viro to cut the Neapolitans off. Missori, who had been out reconnoitring, returned to Caserta at dawn to inform the General of the disposition of the enemy troops at Caserta Vecchia. Between 4 and 5 a.m. on 2 October the *Garibaldini* set out towards San Leucio. Bixio left Fabrizi's brigade to defend Maddaloni, and ordered Eberhardt's to head for Caserta Vecchia. Soon Perrone's column was surrounded, and few Royalists escaped.

Thus concluded the engagement known as the Battle of the Volturno. It was the most important ever fought by the *Garibaldini*, because of its political consequences as well as because of the number of troops involved. Both sides were fighting for all that they stood for. For the Neapolitans, losing the battle meant the end of a kingdom. Had the *Garibaldini* lost, it would have meant the end of their struggle, which hitherto had been crowned with success. A Neapolitan victory would certainly have stimulated the European powers to support the House of Bourbon more actively, and the Piedmont army would have stopped its advance. (However, the true importance of the battle was not publicly recognized until many years later. This was because the new ruling class, the bourgeoisie, could not bear to admit that it owed the unity of Italy to a people's army.)

The Battle of the Volturno is unique in that here for the first and last time the *Garibaldini* fought an essentially defensive battle. The Neapolitans were better equipped, but their leaders, as usual, were lacking in capacity and in resolution. The *Garibaldini* made up for their material inferiority by their competence and, above all, by their officers' ability to control the troops.

Critics were later to comment that the extension of the front was excessive considering the number of troops: 25,000 men were spread out over more than twelve miles. But Sirtori and his General Staff could do no otherwise: to avoid having their communications with Naples cut off, they had to keep control of all the roads which led from Capua and elsewhere to the capital.

The Neapolitans' error was to space their

attacks too far apart in their attempts to make a breakthrough. Garibaldi himself admitted that if the Royalists had concentrated on San Tammaro or on Maddaloni, restricting the movements of the outnumbered volunteers to the environs of Capua, they would have had 'an easy victory'.

The *Garibaldini* suffered 1,634 casualties, with 389 others captured or missing. Neapolitan losses amounted to 1,128 with 2,160 captured or missing.

Garibaldi issued a declaration lamenting the fratricidal battle 'in which Italians fought Italians', and expressing his gratitude to all of his men and especially to the 'Hungarians, Frenchmen and Englishmen, few in number but radiant in valour, who adorned the ranks of the Southern Army, and nobly upheld the martial honour of their compatriots.'

On 26 October 1860 Garibaldi met with Victor Emmanuel at Teano, and formally delivered the conquered territories into the King's hands. The King's attitude towards the Red-shirts may be summed up in the words with which Garibaldi described the attitude of politicians in general: 'They think men are like oranges; you squeeze out the last drop of juice, then you throw away the peel.'

True, Victor Emmanuel offered such rewards as the rank of Major General, the title of Prince of Calatafimi, a fat pension and even a castle. But what Garibaldi really cared about – the continuance of the war and recognition for his men – was not even mentioned. The King refused to inspect the troops, and the proclamation which he sent them did not bear his signature.

Garibaldi refused all the honours offered him, including the nomination of Menotti as His Majesty's *aide-de-camp*. He left Naples for his beloved Caprera, taking with him as booty a sack of seed, some coffee and sugar, a bale of stockfish and a year's supply of macaroni.

The Battle of the Volturno marked the end of the 1860 campaign. The Citadel of Messina still lay in Neapolitan hands, as did the fortress at Gaeta, where Francis II had taken refuge with the last of his courtiers. But the Piedmontese were to enjoy the questionable honour of taking them, after a long and inhuman bombardment.

The campaign ended in a manner which *The Times* described as truly criminal. When Garibaldi left for Caprera, he had entrusted his *Garibaldini* to the King, but it soon became obvious that Victor Emmanuel had no use for this all-too-liberal, vaguely socialist

Neapolitan prisoners at the Volturno.

army. He turned over the problem of the Southern Army to General Fanti, a vigorous opponent of the Red-shirts. And the commission which was appointed to evaluate the qualifications of those of Garibaldi's officers who had applied for a commission in the regular army was to be presided over by General Della Rocca, a typical exponent of the closed and exclusive Piedmont military caste.

The government offered six months' pay in advance to any officer who would hand in his resignation, but to no avail. Only when it became clear that the government had no intention of fighting for the liberation of Rome and Venice did many *Garibaldini* decide to leave military life. They preferred to return to their civilian occupations rather than serve where they were no longer wanted. Others, however, determined to stay in the army, to be available for the conflicts which, they saw, remained inevitable if the Italian question was to be brought to a conclusion.

From the ranks of the *Garibaldini* came three-quarters of the intelligentsia of the new nation; despite their many errors, their contribution to its progress and development was to be a lasting one. In fairness to the government one must point out that it was under considerable diplomatic pressure to dissolve this potentially revolutionary militia.

The question of the Southern Army dragged on for nearly two years. At last it was debated in three stormy sessions of parliament, on 18, 19 and 20 April 1861. The thorniest problem was what to do with those officers who had not resigned but who did not want a commission in the regular army. The discussion was intensified by the presence of many *Garibaldini* who had been elected as Deputies, including Bixio, Cadolini and Garibaldi himself.

Eventually Bettino Ricasoli's motion, which provided for a special corps, separate from the army, was passed 194 to 79. But the provisions were never put into effect. So many *Garibaldini* left the corps that on 27 January 1862 it was dissolved and its members incorporated into the new Italian army.

The Piedmont generals were certainly right when they said that Garibaldi's army had too many officers, particularly in its General Staffs. In the Neapolitan area the cadres were

so swollen with bogus Red-shirts that the rank of major was one of the lowest. These men were hoping to turn the change in regime to their own advantage, without making any military contribution; in fact they only brought chaos. The Sicilians and the Calabrians had been responsible for horrible massacres; some of them were bandits, and regional considerations were often uppermost in their minds, but they gave body and soul to the *Garibaldini*. The Neapolitans, on the other hand, were interested only in a commission – from major up, naturally. It was never clear who they were or how they had acquired their rank: these were typical 'Neapolitan mysteries', as a second-lieutenant of Medici's Division put it. But aside from these last-minute heroes, it is quite true that Garibaldi's army was overstaffed with offi-

Garibaldi meets King Victor Emanuel II at Teano. This scene has always been idealized, but the truth was very different; the King and his court despised the Garibaldini.

cers: in October 1860 they were 7,300 out of 50,000 men. But it is also true that, in Naples itself, 3,000 of them were dismissed when, after the conclusion of the campaign, there was time to check their credentials.

But the real problem was that the regular army could not bear the thought that these motley and unkempt volunteers had conquered half Italy in less than six months. The rancour of the Piedmontese was to last for many years. *Garibaldini* who entered the army had to settle for a lower rank than the one they had earned on the battlefield, and Neapolitan or Austrian officers who entered the same army were often promoted more rapidly, even when their records had nothing special to recommend them. Thus the new Italian army missed an occasion to enlist excellent officer cadres who had been trained in many parts of Europe. And when a few years later (1866) the Italian army found itself at war for the first time, the only divisions to acquit themselves honourably were those led by Medici, Cosenz, Bixio and Sirtori, who had by then entered the regular army.

The intellectual difference, too, soon became evident. Those *Garibaldini* who submitted to the regular army's humiliating entrance examination easily proved their own superior education, to the great embarrassment of the Piedmontese.

When they were certain that the war would go no further, the foreign legions also disbanded. The only exception was the Hungarian Legion, which was incorporated in its entirety into the Italian army, where it remained until 1867.

Not all the foreigners had an easy time of it. When the British volunteers returned home they found themselves abandoned by all, thanks to the London Committee's lack of organization. If the Piedmont government had not intervened, the British *Garibaldini* might have starved to death under the bridges of London. Cavour ordered his embassy in London to see to all their needs: food, lodging, even medical attention.

Thus the great adventure, which in just over five months had conquered a kingdom, dethroned an ancient dynasty, transformed the political configuration of the whole Italian peninsula and set in motion vast mechanisms of social change, ended in homeward voyages, financial crises and parliamentary feuds.

Enriched by the experience morally as well as militarily, the *Garibaldini* now turned their eyes towards other lands and other questions.

Arrival of Garibaldi at Charing Cross, London.

Echoes Around the Globe

After the expedition of the Thousand, the popularity of Garibaldi and his Red-shirts increased enormously. Their very name became a source of hope for oppressed peoples everywhere.

Even in far-off Siberia the *Garibaldini* had admirers and followers who secretly dreamed of a Garibaldian intervention in Russia. Bakunín, the celebrated Russian revolutionary, wrote, 'I can affirm that all the citizens of Irkutsk, almost without exception – merchants, artisans, labourers, and even the civil servants – passionately took the side of liberty against the Tsar's faithful ally the King of the Two Sicilies.' And in 1860 and 1863, 'when the Russian countryside was all in a turmoil, not a few peasants of Great and Little Russia awaited Garibaldi's coming.'

When revolt broke out in Poland in 1863 and it looked as though Garibaldi was going there to fight, ordinary people in Russia reasoned that if Garibaldi was coming to free the Poles, the Polish cause must indeed be just and so the Russians should fight them no longer.

This simplistic argument is a fine example of what the name of Garibaldi meant, in the second half of the last century, to peoples who had never known democratic freedom, and it shows how ardently they longed for the 'Liberator'.

Often, in those years, there were rumours that Garibaldi was about to intervene in Herzegovina, in Greece, in Poland, in Hungary and even in the Ottoman Empire. The chancelleries of Europe trembled.

The details of some of these projects were worked out by 'precursors', even though the majority of the *Garibaldini* stayed in Italy, waiting for precise orders from the General.

We shall attempt to set forth the main events of the years from 1861 to 1866.

At the end of 1860 the *Garibaldino* Zuccoli (who had resigned from the Southern Army) went with a small group of volunteers to fight with the Greeks in a revolt against the Turks.

In 1861 the American Civil War broke out. The secessionists were successful in the early battles, and President Lincoln entertained the idea of enlisting experienced European officers and soldiers. He thought particularly of Italy, where the Southern Army was in the process of being demobilized.

Italian public opinion was unanimously in favour of the Union cause. The press, somewhat far-fetchedly, compared Lincoln's efforts to hold the Union together with the recent struggle for the unification of Italy. But the question which stirred up passions more than any other was that of slavery. Many Italians saw a parallel between the condition of the Negro slaves and that of the subjects of reactionary governments in Europe. Even Jessie White Mario threw herself into the flurry of publications on the question with her study *Slavery and the American Civil War*.

Thanks to the work of recent historians, we have today a good idea of what the real issues were in the war between the states. At the time, however, most people believed that it was being fought for the emancipation of the slaves, and many *Garibaldini* therefore desired to join the Union Army.

Starting in May 1861 Romaine Dillon, *chargé d'affaires* in the United States legation at Turin, received numerous applications for enrolment, particularly from Red-shirt officers and soldiers. Among them were Colonel Francesco Anfossi of the Thousand; Colonel Gustav Cluseret, commander of the French Legion, who was to become a general in McClellan's army; Ulloa; and even some of the Hungarians.

The Washington government, though delighted to have these experienced men on its side, wished, quite rightly, to avoid the internationalization of the war, and it certainly did not want to appear to be recruiting mercenaries. It made it very clear, therefore, that all volunteers were expected to travel to America at their own expense (and the voyage was extremely costly). Upon arrival they would immediately be granted United States citizenship and sent to the front as regular soldiers. It also refused to engage any sort of special corps, such as the one organized by Colonel Cattabene (who had led the ill-fated attack on Caiazzo), even though Cattabene's men were willing to be treated as ordinary Union soldiers.

The reason for so much interest in the Union cause on the part of the *Garibaldini* –

the United States ambassador to the new Kingdom of Italy, George Perkins Marsh, reported that fifteen thousand volunteers could be ready to leave Italy within two or three months – is to be inferred, perhaps, from the last paragraph of Colonel Cattabene's proposal: 'The moment General Garibaldi shall set foot on American soil, the Legion will pass under his command with the name of First Regiment; it will constitute his vanguard.' They were sure he would be.

For some time a rumour had been going around, and had been repeatedly taken up by the press, to the effect that Garibaldi had accepted an invitation from President Lincoln to fight for the North. After the battle of Bull Run, in which the Army of the Potomac had been reduced to a pitiful state, Lincoln desperately needed a skilled and courageous general who could lead the Northern armies to a quick victory. And there wasn't a better man on the market than Garibaldi, who had conquered an entire kingdom in the space of a few months.

It was the consul at Antwerp, James W. Quiggle, who first contacted Garibaldi. 'According to the newspapers', he wrote, 'it is your intention to go to the United States, to join the Northern army in the present conflict. If you do so, your fame will be greater than Lafayette's.' It is unlikely that Garibaldi was much interested in vying with the late Marquis. His conditions for taking part in the war were clear from his reply to Quiggle: 'Tell me whether the purpose of all this is to free the Negroes, or not.' Despite all the speculation on the issue, the emancipation of the slaves had in fact not yet been proclaimed.

Quiggle was unable to carry out such a delicate operation by himself, and the United States government wanted to avoid publicity, so the mission to Garibaldi was entrusted to two seasoned diplomats: Ambassador Marsh, and the Minister in Belgium, Henry Schelton Sanford.

On 7 September 1861 Sanford went to Caprera in a hired boat and had a long conversation with the General. He then sent a detailed report to Washington, stating that Garibaldi would not intervene, as he most

The 39th New York Volunteers, known as Garibaldi's Guard, parade for President Lincoln.

ardently desired to, unless certain conditions were met. He would have to be appointed Commander in Chief of his forces, without which he felt that his presence would serve no purpose, and he would have to be empowered to declare the abolition of slavery. Garibaldi felt that the two sides were fighting purely for material interests and maintained that, as things stood, the war could only be considered an ordinary civil war and that neither side could possibly enjoy the championship of their cause by the European friends of freedom and progress. Sanford expressed his doubts that Garibaldi would ever take part in the conflict unless he was fully convinced that the government and the people of the North were united in the determination to follow a policy which would lead to the abolition of slavery.

Despite precautions, rumours that Garibaldi might be leaving for America soon reached the press – spread in fact by the General's own friends who hoped that the Italian government, for fear of losing him, would decide to settle its account with Austria once and for all. But the government had no intention of impeding his departure; Garibaldi was in fact informed that if he decided upon the venture he would have the King's approval.

Reactions to the report in America were varied. The *World* was enthusiastic, while the *Herald* was opposed to the idea. The *New York Times* wrote, 'We trust that the war will not go on long enough to make his participation necessary.'

In October 1862 Garibaldi replied to yet another entreaty in the usual way: only if the slaves were to be freed. It would be absurd to suppose that it was Garibaldi who induced Lincoln to issue the Emancipation Proclamation. But it is certainly true that Garibaldi brought into the open the fact that emancipation was the logical issue in the American Civil War. The proclamation was published on 1 January 1863. Garibaldi was overjoyed; he wrote to Lincoln, addressing him as 'the Emancipator'.

But in fact Garibaldi never took part in the American Civil War. Many of his followers did, however, although the exact number is not known. Certainly a sizeable group of Garibaldian officers were assigned to the Western Department under the command of Major General John Charles Frémont. And on 28 May 1861, in New York, a volunteer regiment – the Thirty-ninth – was formed, under the orders of the Hungarian Colonel D'Utassy. It was called the Garibaldi Guards, and was comprised of one company of Italians, one of Frenchmen, three of Germans, three of Hungarians, one of Spaniards and one of Swiss.

The Garibaldi Guards wore a *bersagliere*-type uniform: blue jacket and trousers with collar, cuffs, lapels and piping in red distinctive colour, and a plumed hat with the initials 'G.G.' at the front. The regiment fought at the First Battle of Bull Run, at Harper's Ferry and at Gettysburg. The typically Italian uniform was gradually abandoned. Another corps of Garibaldi Guards was formed in Company B of the Ninth Pennsylvania Reserves.

The General's name was also borrowed by the Confederates: a volunteer corps from Louisiana called itself the Garibaldi Legion. But we may be sure that no *Garibaldino* belonged to it.

With the likelihood of his joining the Union army becoming ever more remote, Rome once again became Garibaldi's foremost objective. He had always maintained that whenever the government found itself unable, for political reasons, to promote the cause of national unity, it was the right of the volunteers to take independent action. Cavour had never repudiated this doctrine; sometimes it suited his purpose, as on the occasion when he had used the possibility of a Garibaldian march on Rome as a pretext for his own invasion of the Papal States.

But it took as wily a diplomat as Cavour to succeed in such stratagems, which threatened to disturb the delicate balance in Europe and which clashed with the interests of the all-powerful French Empire. And, unfortunately for Italy, Cavour died of a stroke on 6 June 1861.

He had been ill for some time but, instead of looking after his health, he had buried himself even deeper in his work: national unity

Colonel D'Utassy, commander of Garibaldi's Guard.

had brought with it a vast array of problems which required immediate attention if Italy was to achieve stability. Cavour put all his energy into forging an Italy which could stand up not just to Austria but also to the other great powers, and cope with its own internal political divisions at the same time. He always triumphed, but his health was irreparably undermined by the effort.

The final blow was dealt him by Garibaldi, his bitterest political enemy. In a debate in Parliament the General accused him of having tried to foment a civil war between the Piedmontese and the Red-shirts at the time of the invasion of the Papal States. Pandemonium broke loose, and Cavour was badly shaken. He confessed, 'The wound was made worse by the fact that I had to conceal it.'

The man who replaced Cavour was perhaps the least suitable of all the available candidates: Urbano Rattazzi, the former leader of the Left who now had close ties at Court and enjoyed the favour of the King. He had been a close collaborator of Cavour and tried to apply his methods, though he lacked the dead leader's ability.

What happened next is shrouded in secrecy, but it is certain that Garibaldi set out on the Aspromonte expedition with the approval of the King if not that of the government. Victor Emmanuel himself admitted as much, and foreign diplomats were of the same opinion. Rattazzi's plan was quite simple. Garibaldi was to march on Rome with an army of volunteers recruited in the South; at the same time the Italian Army, unbeknown to the General but with the blessing of Napoleon III, would invade the Papal States on the pretext of protecting the Pope from the Red-shirts. The French, however, were not about to fall for this trick for a second time, and Rattazzi's government was incapable of devising an alternative policy. Thus came about the tragedy of Aspromonte.

Garibaldi arrived in Palermo in June 1862. The city went wild with joy at the presence of its liberator, the descendant of Saint Rosalia. The welcome was so great that the King's sons, who were also in the town, were ignored.

The General's strategy was obvious to all,

and soon the cry 'Rome or death!' was to be heard everywhere, though it had been prohibited by the government, which had pledged to the French not to attack the Pope. But the authorities did nothing to stop the constant demonstrations of popular support, where even the local councillors appeared in their tricolour sashes, and the National Guards paraded before the General as though everything had been approved by the King.

A number of faithful adjutants had meanwhile hastened to the General's side, including Fra Pantaleo, Türr, Corrao, Nullo and Eber (who was once again present as correspondent of *The Times*). Medici, Bixio, Cosenz and Sirtori were absent: they were now serving in the regular army.

Garibaldi recruited three thousand volunteers in a short time. But some of his supporters, who had observed better than he how events were taking shape, now tried to put him on his guard. Lajos Kossuth and György Klapka tried to get him to call off the new expedition, as did Mordini, Cadolini and Fabrizi, ex-*Garibaldini* who had now become Deputies. Medici himself, one of the few men who could influence Garibaldi, warned him that 'the road you are taking leads inevitably to civil war.' Türr received a message from the Hungarian Committee in Turin, urging him not to go against the Sovereign's will; he withdrew his services.

On 3 August Victor Emmanuel himself issued a proclamation, disowning the entire operation and stating that whosoever defied the royal directive would be liable to prosecution under the law. The warning was clear enough, but Garibaldi paid it no attention. How could the King disavow him? The troops he encountered made no attempt to arrest him; on the contrary they were furnishing him with provisions.

The government, in fact, fearing the reaction of the people, had repudiated Garibaldi's mission without actually ordering the Army to stop him. The instructions sent to Admiral Albini, commander of the squadron in the Strait of Messina, show how equivocal was Rattazzi's attitude: 'Take whatever measures may be necessary, but remember that the good of King and Country must come before all else.' Albini thought that the good of the

Garibaldi wounded at Aspromonte. One must presume that this photograph was taken later, probably after his return to Caprera.

country lay in allowing Garibaldi to cross the Strait, and that is what he did. Poor admiral: in the normal course of events he might well have been promoted to Commander of the Fleet. As it turned out, he was obliged to resign his commission. And Garibaldi was arrested.

The tragedy began shortly after the landing in Calabria on 25 August. As the *Garibaldini* marched towards Reggio they were shot at by a small detachment of *bersaglieri*. In order to avoid a conflict, they withdrew to the mountains of the Aspromonte range. It was a rude awakening. They marched all night in torrential rain; enthusiasm gave way to depression, and then to fear, and there were many desertions. There were only five hundred volunteers left when, at Santo Stefano d'Aspromonte at 3 p.m. on 29 August 1862, they found themselves face to face with two line regiments and two battalions of *bersaglieri*, sent out to stop them.

Garibaldi ordered his men not to fire no matter what happened, and he set out, alone, to confront his adversaries. But as soon as he was in the open, he was shot at. One bullet struck him in the left thigh, and another in the right foot. Enrico Cairoli, crying 'Viva l'Italia!', ran forward and dragged him to safety. Enraged at the sight of their wounded leader, the *Garibaldini* began to return the fire.

The encounter only lasted ten minutes, but it was long enough to kill twelve (five *Garibaldini* and seven *bersaglieri*) and wound thirty-four (fourteen *bersaglieri* and twenty Red-shirts). Then silence fell. The antagonists stared at each other aghast – so much for their two years of unity!

A lieutenant called Carlo Rotondo stepped forward from the government ranks and, in an arrogant tone, demanded that Garibaldi surrender. 'That is no way for an envoy to speak', cried the General, 'Disarm him!' The scene was repeated with a major of the *bersaglieri*. Finally, Colonel Pallavicino, commander of the royal forces, approached with his head uncovered. 'I must perform an unpleasant duty', he said, and Garibaldi

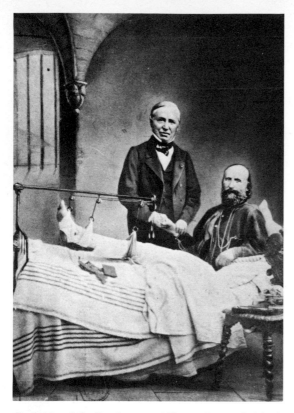

Garibaldi and the French surgeon Nélaton, photographed in the Fortress of Varignano. Nélaton was one of the internationally famous surgeons who rushed to Garibaldi's bedside to attempt to remove the bullet and avoid amputation of his leg. Garibaldi was to remain a near cripple for the rest of his life.

surrendered. He was black in the face as Ripari dressed his wounds. He smoked nervously and would look at no one, neither at his own men (among whom there was his son Menotti, who had also been wounded) nor at the *bersaglieri* (who included Eberhardt among their ranks).

It took all night to carry the wounded General down from the mountains on a makeshift stretcher. It was a painful journey, though his men did what they could, pouring cool water on his wounds and providing cloaks to keep him warm. When they reached the sea he was put aboard the steam frigate *Duca di Genova*. While he was being taken on board he encountered General Cialdini, who had challenged him to a duel the year before and who now refused to exchange salutes. As Indro Montanelli has said, 'The generals of the Piedmontese army seldom won. And when they did, they were poor winners.'

Garibaldi was shut up in the Varignano fortress at La Spezia. Nobody knew what to do with him: should he be put on trial, should he be released? Piedmont military circles wanted to make an example of him – a court-martial would give them a chance to have their revenge on the Red-shirts. They spoke of Aspromonte as though it had been a major operation, handing out 76 medals and decking Pallavicino with honours.

Meanwhile the fortress was fast becoming a place of pilgrimage. Supporters stood outside night and day waiting for medical bulletins. The Italian government made itself look even more ridiculous by surrounding the building with an infantry regiment.

The leg wound healed quickly, but the wound in the right foot was more serious: the bullet was lodged in the ankle-bone. No less than twenty-three surgeons, including the Englishman Partridge, the Frenchman Nélaton, the Swiss Zoply and the Russian Pirogoff, examined the patient, but none of them was able to extract it, and it was feared that the foot might have to be amputated. The surgeons' constant probing was excruciatingly painful, but Garibaldi bore it all without complaint.

Meanwhile Committees for the Liberation of the General were being formed in Leipzig, in Stockholm, in Paris, in London and throughout Europe. The press singled out the Emperor of the French (who, it was thought, had instigated the arrest) for its attacks. The *Daily News* went so far as to write, 'If Napoleon is tired of living, just let him touch one hair of Garibaldi's head.'

On 11 October he was officially released, but he was not well enough to leave the fort until the 22nd. He was brought to the Hotel Milan, where the doctors' consultations continued. His torments went on until 23 November when, after eighty-seven days, the bullet was extracted by Professor Zanetti of Florence. Garibaldi was gagged to prevent him from screaming; Jessie White Mario held his hand. Doctors Ripari, Basile, Albanese and the Belgian Jean-Baptiste Allart assisted Zanetti.

The operation was over, and Europe rejoiced. The general's boot and stocking, with their respective bullet-holes, were placed in a glass case in Rome, where they may be admired to this day.

On 20 December Garibaldi was taken to Caprera to complete his convalescence. He was confined to his bed until January 1863; had to use a bath-chair until June, and crutches after that. By Christmas he was walking again, though he was to use a cane for the rest of his life.

Yet another epilogue to the tragedy of Aspromonte showed that the Italian government was also a poor winner. The *Garibaldini* dead were denied a burial and another seven (mostly from the 25th Battalion of *bersaglieri*), after a summary trial on charges of desertion, were executed. The remainder were imprisoned in the fortress of Vanadio in Piedmont, where, thanks to General Staff Captain Giuria's disregard for his orders, ten of them died of maltreatment and deprivation.

Many of the Red-shirts, however, seemed to draw new strength from the whole sad affair. In fact one of them, upon being released from the government prison, immediately went off to fight for a new cause: the liberation of Poland.

Poland had always had to fight for its independence against the expansionist policies of Russia, Prussia and Austria. It had been partitioned by them during the eighteenth century and had ceased to exist as a political entity. In 1807, with the creation of the Duchy of Warsaw, Napoleon I had partially restored its independence; but the Congress of Vienna had once again assigned the West to Prussia and the South to Austria. The Duchy remained nominally autonomous under Russian sovereignty, but after the unsuccessful revolt of 1830–1 it was made a province of the Russian Empire.

But the Poles never gave up their struggle, and in 1863 another great revolt broke out. It too was unsuccessful, and as a result the Polish people were more thoroughly enslaved than ever.

Public opinion in Europe had always been sympathetic to the Polish cause, and when Garibaldi appealed to the world to not abandon Poland, committees of all sorts sprang up everywhere to denounce the oppressors and provide aid for the oppressed. The war-cry of the Poles who had fought with the *Garibaldini*

Francesco Nullo, about 1862.

in 1848–9 had been 'Your liberty and ours!' The Red-shirts could hardly remain insensible to the revolt in Poland now, so they began to organize an expedition.

Despite his wound Garibaldi offered his sword to Langiewicz, one of the leaders of the revolt, who had fought with him in 1860. But his offer was rejected: the Committee at Warsaw was counting on the support of all classes of Polish society, and they feared that Garibaldi might prove to be a divisive influence.

But one of the *Garibaldini* set out for Poland all the same: Francesco Nullo, 'Checco' to his friends, a slightly snobbish gentleman from Bergamo, described by Abba as 'the handsomest of all the Thousand'. The founder of a linen mill of international fame, Nullo divided his time between his successful business activities and the liberal cause. He was born on 1 March 1826, and by the age of twenty-two he had taken part in the First War of Independence and in the defence of Rome as one of Masina's Lancers. In 1859 he

A rare photograph of some of the Garibaldini *prisoners of the Russians during the expedition in Poland. From the left, standing: Emile Andreoli, Alessandro Venanzio, Charles Richard, Lucio Meuli. Sitting: Giacomo Meuli, Giuseppe Clerici, Ambrogio Giupponi. Foreground: Ernesto Bendi and Luigi Caroli, who was to die in a Siberian prison camp.*

joined Garibaldi's Guides, and by the end of the campaign he had earned the rank of lieutenant. In 1860, at the head of 264 fellow Bergamasks, he had gone to Sicily with the Thousand: it was he who led the charge at Ponte dell'Ammiraglio, and he went on to become a lieutenant colonel. In 1862 he was with Garibaldi at Aspromonte. And now once again he interrupted his commercial affairs and hastened to Poland.

The volunteers were very much reduced in number: twenty-seven Italians, eight Frenchmen and three Hungarians. But they were all very experienced – they had taken part in the wars of 1848–9, 1859 and 1860, and six of them had belonged to the Thousand. All, that is, except Luigi Caroli, another rich man from Bergamo, who had led a decadent

life (and had had a liaison with Garibaldi's second wife, Countess Raimondi – a sordid affair which had tragic consequences for all three).

To reach Poland they had to cross the Austrian Empire. To avoid the suspicion of the police they went in small groups, travelling by way of Venice, Trieste and Vienna. They were to meet in Cracow on 1 May. Here ten of them were arrested by the Austrian police, and repatriated.

Aiace Sassi was fortunate, and managed to escape from the moving train, and returned to Cracow. He joined Rochebrune's French Legion, which was dispersed in an encounter with the Russians on 4 May. Giambattista Bellotti, who was the brother of Nullo's fiancée, persuaded his captors to release him in Switzerland. After many difficulties he reached Poland again, and joined Colonel Wirzbiki. He was killed in battle in July 1863, at Growno.

After the arrests, Nullo's little legion was reduced to twenty-six men. But in Cracow they were joined by six hundred Poles under the thirty-year-old Józef Miniewski, who had been made a general by the Warsaw Committee in recognition of his substantial financial contributions to the Polish cause. On the evening of 2 May they crossed the border without incident. (The Austrians, in fact, were pleased to see these revolutionaries leave their territory.) They marched all night through marshes and forests. After nine hours they came to a clearing where they found the chests of buried arms and uniforms which the Warsaw Committee had left for them. There was even a supply of red shirts.

The Polish force consisted of four companies and a small cavalry squadron of fourteen men. Many of them were mere youths, and none had any military expertise. The Red-shirts had plenty of that, but as none of them spoke Polish they were obliged to remain a separate group. Their flag, which had been given to them by Madame Lewicks at Cracow, bore the image of Our Lady of Czestochowa, the patroness of Poland.

At dawn on 5 May 1863 (the anniversary of the embarkation at Quarto), they arrived at Krzykawka, a few leagues from the city of Olkusz. They were resting along a country road embanked on both sides so as to form a kind of natural trench, when out of a nearby wood came a burst of rifle-fire. It was the vanguard of Prince Szachowskoy's Russian troops, who had been hunting for them. Lieutenant Elia Marchetti was wounded, as was his friend Febo Arcangeli, who had rushed forward to help when he saw him fall.

But the Russians did not seem to have decided on an all-out attack, and ammunition was precious, so Nullo gave the order to cease fire. The Poles, however, were eager for action, sprang out of the ditch, and charged. The enemy, who were planning an ambush, pretended to retreat into the wood. Nullo guessed what they intended. He mounted his horse and, dashing in front of the Poles, ordered them back to the trench. As he watched them doing so his horse was struck by a bullet; it fell and his leg was caught beneath. The Polish interpreter Zajeczkowski and the French captain Camille Didiers rushed forward to drag him to safety.

The abortive charge and the sight of the fallen Nullo demoralized the Poles, who had been unaware of the danger. Partly to encourage them and partly to get a better view of the enemy's movements, Nullo leapt on to a nearby mound. An instant later he fell spinning to the ground, without uttering a sound.

Nullo's death was a grievous blow to the volunteers' morale, and the inexperienced Miniewski didn't know how to deal with it. The legion retreated – in good order, at first, but when at the edge of the wood they were greeted by a volley of rifle-fire from the Russians – who were waiting for them – they gave way to panic. Many of the young volunteers discarded their weapons and took flight; cut off from the rest, they were an easy prey for the Cossacks. Some of the veterans also fled, and in the end only a small group managed to stay together.

The Russians surrounded them and were about to massacre them all, when Prince Szachowskoy ordered otherwise: he had admired their courage, and now spared their lives. Luigi Caroli, Febo Arcangeli, Alessandro Venanzio, Ambrogio Giupponi, Giuseppe Clerici, the Meuli brothers, Ernesto Bendi, Emile Andreoli, Luis Alfred Dié, Charles Richard, Josef Czerny, Ritter, Leczinski and Captain Krasuski were taken prisoner. They were sent before a court-martial, which condemned them to be hanged, despite their protests that as soldiers they had the right to die before the firing-squad. But the sentence was then commuted to hard labour in Siberia, and they spent years of infernal hardship in the salt-mines at Kadaya. These 'political' prisoners were granted amnesty on 7 December 1866. But not all of them reached home: Krasuski was torn to pieces by wolves in an escape attempt; Caroli died of exhaustion. And many of those who did return never recovered their health.

That was the end of the Polish campaign of the *Garibaldini*. On a practical level it accomplished nothing whatsoever. Morally, however, it helped perpetuate the fame of the Red-shirts' devotion to international liberty.

To this day, Nullo's memory is venerated by the Poles. There are monuments to him everywhere, squares are named after him, and the 50th Infantry Regiment bears his name. The only record of the others, though, is a caricature drawn by Krasuski: they are shown marching, with their feet in chains, each with a musical instrument in his hands.

In 1864 Garibaldi was invited to go to England. It was not the first time, but in the past he had always refused the offer, knowing that, while the British government regarded him with favour, it was also wary of the visit of a 'demagogue' who stirred up revolts in countries with which England was on friendly terms. Now, in fact, the news of his coming set the government in an uproar, though it obviously could not prevent the visit.

But the British were not the only ones to be upset. The news that Garibaldi was leaving Caprera caused much alarm among the Italian establishment. The stock-market fell, and provincial magistrates asked the central government for instructions as to what measures to take should he land on their territory. Naples even requested that gun-boats be sent to impede an eventual landing in these areas.

Unaware of the fuss he was causing, the lame, fifty-seven-year-old General boarded a steamer belonging to the Peninsular Oriental Company. It was en route from Marseilles to Malta and had made a special stop at Caprera to pick him up. With him were Mr and Mrs Chambers, the British couple who had persuaded him to go to London, his sons Menotti and Ricciotti, his doctor Basile, Basso Mordini and his secretary Guerzoni. At Malta they boarded the *Ripon*, bound for Southampton.

Exactly why he went to England is not known – Garibaldi hated popular demonstrations in his honour, and he certainly knew the sort of acclamation that awaited him. He gave three different explanations for the visit depending on whom he was talking to: he was seeking British support for the liberation of Greece, Poland and Venice; he wanted to intervene in favour of Denmark in the Schleswig-Holstein question; he was attending a summit-meeting of the world's revolutionaries. The truth will never be known, but given his propensity for enthusiasm it is likely that someone had hinted at possible support for one or other of these causes.

The *Ripon* docked at Southampton on 3 April 1864. Despite the pouring rain the pier was crowded with people come to welcome Garibaldi. The ships in the port were decked with flags, while the British and Italian colours were flying everywhere in the town. The admiration of the British for Garibaldi was quite sincere, but it had its absurd aspects. Red shirts became fashionable ladies' apparel and children wore 'Garibaldi suits'. His popularity was exploited in every possible way: there was a Garibaldi polka, a Garibaldi waltz, a Garibaldi biscuit, a Garibaldi cravat-pin and even a Garibaldi perfume, which was advertised as 'irresistible' and was available in two- and five-shilling bottles.

The reasons behind the fad are clear enough. No one could be insensible to the myth of the shy hero with countless dramatic exploits to his credit, the man of the people risen to the peak of power and success. His charisma was considerable, and we may be sure that the blond blue-eyed warrior troubled the dreams of many a Victorian lady. The working classes saw him as a champion of their rights, the man who could stand up to kings and emperors but who remained proud of his own humble origins and who, in a census, stated his occupation as 'peasant'. His popularity had political reasons as well: he was, after all, the enemy of Napoleon II and of the Pope, neither of whom had many admirers in England. No wonder that people lost no opportunity to cry 'God bless you, Garibaldi!'

Standing on the bridge of the *Ripon*, Garibaldi waved his hat in reply to the hosannas of the crowd. But as soon as he went ashore he was met by the Duke of Sutherland, Mr Seely and Signor Negretti of the welcoming committee, who immediately spirited him away, despite the protests of the workers, who considered him one of themselves and resented his being monopolized by the grandees. Among those who paid their respects were the Prince of Wales, Gladstone (who was then Chancellor of the Exchequer), Tennyson, Florence Nightingale (with whom he had been corresponding for some time) and the schoolboys of Eton, who honoured him with three cheers. The fleet treated him to a mock sea-battle at Portsmouth, as though he were King of Italy. His friend Herzen, a

Russian political exile who had been in London since 1847, has left an amusing description of the homage he received:

'The door opened and a Master of Ceremonies improvised for the occasion, with a list in his hand, commenced to call out the names and titles of all those who entered: the Right Honourable So and So ... the Honourable ... Lady ... Esquire ... His Lordship ... Miss, etc., etc. There was no end to it.

'With each name there sailed in through the door old and young crinolines, aerostats, grey heads and bald heads, little old fat ladies, lean but vigorous giraffes missing their hind legs who, as though they weren't tall enough, tried to make themselves taller by propping up the upper portions of their heads on enormous yellow teeth. ... Each male guest came with four or five ladies, and this was a good thing: they occupied enough space for fifty persons

Presentation of the Freedom of the City of London to Garibaldi at Guildhall.

and thus prevented the hall from becoming overcrowded.

'They approached Garibaldi by turns; the men shook his hand energetically, then flinched as though they had stuck a finger in boiling water.

'A few spoke a few words to him, but most kept silent and went away in silence. The ladies kept silent as well, but they stared at him so long and so passionately that numerous infants with his features will certainly be born this year. Since it is already customary to dress children in red shirts, the cloak will be the only problem.'

On 11 April half a million Londoners came out to celebrate his arrival. 'People waited for hours, on the roofs, on balconies, at windows, everywhere. Garibaldi arrived at Nine Elms Station at half-past two; not until half-past eight did he reach Stafford House, where the Duke of Sutherland awaited him with his consort.' It was a truly memorable reception.

'At Westminster Bridge, near Parliament,

the crowd was so dense that the coach, which was moving at a snail's pace, had to halt completely. A cortège a mile long, complete with flags and music, somehow got through. The people mobbed the coach amidst loud hurrahs: everyone wanted to shake the General's hand or kiss the hem of his coat; they were all shouting "Welcome!".'

Garibaldi was virtually held prisoner at Stafford House until 22 April. No foreigner, not even a head of state, had ever been subjected to such a round of ceremonies, balls and banquets. But the activities in his honour, as his engagement-book shows, kept him far removed from the common people.

On 12 April, the morning after his arrival, he received the homage of the inhabitants of the neighbourhood of Stafford House. Then he went to lunch with the Dowager Duchess of Sutherland. The guests were Lord Granville, Lord Russell, the Duke and Duchess of Argyll, Gladstone and his wife, and the Earl and Countess of Clarendon. Outside the Life Guards' band played Garibaldi's 'anthem' non-stop. In the evening there was another banquet. On the following day he visited the cannon-factory at Woolwich (where the workers, at last, could approach him and demonstrate their affection). That evening there was a banquet for forty, where the General was presented to the cream of the British aristocracy. On the next evening there was a gala at Covent Garden, and here he was buried in flowers. In a ceremony at the Guildhall he was given the Freedom of the City of London.

Though grateful to his hosts, Garibaldi scarcely enjoyed this series of festive occasions, official luncheons, hosannas and late nights – and he could not bear English coffee, preparing his own in private.

Not everyone in England shared in the general euphoria; a few even protested against the Garibaldi-mania which had swept the country. Queen Victoria thought it all rather excessive. Bishop Manning warned his flock against 'that representative of the Socialist revolution in Italy, whose theories I need not delineate'. Disraeli refused to meet him, and the Austrian ambassador expressed his astonishment that an *Unwälzungsgeneral* (revolutionary general) should receive such a welcome. Karl Marx called the whole affair 'a deplorable piece of buffoonery'. But ninety per cent of the population, and especially the working classes, declared themselves for Garibaldi.

On 17 April he received a visit from Dr Fergusson, the Queen's physician, who found him tired and ill. It wasn't true, but it was a good excuse to send him home. Garibaldi conferred with Palmerston, and agreed to leave, setting out on the 22nd. Crowds lined the streets, begging him not to go.

The government, which was suspected of having sent him away, had to face a great deal of public resentment. The charge was brought up in Parliament, and Palmerston and Gladstone found themselves in an embarrassing situation.

Garibaldi's final visit was to Peard, who was living in retirement in Cornwall. Then he sent a message thanking the government and the population for their hospitality, and departed for Caprera.

None of his hopes had come true. As Guerzoni said, 'Garibaldi obtained everything from the British, except what lay nearest his heart.' He spent the next two years at Caprera cultivating his garden and looking after his animals.

But that 'idle and useless life' was drawing to a close.

A photograph of the meeting organized near London by the revolutionary Herzen, in which the crème de la crème *of the European revolutionaries participated. No major programmes, so feared by the security services of the time, were agreed upon.*

The battle of Vezza d'Oglio by Gerolamo Induno.

The Great Defeat

In 1866 Italy had a right to be pleased with itself. In the course of a few years' struggle against great powers and international interests it had achieved independence and nationhood. Eighty per cent of Italian territory had now been unified. But to complete the process, two cities would still have to be liberated: Venice (with its hinterland extending to the Alps) – and Rome.

The freedom of Rome was still an extremely problematic goal, since Napoleon III had persevered in his rôle as guarantor of the Pope's temporal power and Victor Emmanuel was bound to the Emperor by profound and loyal friendship. The Venetian question was simpler: Italy was still the sworn enemy of Austria, and had been trying to undermine its power since 1861 by fomenting revolts in Hungary and the Balkans, though none of these had been successful.

A solution to the Venetian problem seemed to present itself in 1866, when Italy entered an alliance with Prussia. Since 1859 Prussian Chancellor Otto von Bismarck had been seeking to obtain for his country a rôle in Germany analogous to that of Piedmont in Italy, by taking advantage of the complications which Italy had unleashed in Europe. Germany, like Italy, was in fact divided into numerous small states loosely united in a Confederation led by Austria who, naturally, controlled everything according to interests. Prussia also belonged to the Confederation, where it found itself in an ambiguous situation. On the one hand, it was subaltern to Austria; but on the other, it was itself considered a major power, as a result of its part in the defeat of Napoleon I, and it was often appealed to in international disputes.

Bismarck felt he was now ready to make the dreams of millions of Germans come true and establish a 'Greater Germany' – with Prussia, of course, at its head. The price of such a project would be conflict with Austria.

Many German states were loyal to the Austrian Empire, and Bismarck therefore needed allies. One country which had everything to gain from a war with Austria was Italy. It appeared to be strong, and not only did it have an eye on Venice but also felt the need of more effectively defendable frontiers with the Hapsburg Empire. Thus came into

General La Marmora, the brother of the founder of the famous bersaglieri, *who died in the Crimean War.*

being the Italo-Prussian alliance, which was ratified on 8 April 1866.

But Italy had changed since 1860. It had lost much of its momentum in the struggle for independence, and now many internal contradictions – brought about by the too rapid unification of a land where radically different mentalities and administrative traditions existed side by side – were coming to light.

The phenomenon of political banditry had just been stamped out: it had gone on for five years, and half the army had been required to restore order. It had been a very divisive problem, and many Italians were left embittered. The public debt continued to mount. The army was 400,000 strong, but in reality it was a shambles. The various pre-Unification armies had officially joined in 1861, but they were not yet completely amalgamated. Many officers still felt tied to deposed ruling houses, while the Piedmontese tended to form a caste of their own; they divided up all the important commands amongst themselves, thus fostering envy and dissent. Personal rivalries kept the generals at loggerheads, and there was much bad feeling between those who had fought in

Photographs of Austrians in the Peschiera and Mantua fortresses during 1866 war.

revolutionary campaigns and those with Court backgrounds. The ordinary soldiers, on the other hand, were divided by linguistic differences, which constituted a serious obstacle to the formation of an *esprit de corps*.

In short, Italy was not really ready to go to war. And the clash with reality would give rise to what, in the future, would be its most serious psychological defect: lack of confidence in itself. Yet when Austria, hoping to take the wind out of the sails of the Italo-Prussian alliance, offered Italy the Veneto in exchange for its neutrality, it was the upper echelons of the military and the ruling class of the country who refused. They were set on proving their mettle as a nation.

Prime Minister at the time was General Alfonso La Marmora, a man utterly without political sense, though he had for years been a close collaborator of Cavour. Not only did he fail to seize the political advantages which the alliance with Prussia offered – such as the entire Veneto, gratis and without a war – but he aggravated the error by taking command of the military operations himself. He refused to co-ordinate his own strategy with that of the Prussians. Bismarck wanted him to open a third front by sending the *Garibaldini* to Dalmatia, where they could incite the population to revolt and then march on Vienna. La Marmora replied that stirring up revolts was a shameful business, 'contrary to every principle of humanity and morality and political wisdom.' The German plenipotentiary Von Bernhard was so staggered by this that he commented, 'I cannot repress the painful suspicion that this man is not equal to his task. He does not, in fact, appear to understand the real nature of the problem before him.'

La Marmora got his operations under way. But because of personal rivalry he did not inform General Cialdini, who was in command of the Army of the Po, to the south of the Austrian front. The only important engagement between the Austrian and Italian armies was the battle of Custoza (24 June 1866). General Govone and Prince Umberto resisted the Austrian attack tenaciously, but they were outnumbered. All day long they called desperately for reinforcements, but La

Marmora failed to order General Della Rocca, who was sitting blithely in the café at Villafranca, to send help. Von Moltke wrote later that Govone should most certainly have been given the necessary support. But the generals do not seem to have grasped this; Govone was one of the few who was really intent on victory.

Only a small part of the army – five divisions out of twenty – was used at Custoza. The day ended disastrously. La Marmora did not even try to get the situation back under control, though the enemy was exhausted and practically without reserves. Instead he retreated, immobilizing the army (which was by now ready for a counter-attack), and throwing the entire nation into a panic with a message in which he announced to the astonished Austrians that they had won 'a great victory'.

La Marmora should never have been placed in command. He had been away from the army for two years, a long time when one considers the profound changes which had been taking place. The performance of the other generals was not much better – later they were to exchange sterile accusations, each trying to blame the defeat on the others. The only officers in this war who gave an honourable account of themselves were the division generals Medici, Bixio, Sirtori and Cosenz, and one former Neapolitan general, Pianell.

The Navy only made matters worse, suffering a defeat at Lissa on 20 July, again because of the indolence of the high command.

The Italy of the Establishment thus failed its first military test. When, after the Prussians routed the Austrians at Sadowa (3 July 1866), the participants in the war sat down at the peace table, all that Italy had to show for itself were the victories won by the despised *Garibaldini*.

Only four years had gone by since Aspromonte, but when Fabrizi, in the government's name, went to Caprera to offer the General command of the volunteers, Garibaldi accepted immediately. 'I forgive wrongs quickly', he wrote.

As usual there was a lot of opposition to the 'Italian Volunteers Corps', which was the name given the *Garibaldini* in the Third War of Independence. Indeed, if public opinion had not been so strong in their favour, and if the Italo-Prussian agreement had not specifically mentioned them, the Red-shirts might not have taken part at all. As it was, the army chiefs did what they could to slow down recruitment, in a 'persistent effort at sabotage'. Garibaldi wrote that he could have raised 100,000 volunteers. The figure seems exaggerated, but it is true that of the 40,000 men who tried to enlist more than half were sent home again. Nevertheless, their number rose to 33,000 during the course of the campaign, as a considerable number of volunteers joined the regiments directly, bypassing the Regular Army's recruiting centres.

Once again the volunteers were badly treated and badly equipped. They were issued old rifles, and at first they were given no cannon at all, because they might lose them. Their leather pouches were defective, so that their ammunition frequently got wet; there was even a shortage of uniforms. But once again Garibaldi could count on a tried and true General Staff, made up of old comrades-in-arms like Fabrizi, Bertani, Mosto, Missori and Cairoli, and young but experienced officers like Menotti Garibaldi and Stefano Canzio, the General's son-in-law who now joined their ranks.

Bismarck's plan was rejected and the Red-shirts were assigned to the far left flank of the army in the hilly area around Lake Garda. It was not a key sector, and yet here the *Garibaldini* – under a fifty-nine-year-old General, half-crippled and plagued by infirmities, who directed operations mostly from his carriage – managed to win the only victories of any importance in the entire campaign.

'Be eagles', said Garibaldi, and the Red-shirts were: without giving the enemy time to catch their breath they captured the mountain heights from them one by one. Thus they won at Monte Suello, at Caffaro, at Forte Ampolla and finally at Bezzecca, in a hard day's fighting in which the *Garibaldini* alone lost 2,382 men.

After the victory at Bezzecca the road to Trento and to Austria lay open. What stopped them was not Franz Josef's army, but a telegram from La Marmora ordering the General

A vivandière Garibaldina *in the 1866 campaign. Very often the women followed the* Garibaldino *army, taking an active part in the fighting.* (Above)

Colonel Giuseppe Missori. As a 19-year-old he fought in the five-day battle of Milan. In 1859 he joined the Garibaldini *as a Mounted Guide, later taking over from Simonetta as the corps commander. He remained with Garibaldi until the end of the Roman campaign of 1867 and retired to private life. A good officer and a heroic soldier, he saved Garibaldi's life at Milazzo, although his military capability was limited to battalion commander.* (Below)

to withdraw immediately from the frontiers of the Tyrol.

Peace had come. The order, however, was not only to halt, but to give up much of their conquered territory. A few hours later, Garibaldi replied, 'I have received the dispatch. I obey.' The laconic message gave no idea of the rage of the *Garibaldini*, who had advanced steadily at great cost to themselves (even Garibaldi was wounded), storming every mountain peak in their path, and were now compelled to stop, only a few miles from Trento – the city which, forty-nine years later, was to cost Italy three more years of war and 600,000 dead.

Once again Jessie White Mario was a witness, and she has left us a vivid description of how the order was received by the *Garibaldini*: 'I saw them break their swords, shatter their bayonets. Many threw themselves to the ground and rolled in earth still soaked in their brothers' blood.'

After the war the *Garibaldini* went home, full of rancour towards those who had stopped them. Once again the government was preparing to play a cruel trick on them and they, ingenuous as ever, would once again be taken in.

On 15 September 1864 Italy had signed a convention with France in which it repudiated the claim that Rome was the natural capital of the new Italian State, and transferred the seat of government to Florence. Napoleon III, in turn, withdrew his troops from the Eternal City.

The historian Gregorovius, an impartial observer of these events, wrote, 'It is a serious crisis indeed; Italy is playing to break the bank. Either Cavour's plan [to make Rome the capital] will succeed, or the country will plunge into anarchy.' Italy, in fact, could not with impunity move the capital to Florence. Turin was the cradle of the Savoy monarchy and had been the heart of the entire independence movement. If it was no longer to be the capital, then the capital would have to be Rome, around whose name all the propaganda of the *Risorgimento* had revolved. The King had accepted the idea in public, though privately he had no intention of leaving his beloved Turin. But the move was imposed upon him. The Left were in favour of it because they thought it would 'Italianize' the new State, which was in danger of becoming an enlarged version of Piedmont. The military thought that Turin was dangerously exposed to invasions since the cession of Savoy. And Napoleon III, in his thankless rôle as Rome's Cerberus, hoped that around the new capital there might grow up such a series of interests as might cause people to forget the 'Roman question'. And so, against his will, the King gave in.

Most people saw the agreement with France as containing the germ of a peace be-

tween the young nation and the Pope who, a few years previously, had excommunicated virtually half of Italy. But Gregorovius wrote, 'I do not believe that the Papacy will be reconciled; it will not cease to reclaim its lost provinces.' And he was right. The politicians were well aware that a reconciliation with the Pope was impossible, not only because of the territories which had been taken from him in the wars of 1859 and 1860, but also because of the Italian laws which had secularized church property. But they hoped that, with the French troops out, they might provoke a revolt in the Papal State which would justify their own armed intervention and, ultimately, the annexation of Rome.

It was the only course open to Italy; any other would lead to war with France, and this would play into the hands of all those interests which opposed her unification. The work of many years would go up in smoke. The French, for their part, aware that the Italians could hardly be expected to renounce their ideal altogether, substituted the 'Antibes Legion', made up of veterans of the French

Pius IX and his personal court in about 1862.

army, for the Observation Corps in Rome.

The Throne of Peter was still occupied by Pius IX. Over the years he had grown more serene in appearance, but remained as staunch as ever in his defence of a temporal power which by now had become an anachronism. He persisted in refusing to look beyond the drowsy walls of his parasitical city thronged with priests, monks, nuns and the so-called 'black aristocracy'. Half its population lived on alms or on public assistance, while all about it the world was changing rapidly and new problems were vexing the conscience of humanity.

The ruling circles of the Church were principally concerned with protecting their vested interests; but a few minds among them were aware that times had changed, and they realized that the temporal power was an obstacle to the reconciliation of 'liberal sinners' to the Church. Pius IX replied to the hesitant efforts of these liberal Catholics in December 1864, with the encyclical *Quanta Cura* and the appended 'Syllabus of Errors', in which he confirmed his condemnation of all the basic tenets of liberalism: religious tolerance, freedom of conscience and of the press, and 'destructive' – by which he meant 'democratic' – legislation. He condemned, at the same time, socialism, rationalism and Bible-study groups, going so far as to affirm that freedom of discussion endangered the soul and that he, the Pope, could never 'reconcile and adjust himself to progress, liberalism and modern civilization.'

The Syllabus, in other words, was a round condemnation of all that was democratic and progressive, and of the very foundations of the Italian *Risorgimento*. It aroused enormous indignation. Crispi declared to Parliament, 'Christianity must purge itself of the vices of the Church of Rome, or it is doomed to perish.'

The government, which clearly was not aiming at a pacific conclusion to the affair, took advantage of the wave of anticlericalism provoked by the Syllabus by dissolving 25,000 religious organizations (in addition to the 13,000 which had already been dissolved) and confiscating their possessions. This produced a further stiffening of the Church's attitude. In the Papal State fear and suspicion reigned.

The police stepped up their activities, and arrests and searches became the order of the day.

An 'International Congress for Peace' was convened at Geneva the second week in September 1867. It was a failure, partly because of the spies sent by the various warmongering nations, suspicious of this strange conference composed mainly of republicans, but mostly because the delegates themselves were 'more belligerent than pacifistic', as Dostoievsky, who was present, asserted. Its organizers, in fact, were old revolutionaries, mostly veterans of liberal risings and wars of national liberation, who now identified themselves with the socialist movement. Garibaldi's presence at this 'pacifist' congress was of course essential. As early as October 1860, in fact, the General had sent a memorandum to the European powers, calling for general disarmament and for international arbitration of disputes.

He arrived at Geneva on 8 September, accompanied by Benedetto Cairoli, Jessie White Mario and other loyal followers; many of them, such as Türr, destined to become vigorous supporters of the movement. On this occasion Garibaldi showed more political good sense than usual – for once his tendency to adhere to sacred causes which would have tragic consequences for him and his men did not get the better of him. In his address on 9 September he avoided taking an extreme position, so as not to affront the Austrian and German delegates, who were none too radical, or the French, some of whom were admirers of Napoleon III. But the speech did not please the die-hard republicans who had been more eager than anyone else to have him participate. In fact, he alienated them definitively with such statements as, 'I am not one of those who want to overthrow monarchies to found republics, but rather one of those who want to abolish absolutism and establish on its ruins the reign of liberty and justice.'

After delivering this rather moderate speech, however, he presented a motion which took many of the delegates aback, especially on account of his somewhat naïve attack on the Church (which had become Garibaldi's particular aversion) and because of his dated conception of God as Reason.

Other parts of it, though, are genuinely progressive, and the last clause in particular expresses the essence of the Garibaldian political philosophy.

We reproduce the entire text of the motion, leaving the reader to form his own judgment:

1. All nations are sisters.
2. War between them is impossible.
3. Disputes which arise between nations should be settled by a Congress [a sort of United Nations *avant la lettre*].
4. Members of the Congress shall be nominated by the peoples' democratic societies.
5. Each people shall have the right to vote in the Congress, regardless of the size of its representation.
6. The Papacy, being the most pernicious of sects, is hereby abolished.
7. The Congress shall adopt the religion of God, and each Member shall undertake to propagate it. By religion of God I mean the religion of Truth and of Reason.
8. The priesthood of revelation and of ignorance shall be supplanted by the priesthood of Science and Intelligence.
9. Democracy is the only remedy for the pestilence of war.
10. The slave alone has the right to make war on the tyrant; this is the only circumstance in which war is justified.

Naturally the motion was not carried – not so much 'because it was more radical than Luther and Calvin', as because it was ahead of its time: this was a period when nationalism, with all the tragic consequences it would have for the world, was still very much on the rise.

Despite his proposals Garibaldi could hardly claim to be a dyed-in-the-wool pacifist. At that very moment – and everyone, of course, knew it – he was busily organizing an expedition to achieve what was now his most obsessive aim, the liberation of Rome.

On 12 September, without waiting for the vote on his motion, he left the Congress.

Since January 1867 Garibaldi, contrary to his usual practice, had been actively engaged in politics, haranguing all Italy with inflammatory, rabidly anticlerical speeches on the Roman question. The response was enthusiastic. At Siena, at a banquet held in his honour by the Accademia dei Rossi, he made a remark which rapidly spread by word of mouth: 'When the cool weather comes, we shall take action.'

The prime minister in 1867 was Urbano Rattazzi, the politician who had sent troops against Garibaldi at Aspromonte. Now, as five years previously, he had to deal with a Garibaldi who was stirring up popular sentiment with the cry 'Rome or death'. He felt he must do something to counteract him, but the political situation was not propitious for rash gestures. The recent war had been humiliating for Italy, even though it had led to the annexation of the Veneto, and public confidence in the government was at low ebb. After Cavour's death parliamentary strife had produced a long series of short-lived governments. Parliament, for that matter, was divided on the Roman question. Some deputies wanted to see it resolved at once; others believed that Italy's social problems should have priority.

Victor Emmanuel II, still unwilling to go against Napoleon III, was opposed to any sort of adventure. Rattazzi hoped for a political solution to the problem. He intended, if the French would let him get away with it, to repeat the manoeuvre which had already gone badly for him, and for the *Garibaldini*, at the time of Aspromonte: to allow the Red-shirts to march on Rome and stir up a revolt which would in turn justify the intervention of the Italian army.

But Rattazzi knew that Napoleon, who relied on the support of French Catholics, was opposed to the plan. He also knew that a division commanded by General de Failly was stationed at Toulon; it was prepared to set out at a moment's notice, and could be at Civitavecchia within twenty-four hours. Nevertheless, he encouraged Garibaldi to move, assuring him that France would permit the liberation of Rome. He convinced his government and the civil service of the same thing, and had a functionary called Cirillo Monzani draft a proclamation, dated 16 October 1867, announcing the conquest of Rome.

(Some claimed later that the instigator of

Menotti Garibaldi, the General's first son, was his closest collaborator. After the French campaign he abandoned military life for politics and became a left-wing deputy.

the scheme was not Rattazzi, but the King, who had been looking for a pretext to get rid of the Red-shirts ever since they had become so involved in social problems.)

The background of this brief and tragic campaign is extremely complicated, and all sorts of conjectures are possible. A few things are certain, however: Garibaldi was defeated; the King was not such a 'gentleman' after all; and the prime minister was an inept politician who, when the moment of truth arrived, could think of nothing better to do than to resign so as not to be responsible for the consequences.

The generous and ingenuous Garibaldi agreed to Rattazzi's plan. Perhaps it was on this occasion, rather than in 1866, that he ought to have written 'I forgive wrongs quickly'. But in any case, in his view, the Roman question could be resolved only by the Italian people. He therefore got his campaign underway, and when Rattazzi finally realized how dangerous it was and tried to stop him, it was too late: the Red-shirts were on the march towards their first great defeat.

When he returned from Geneva Garibaldi put the finishing touches to his plans. The Red-shirts were already mobilizing, and it was taken for granted that the people of Rome would revolt as soon as the expedition approached the city. The Roman Revolutionary Committees were asking for arms and money.

The French protested as soon as they heard of Garibaldi's preparations. Rattazzi did nothing to stop him at Florence, or at Arezzo, where there was a huge demonstration in his favour. But on the night of 24 September, while the General was a guest of the engineer Luigi Angelucci at Sinalunga (a village near Siena), he was arrested and taken to Alessandria, where he was shut up in the fortress. Word of his arrest spread like wildfire, and protest meetings were held all over Italy. When he passed through Pistoia, in custody, some priests were thrashed by the crowd, and even the army – normally so loyal to the monarchy – seemed to take his side. At Alessandria the soldiers of the garrison flocked beneath his window and shouted 'To Rome! To Rome!'

Though Rattazzi received many letters congratulating him on his 'courageous move', he knew quite well that he could not keep Garibaldi in prison for long. So he had him taken by ship to Caprera. Here the General was requested to pledge, on his word of honour, that he would not try to escape. He refused. The island was surrounded by eight warships, with instructions to keep him there at all costs.

But the absence of their leader did not put a stop to the mobilization of the *Garibaldini*. They organized three columns: one to the north-west of Rome (between Pitigliano and Arcidosso) under Acerbi; one to the north-east (between Narni and Terni) under Menotti; and one to the south-east (between Naples and the Molise) under Nicotera. But the columns were amalgamations of disorganized and completely undisciplined bands of men (one of the negative features of the campaign).

This time there were few military experts in the ranks. Menotti took over the general command in his father's absence, but he was unable to keep the other columns completely under control. Capable soldiers, such as Missori, Frigyesi, Salomone, Francesco Vigo-Pellizzari, Guido Evangelisti and Francesco Biderchini, took part in the campaign, but there was certainly no one of Bixio's or Türr's stature. Most of them were rabid anticlericals, more concerned with 'hoisting the tricolour on all the church steeples' (to frighten rural parish priests) than with providing the Red-shirts with adequate structures and services.

The commanders of the three columns did not show much ability, either military or political. Acerbi had taken part in several of Garibaldi's campaigns and had even served as General Commissary of the Thousand, but he was incapable of leading his troops in action. Only a timely victory of Garibaldi's at Monterotondo prevented him from fleeing the region of Viterbo at full speed.

Nicotera was more of a politician than a soldier; at the time he was already a deputy and in the future he was to head several ministries. His military experience was limited to the defence of Rome in 1849 and to the Trentino campaign of 1866. Certainly he was not up to the responsibility of commanding an independent column. His troops were the most disorganized of all: not only were they defeated repeatedly but they were often without food. Later, when the King disavowed the expedition, Nicotera deserted the ranks of the *Garibaldini*.

Worst of all, these commanders did not join forces with Garibaldi when he came to take over the leadership of the Red-shirts, but neither did they take advantage of the opportunity before them when the Papal troops concentrated their offensive on the column led by Garibaldi.

Menotti's column was the best of the three. The General's elder son was a capable officer – at the age of nineteen he had served with the *Cacciatori delle Alpi*, and was now always at his father's side. But he was no strategist, and from the beginning he too committed a series of unbelievably silly errors.

An initial band of forty men entered Papal territory on 28 September 1867, but they were immediately dispersed at Ronciglione. Other bands met the same fate at Acquapendente, at San Lorenzo, at Nerola, at Moricone, at Montemaggiore, at Ischia di Castro, at Farnese, at Bagnoregio and at Subiaco.

In short, from 28 September until 23 October, when Garibaldi arrived, the Red-shirts were always the losing side. Only Menotti had a victory or two to his credit. He and his column occupied Montelibretti after some difficult fighting. There they were attacked by Colonel Anastase de Charette's Zouaves, and after a fierce struggle the *Garibaldini* forced the Zouaves to retreat. But then, inexplicably, Menotti himself ordered a retreat. The bridgehead he abandoned was retaken, a few hours later, by fifty Papal gendarmes.

'And so Menotti, Acerbi and Nicotera, all three on the same day, had to pay for their impetuosity. Their error was brought home to them: they had supposed that everything could be extemporized in a few hours and that they could beat the enemy merely by showing their face.' Thus did Felice Cavallotti, a *Garibaldino* of long standing and a member of parliament, express himself.

Their principal error was the excessive fragmentation of their offensive. By attacking in such small groups they allowed the powerful Papal 'mobile columns' to defeat them with ease, thus undermining the self-confidence they would need for the final confrontation. A mass attack, on the other hand, would have demoralized the enemy and given Napoleon III an excuse to resist the pressure he was under from the Catholics to intervene in the war (the French troops did not arrive, in fact, until a month later).

After the fall of the Roman Republic, the Papal State had relied on French military support and had not gone to much trouble to rebuild its own army. But when the Pontifical government saw, in 1859, that Napoleon III did not try to stop the annexation of the Romagna by Piedmont, it realized that it would have to defend itself in the future, and it did its best to make up for lost time. Monsignor de Mérode, formerly an officer in the Belgian army and now First Minister at Arms, reorganized the Pontifical army, but the Pope's cause did not meet with much enthusiasm from the populace and Mérode

Pontifical Zouaves. The corps, supposedly created on the lines of the famed French Zouaves, was mainly composed of foreign Catholic fanatics. The officer in the middle is Colonel de Charette.

A company of engineers during the manoeuvres at Campi d'Annibale.

had to rely on foreign volunteers, who enlisted on account of their religious convictions.

In fact, when one examines the muster-rolls of the various Pontifical battalions and regiments, one is struck by the huge number of names originating in Catholic lands such as the Vendée, Brittany, Belgium, Austria, Ireland, Bavaria and French Canada; many of them are prefixed by 'de' or 'von'. A kind of religious-conservative International, a survival from the period before the French Revolution, was preparing for a collision with that 'socialist' world which had emerged in the nineteenth century and which was to come into its own with the Paris Commune and with the October Revolution.

After their defeat by Piedmont in 1860 the Papal forces were reorganized into the following units: one infantry regiment, one battalion of chasseurs, one battalion of *carabinieri*, one regiment of Dragoons, one legion of gendarmes, artillery and engineers, plus a series of small corps such as the *Zampitti* (a sort of rural police-force) and the Volunteer Reserves. At the head of the whole army was General Hermann Kanzler, a German from Baden who had been in the Pope's service for years and who had distinguished himself in 1848 and 1860.

Though Garibaldi was a prisoner on his island, he soon came to hear of the errors being committed by his men, and realized that he must get away and take matters in hand. Garibaldi's escape from Caprera, in October 1867, is like a chapter from an adventure novel by his friend Dumas. It was recounted in the European press with amazement, admiration and dismay.

His first attempts ended badly. On 8 October he tried to slip away aboard the mail-boat for La Maddalena, an island a few miles away, but the boat was stopped by one of the warships and Garibaldi was taken back to

Kanzler (in the centre) and his General Staff shortly after the victory at Mentana. Behind Kanzler on the right is De Charette, and, sitting to the left, Colonel Allet, commander of the zouaves.

Caprera. Next, Stefano Canzio tried to smuggle him out in a fishing boat; this time the navy actually fired on them. Teresita, who was aboard, and who resembled her mother, called out to the naval officers, asking if they meant 'to take out their defeat at Lissa on women'. Again, the attempt was a failure.

The navy had of course impounded all the boats on Caprera. But they had overlooked a leaky little dinghy, just big enough for a single man: no one would ever have thought it seaworthy.

For two days Garibaldi pretended to be ill and stayed shut up at home. On the night of 17 October, in a heavy fog, he put out to sea in the tiny craft. Rowing silently with one oar he managed to slip between the warships, passing so close that he could hear the sailors talking, and he was afraid that a big wave would send him against one of the ships' sides. He rowed to La Maddalena, where Susini and Basso were waiting for him at the house of English friends called Collins. The next day, disguised as a fisherman and with his beard dyed black, he landed in Sardinia with his two accomplices. There Canzio was waiting for him with a sloop. They crossed the Tyrrhenian Sea and landed at Leghorn on 19 October. The next day, at noon, Garibaldi was in Florence.

Rattazzi had arrested him at Sinalunga without hesitation, but he was not going to try it again: too many people in Florence were prepared to defend the General whatever the cost. In any case Rattazzi had just submitted his resignation and had designated as his successor General Cialdini, who was even less prepared than he to take such a risky action. Cialdini attempted gentle persuasion, but there was bad blood between the two men and Garibaldi would not listen. He went on to Terni, where he met with Crispi. He sent instructions – which were not obeyed – to Acerbi and Nicotera, ordering them to join forces with him. At Passo Corese, on 23 October, Menotti turned over to him the command of the entire Volunteer corps, which now numbered nearly seven thousand men, though some of these were with Nicotera and with Acerbi.

Meanwhile, confusing and contradictory reports were arriving from Rome, where an insurrection had been scheduled for the 22nd. There were (as one might have guessed) two Revolutionary Committees in the city, one republican and one favourable to the Italian monarchy. Neither had done much more than to organize a few half-hearted demonstrations, publish a few pamphlets, or distribute bogus photographs showing former Queen Sophie of Naples in pornographic poses. Instead of preparing for a conflict, they talked politics in the salons, making no pretence of secrecy – so that all Rome knew that on the evening of 22 October the populace was to rise in revolt. Gregorovius spent that evening at a public-house, the 'Osteria del Falcone'; he tells us how two of the regular customers, young men with whom he was on friendly terms, explained to him in minute detail exactly what was supposed to take place. The gendarmes, of course, were on hand to wait for the revolutionaries as they assembled, but they made very few arrests: a sudden cloudburst had convinced most of the insurgents to postpone their action. The Revolutionary Committees issued no orders and distributed no weapons. In fact, when they realized that the Italian army was not about to intervene, they resigned: most of them feared the Redshirts – who by now were wholly identified with the Left – far more than the Papal police.

Garibaldi and his men were left without support. The few episodes of revolutionary violence which took place in Rome did nothing to rouse the city from its somnolence. Someone threw a bomb at Castel Sant'Angelo, and there was an attempt to blow up the new Serristori barracks. At the moment of the explosion there was no one in the barracks except for the brass band, but the troops came back in time to arrest the dynamiters – Giuseppe Monti and Gaetano Tognetti – who were sentenced to the guillotine. Other actions were the work of emissaries of the *Garibaldini*. Francesco Cucchi tried to storm the Capitol, but with such a small group of followers that even the few guards on duty were able to turn them back. Guerzoni was meant to force the gate at Porta San Paolo to allow some arms to be got into the city, but he too failed for lack of sufficient help.

Enrico and Giovanni Cairoli also tried to supply arms to the insurgents, and so doing they brought their family's tragedy to its conclusion in the abortive exploit of the 'Seventy of Villa Glori'. Nicola Fabrizi, an old revolutionary (he was then sixty-two years of age) and not taken in by all the facile predictions of success on the 22nd, advised them to send the weapons by rail, camouflaged. But this did not seem feasible, and the brothers decided to convey the shipment down the Tiber themselves. Well aware of the risks of the mission, they personally selected their associates and an élite corps of 76 men was formed.

They loaded the weapons on two barges, and set out at 3 p.m. on 22 October. Shortly after sunset the river's current brought them to a spot near Monte Antenne, a mile or so from Porta del Popolo. Here they landed as planned; but nobody from the Revolutionary Committees was there to meet them.

The insurrection should have begun by now, but no sound of shots or shouts could be heard coming from inside the walls. The Cairoli brothers were worried. They and the others hid in the vegetation along the river, sending one of their number into the city to reconnoitre. In the morning they learned that the insurrection had failed; they were advised to hide out until nightfall, when another attempt would be made. They moved the weapons to a nearby hill where, in the midst of a large park, stood 'a charming little house' belonging to a Signor Glori. Here they would wait until dark. But at 4 p.m. the Pontifical troops arrived, some four hundred of them, including Zouaves and Foreign *Carabinieri*. The 'Seventy' ought to have fled, but they decided to hold out: a heroic decision, but one which, however, led to a needless sacrifice of lives.

The group led by Giovanni, stationed at the edge of the park, bore the initial brunt of the attack. The Papal forces, armed with Remingtons, had advantage over the *Garibaldini* with their left-over National Guard rifles. Enrico saw that he would have to come to the rescue. 'Bayonets!', he ordered. Many of his men were mown down by the enemy fire, but the Pontificals fell back. The *Garibaldini* caught up with them, and a hand-to-hand battle was the result. Enrico leapt at Captain Meyer and nearly overcame him, but the Zouaves rushed to the defence of their leader.

Enrico was surrounded and, wounded several times, he fell at the foot of an almond tree (which stands to this day). Sergeant Hoffstetter administered the *coup de grâce* with his bayonet. Giovanni, who had also been wounded, ran to cradle his brother's head in his arms. Enrico murmured, 'Say good-bye to Mamma ... our friends ...' Giovanni was never to recover, either from his wounds or from the memory of being bathed in Enrico's life-blood; he died the following year.

The struggle had only lasted half an hour, and the *Garibaldini* had lost twenty-five comrades in addition to their leaders. But the Pontificals had retreated. The survivors spent the night in the villa, taking care of the wounded and dreading another attack. They held a meeting at 6-o-clock on the morning of the 23rd, and a number of them decided to rejoin Garibaldi. When the Pontificals returned with a large force at ten-o-clock they found only the dead, the wounded and the few men who had stayed behind to look after them.

Guillotine in via dei Cerchi, Rome.

Death of the Cairoli brothers during the fighting at Villa Glori.

Two other tragedies came after the skirmish at Villa Glori: the defence of the Ajani Woollen Factory and the massacre of Villa Cecchini.

Giulio Ajani's premises had for a long time served as a secret factory of 'Orsini bombs' (i.e., hand-bombs of the type invented by the revolutionary Felice Orsini), and as a weapons depot. After the abortive insurrection of 22 October the police began to search Rome building by building, hunting down subversives. On the 25th they presented themselves at the Ajani house. Inside were Giuditta Tavani Arquati, a forty-seven-year-old *pasionaria* and mother of nine, the guiding spirit of this group of revolutionaries; her husband Francesco; their youngest son (fourteen-year-old Antonio); and about twenty-five other persons. (The exact number is uncertain because a certain Rinaldo Marinelli, who was compromised in the affair and arrested, furnished the police with the names of all those who survived the massacre, hoping thereby to save his own skin. But not even the police

considered his information trustworthy.) When they were ordered to open up, Antonio threw a bomb from the roof, killing several gendarmes. There then arrived the Third Company of Zouaves, who had been in the nearby Piazza di Santa Maria in Trastevere. They surrounded the house and demanded that the revolutionaries surrender. Giuditta cried 'Nobody's coming in here', and started shooting. The exchange of rifle-fire lasted an hour.

Seeing that the household was determined to hold out, the Zouaves set fire to the building. Someone then began to wave a white flag from a second-storey window. The Pontificals broke into the house, and a young man called Angelo Marinelli hurled a bomb down the stairs into their midst. It did not explode. Sergeant Arnaud of the Zouaves rushed at him with his bayonet; his rifle went off at the same time, and Marinelli was killed instantly. That was the beginning of the massacre. The Zouaves, wild with rage, slashed the rebels with their bayonets and clubbed them with their rifle-stocks. Giuditta stood with her husband and son, pistol in hand, crying 'Stay

163

with me – we'll live or die together.' They died: husband, son, and finally Giuditta, with a bayonet in her abdomen. Those who managed to escape hid in houses nearby; some were denounced to the police by 'Christian' informers, and were arrested and executed on the spot.

According to the official report filed by the gendarmes, thirteen revolutionaries were killed and four wounded. But three of the wounded died, so the victims were sixteen in all.

Villa Cecchini was the rebels' last refuge, and there the same scene was repeated. Colonel Charette of the Zouaves sums it up neatly in his report: '*La plupart des garibaldiens furent passés au fil de la baïonnette.*'

The failure of the revolt and the indifference of the Roman people – as Gregorovius wrote, 'The passivity with which Rome awaits its destiny is a great enigma' – were a source of worry for Garibaldi. He had based his strategy, as usual, on the assumption that he would have abundant popular support; without it he could do nothing. He knew from experience that a voluntary militia will grow rapidly when it has the good will and the enthusiasm of the masses on its side, but it will shrink just as rapidly when it has to contend with the apathy or, worse, the hostility of civilians.

In fact, news of the setback at Rome had already cooled the ardour of many of the volunteers; indiscipline and desertions increased. Clearly, a victory was needed now: one which would confirm the legend of the Red-shirts' invincibility and inspire the masses to revolt.

On 23 October Garibaldi moved to attack Monterotondo. The Papal garrison there was not numerous, consisting of two companies of the Antibes Legion, one of Foreign *carabinieri*, one section of artillery, one Dragoon platoon and some gendarmes. But the town was well protected by a solid circuit of walls.

On the 24th the *Garibaldini* occupied the railway station at Monterotondo, tearing up the tracks and cutting off the telegraph line.

On the 25th they attacked the town, concentrating particularly on the gate known as Porta San Rocco. The Pontificals defended it bravely. Only around two in the morning did the *Garibaldini* manage to set fire to the gate

and enter the town. The Dragoons surrendered; the other Pontificals shut themselves up in the Castle and continued to resist. But at 9 a.m. the following morning they hoisted the white flag. Garibaldi took possession of two cannon and of seventy rounds of ammunition, which he turned over to his son Ricciotti. The expeditionary corps finally had its artillery.

The battle of Monterotondo was a victory, but it further exposed the latent defects and the indiscipline of the Red-shirts, as the following example will show. When the *Garibaldini* attacked the town, they left their wounded in the railway station – but they did not leave sufficient troops to protect them. A battalion of Zouaves approached Monterotondo, intending to bring relief to the garrison. When they saw that the town was surrounded they turned back to the station, and vented their fury by massacring the defenceless *Garibaldini* they found there.

Nevertheless, the taking of Monterotondo touched off a wave of enthusiasm throughout Italy. The new prime minister, General Menabrèa, was obliged to order General Cadorna to advance 'peacefully' into Papal territory to restore order. It looked as though Rattazzi's plan was going to work after all.

But too much time had been lost. On 26 October De Failly's division of 20,000 men set sail from Toulon: the spectre of 1849 had reappeared. When he learned of the French intervention, the King disowned the *Garibaldini*, declaring that they had been 'seduced and led on by a political faction which has not got my authorization or my government's.'

Rome prepared for a dogged resistance; the walls were fortified and armed with guns, while all the Pontifical troops hastened to the defence of the city.

Garibaldi tried to surround the city with mobile units, but this was a wasted manoeuvre. He moved men from the Via Salaria to the Via Nomentana, and then to the Via Tiburtina, thus leaving the enemy too much leeway. He occupied Castel Giubileo, not far from Rome. On 29 October he arrived at Tivoli.

Meanwhile the French had landed, and De Failly was already at Rome. Kanzler's force

Massacre in the Ajani house, by Carlo Ademollo.

of fifteen thousand was thus reinforced by twenty thousand well-trained and well-armed Frenchmen. And they were concentrated in one small area, whereas the *Garibaldini* were spread out along the three highways named, as well as along the Via Prenestina and the Via Casilina. Garibaldi decided to regroup all his troops in a good, easily defendable position like Monterotondo, build up his strength, and beat the Pontificals and the French separately.

He ordered a withdrawal to Monterotondo. But the order irritated the volunteers. That night – partly because of the King's disavowal and partly because many were convinced that the campaign was coming to an end – two thousand of them failed to report for roll-call.

In Rome, the two allies were not at all in agreement as to what course of action to pursue. De Failly wanted to keep all the troops in Rome as a deterrent and to attack the *Garibaldini* only when the occasion should arise; he seemed more concerned with avoid-

ing any conflict with the regular Italian troops (who were now stationary at the frontiers) than with defeating the Red-shirts. Kanzler, on the other hand, wanted to 'come down on them like a thunderbolt, take [Garibaldi] by surprise, and inflict on him, before the whole world, a severe and well-deserved punishment.' Kanzler evidently feared that if the various volunteer columns were allowed to regroup and penetrate more deeply into Roman territory, the much-feared rebellion might become a reality.

Kanzler put his view across. On Sunday 3 November the troops were assembled at the Macao barracks. Kanzler set out from Porta Pia at 4 a.m., heading for Mentana. The Franco-Pontifical army consisted of seven thousand men, divided into two columns. The Papal troops were headed by General Raphaël de Courten, and the French by General de Pohles. A considerable number of pro-Papal volunteers joined the combatants: Colonel de Charette has left the register of their names and, glancing at it, one gets the impression that the entire nobility of Europe had rushed to Rome to put down the subversives and uphold a temporal power which cataclysms, schisms and revolutions had never managed to shake. Among the more illustrious names are those of the Count of Caserta, brother of the former King of Naples, with his *aides-de-camp* Ussani and Afan de Rivera; Baron Sonnenberg, commander of the Swiss Guard; Lieutenant Colonel the Count Carpegna; Count Victor de Courten, brother of the General, enrolled for the occasion in the Foreign *Carabinieri*; De Christen, commander of the Foreign Chasseurs; the Vicomte de Saint-Priest; the Duc de Lorges; Benoît d'Azy; de Saint Maur; de Luppé; Vrignault.

According to Garibaldi's orders, the Red-shirts were to leave Monterotondo at 6 a.m. and advance upon Tivoli once again. Menotti's corps should have been the first to set out, but the men were practically barefoot and Menotti asked for a delay so that he might distribute a large shipment of shoes which had arrived the night before. This took a long time, and it was nearly noon before the columns got underway. The defeat which followed has often been attributed to those six hours' lost time. But the truth is that in this campaign the *Garibaldini* never approached their former standard. Even the performance of tried and true leaders left much to be de-

sired. Ciotti, for instance, had occupied Mentana on the previous evening; at dawn he set out for Tivoli as per orders received, because no one had taken the trouble to inform him of the delay at Monterotondo.

The *Garibaldini* left for Mentana about 11.30 a.m. But before they reached it their vanguards were assaulted by the Papal troops, who had, in Ciotti's absence, occupied the town without difficulty.

The Zouaves rushed to the attack, but then the main body of the *Garibaldini* appeared, and drove them back. The Red-shirts occupied Mentana again; the Pontificals counter-attacked in force. At the first charge, the *Garibaldini* under Lieutenant Colonel Missori, Major Antonio Burlandi and Captain Karl Mayer held their ground, but with the second, the enemy succeeded in driving many of them from the town.

The Papal forces fought valiantly. The Zouaves, especially, led by Colonels Allet and de Charette, were unstoppable. For a while it seemed that the battle was lost, but then – thanks to the two cannon they had captured at Monterotondo – the *Garibaldini* managed to slow down the enemy attack. At this point they lowered their bayonets and commenced a counter-attack of their own. The fighting was particularly ferocious near Villa Santucci and at the Castle. The Papal troops were beaten

Battle of Mentana.

Retreat from Mentana, by A. Tanzi.

back and Mentana was once again in Garibaldian hands.

At 3 p.m. the battle was going in favour of the *Garibaldini*, who were on the point of mounting an enveloping movement against the enemy flank, and it might have been decisive. But 'then another, unseen enemy descended upon us, thinning our ranks. . . . We sought the enemy within the range of our rifles, but in vain; the only sign of them was the death they scattered amongst us. . . . We fired back, but our bullets had not half the range of theirs . . .'

It was the French army's *chassepots* which proved decisive. Kanzler had sent all his reserves to the front lines to no avail; then he called in Pohlés' column. In an instant the French were subjecting the *Garibaldini* 'to rifle-fire so dense and so deadly that they had no choice but to withdraw immediately.' Garibaldi ordered his artillery to fire, but their seventy rounds were now used up; cartridges were running short as well. The only other solution was the customary bayonet-charge, but the troops could not ad-

vance in the face of such a volume of fire. The French now tried an encircling manoeuvre, and the *Garibaldini* began to fall back. Soon the retreat turned into a headlong flight in the direction of Passo Corese. Never had the *Garibaldini* been so thoroughly routed.

Garibaldi did everything he could to stop them, but it was hopeless. He himself was about to charge into the face of death when Canzio, seizing his horse's reins, cried, 'Who do you want to die for, General? Who for?', and dragged him away. He seemed to have aged twenty years, and his rheumatism was giving him trouble. But he refused the carriage ordered for him.

'It's the first time they've turned their backs on me', he said to Guerzoni. His friends tried to rationalize the defeat: it was the fault of the *chassepots*, of the shoes, of the undesirable elements who had enlisted, of the 'amateurs who thought they could walk into Rome and enjoy an easy triumph'. They blamed the King, the government and the Mazzinians. The recriminations were endless, as each sought to shift his share of the responsibility to another's shoulders. But they were all responsible to some degree, including the General: he was sixty now, half crippled by his wounds and by rheumatism, conducting his battles mainly from a carriage, so that he could hardly hope to stir his men's hearts, as he had once done, by his mere presence among them. And his General Staff was no longer up to its task.

Six hundred of his *Garibaldini* were killed in the Roman Campaign of 1867, and 1,700 were taken prisoner. After Garibaldi's defeat the other columns withdrew from Papal territory as well. The *Garibaldini* were now faced with imprisonment once again. The Italian army, in fact, was waiting for them at the frontier, to disarm them and place them under arrest; but most of them were escorted to their homes.

Garibaldi, however, was arrested at Figline, on a train bound for Leghorn. The little station was occupied by a unit of *bersaglieri* and a platoon of *carabinieri*. The General got off the train and Lieutenant Colonel Camozzi, who was in command, notified him in the name of the Government that he was under arrest. Guerzoni has recorded the heated dialogue which followed; it was also witnessed by Francesco Crispi, who had come to greet the General, and by others who were travelling with him:

'Have you a regular warrant for my arrest?' asked Garibaldi.

'No,' replied Camozzi, 'but I have orders to arrest you.'

'You are aware that you are committing an illegality. I am guilty of no act against the Italian State or against its laws. Nor have you caught me committing any crime. You have no right to arrest me, and I refuse to yield to an act of violence.'

Camozzi wired Florence, requesting that his orders be revoked. But no answer came. After an hour he announced that he would have to carry them out. So Garibaldi was taken away by four *carabinieri* and conducted to the fortress of Varignano, where he had been imprisoned after Aspromonte. Canzio and other members of his family accompanied him. But an amnesty came almost immediately; the government did not want to have to face the protests and the disorder which news of Garibaldi's arrest would certainly evoke.

Despite the Franco-Pontifical victory at Mentana the days of the Pope's temporal power were numbered. It was a useless burden for the Church, one which contradicted its true nature. Rome would soon become the capital of the Kingdom of Italy.

Garibaldini *tombs along the Mentana road.*

French soldiers photographed at the Capitol in 1867.

The battle of Dijon by De Albertis.

Rally Round the General

Between 1860 and 1870 Napoleon III attempted to put into practice some of the ideals which had been instilled in him in his youth by his Jacobin tutor Le Bas. But he went about it in a contradictory manner: thus, while he gave official recognition to labour organizations and sanctioned the right to strike, he also sent in the army to protect the interests of capital. It must be said to his credit, however, that he laid the basis of modern, industrial France.

The Emperor's liberal ambitions aroused a great deal of opposition at court, where a powerful conservative faction had grown up around the Empress Eugénie. It was she who influenced Napoleon to embark upon disastrous military operations, such as the Mexican expedition of 1862–7, which marked the beginning of the end for the Second Empire. His colonial conquests in Asia could not make up for such failures.

Though France had entered a phase of political decadence, Bismarck's Germany was very much on the rise. But the economies of both countries were expanding, and in this fact lay the germs of conflict. A number of disputes nearly came to a head during the years 1867–8, and only the mediation of other European powers succeeded in exorcising the threat of war.

A newspaper of the period wrote, 'Fate seems to have willed that the two great races which until now have alternated as masters of Europe should be incapable of living side by side in peace. They are destined periodically to clash with all their might, as they attempt to seize the supremacy one from the other.'

In 1870 a problem arose which at first did not seem especially serious. But, thanks above all to the intransigence of the Empress, it was to lead to war. Spain had just come through yet another civil conflict (1868–70); the Queen, Isabella II, had been dethroned; and now the country was looking round for a new monarch. In 1870, after various European princes had been consulted, the crown was offered to – and accepted by – Leopold von Hohenzollern, nephew of the King of Prussia. But this solution met with strong opposition in France, especially from the Empress's faction. Eugénie was a Spaniard by birth, and her view of the matter was strictly personal.

Napoleon III.

An anti-German campaign was launched; its basic principle was that 'the government must not permit a foreign power to place a prince upon the Spanish throne, as this would offend the honour and dignity of France.'

Leopold bowed to French pressures and renounced the crown; the advocates of war were left without a pretext, and the whole incident seemed destined to blow over. But the section of the press which spoke for the Court continued to write, 'War, at the present moment, is for us an imperative dictated by the interests of France as well as by dynastic exigencies.'

Bismarck believed that war would be profitable for Prussia politically and economically, and he skilfully turned the situation to his own advantage. When the French demanded that the King of Prussia renounce all claim to Spain for the future as well as for the present, he broke off negotiations with Benedetti, the French ambassador, and on 13 July 1870 he issued a *communiqué* so brutal in tone that –

The Empress Eugenie.

just as he intended – it 'had effect of a red cloth upon the Gallic bull.' In fact, the French newspapers came out with huge headlines, 'To Berlin! To Berlin!' War had come.

Those were the days in which the pro-government papers could still write 'Never has France been so prepared for war as at present.' But they spoke too soon. When later, during the parleys for the capitulation of Sedan, Von Moltke said to the French general Wimpffen that France had conducted the war 'presumptuously' and 'without method', he was only stating a fact.

In fact France's lack of military preparation resulted in a staggering series of defeats which culminated at Sedan on 2 September 1870, when the Emperor himself was taken prisoner along with 170,000 men.

Two last bulwarks remained in French hands: Paris and Metz. The eyes of the nation were upon those cities, and its heart beat with them.

The rapid collapse of the Second Empire and the capture of Napoleon III transformed the political situation in Italy: the Papal State had lost its protector. An Italian paper wrote:

'Within a few days the French will be gone from the Patrimony of St Peter. [And indeed, the Observation Corps was soon recalled to France.] The Pope will be left to face his subjects. This is a most advantageous situation, one which will probably lead to the definitive solution of the Roman Question, if only our government finds a way to act with the necessary prudence and boldness.'

But parliament was split down the middle. One faction, headed by the King, favoured an immediate intervention in the war on the French side, out of loyalty to the alliance with Napoleon III. The other faction maintained, more realistically, that Italy's debt to France had been more than repaid with the cession of Nice and Savoy and that any moral obligation had come to an end at Mentana.

Eventually the King capitulated. On 11 September Italian troops invaded Pontifical territory. On the 20th they broke through the walls at Porta Pia, and entered Rome, which thus became capital of Italy.

Garibaldi did not approve of the operation, though he himself had twice marched on Rome and had fought for its liberty: he thought it unfair to take advantage of other people's misfortunes. Thus once again he demonstrated his political *naïveté*: obviously the Italian move was dictated by common sense and political logic. His maligners said later that his silence about the event was due to the fact that his own presence had not been requested. But in all probability the General, at that moment, had entirely different problems on his mind.

Two days after the capitulation at Sedan, on 4 September 1870, the people of Paris had burst into the Assembly and proclaimed the Third Republic.

Garibaldi had always had a complicated relationship with the French. On the one hand he could not forget the Roman Republic and Mentana; on the other hand he was aware that France had given birth to the Revolution of 1789, the historical turning-point which had been a source of inspiration for him. And

French republicans had always given him their help and support.

Napoleon III had been the principal object of his aversion – when he heard of the defeat at the French army he remarked that Germany had rendered a great service to humanity. But then came the news that a republican government had been established and that the Germans were advancing on the capital. This changed matters: now that there was no longer a tyrant to be overthrown, the territorial integrity of France was something to be defended. Impetuously, on 7 September he sent a telegram to the French National Defence Government: 'All that is left of me is at your disposal: put it to use.'

Not everyone in Italy understood the General's attitude, or his distinction between an imperialist France which had invaded and interfered with other nations and a republican France which was fighting for its own liberty. *L'Opinione* wrote:

'General Garibaldi's behaviour is most extravagant. Hardly more than two months ago, when this war began, he wrote a letter calling for a German victory and sought to stir up Nice in the hopes of taking it from France. Now he is at Tours, to offer France the gift of his abilities and his fame.'

Neither did all the French understand. As late as 1882 the newspaper *Le Grelot* published a front-page cartoon with the caption '*La dernière pensée de Garibaldi*': it represented the General defecating upon France the words with which he had greeted Napoleon III's defeat.

For that matter, not all of his own comrades-in-arms understood him. He issued the following appeal:

'Yesterday I called for war to the death against Bonaparte. Today I say: uphold the Republic with all the means at your disposal. Though I am an invalid, I have offered my services to the Provisional Government in Paris, and I trust that it will not be impossible for me to do my duty. Yes, citizens, we must consider it our sacred duty to succour our brethren in France. Our aim, certainly, shall not be to combat our German brethren, the agents of Providence who have cast down into the dust the nightmare of tyranny which was oppressing the world. We shall go to sustain the only system which can assure peace and prosperity among nations. I repeat: we shall sustain with all our force the French Republic which, wise in the lessons of the past, will always be one of the greatest pillars of human regeneration.'

But many of the 'old guard' had never got over the bitterness of the defeats of Rome and Mentana; staunch republicans though they were, they could not bring themselves to fight for France. When the news came that Garibaldi had landed at Marseilles, only a few thousand Italians could bring themselves to join him.

France began recruiting troops for the General. Colonel Philippe Bourdon, an old comrade from the days of the Thousand, went to Caprera to escort him to Paris. They sailed on 6 October 1870. Half the Italian fleet was standing by, but this time there was no need to elude the gunboats by subterfuge. The government was quite delighted that Garibaldi was going so far away to look for a

Napoleon III surrenders to Bismarck. After a brief imprisonment in Germany the ex-Emperor took refuge in England, where he died in 1873.

The storming of Rome. On 20 September 1870 the Italian troops, on the orders of General Raffaele Cadorna, broke through the walls of the city near Porta Pia and entered the city, thus completing the unification of Italy.

fight, especially since he would be taking with him some of those rabid republicans and socialists who were now demonstrating in the streets for workers' rights.

He landed at Marseilles on the evening of 7 October and received a hero's welcome. As soon as the city learned that his ship, the *Ville de Paris*, was in the port, an immense crowd, including the municipal authorities, came down to the pier. In reply to the mayor's speech Garibaldi said, 'This is the second time I have come to Marseilles. The first time, I had been condemned to death by my country's oppressors and you generously gave me asylum. Now I have come to repay my debt to France, to co-operate in freeing her territory from the Prussian hordes and in raising once again the glorious banner of the Republic.'

Not everyone echoed the hosannas. Isaac-Moïse Crémieux, the Keeper of the Seals in the National Defence Government, had said a few days earlier, 'Oh, Garibaldi! If we could have him come to Paris, what an effect he would produce!'. But now he exclaimed, 'He's really coming ... As though we hadn't enough troubles already!'. And certainly there was some truth to what he said: Garibaldi created problems wherever he went, and the French had no need of those. The possibility of a Bonapartist restoration was becoming more concrete; the coming revolt of the Communards was in the air; and the Prussians were closing in on Paris. But Garibaldi was by now a living symbol, and the French welcomed him with open arms.

The journey to Tours, where the Triumvirate – Crémieux, Alexandre-Olivier Bizoin and Clément Laurier – had established the seat of the government, was a triumph. But there was no time to lose in rejoicing: the situation was desperate. A newspaper wrote, 'We are grateful to the hero of Marsala and Messina for having offered to place his fearsome sword at the service of our National Defence. But if he wants to lay a serious claim to our gratitude, he must take his place without delay upon the field of battle. Then indeed he shall have our applause and our acclamations.' But of course, as soon as he did decide to take his place on the field of battle it became apparent that even in that emergency many Frenchmen feared him more than they did the Prussians.

Garibaldi arrived at Tours on 9 October. Minister of the Interior Léon Gambetta was waiting for him: he had made the journey from Paris in an aerostatic balloon. He thanked Garibaldi for his generous aid, and invited him to go to Chambéry to take command of – three hundred volunteers! Garibaldi was mortally offended by this ridiculous offer; he wrote Gambetta a violent letter, announcing that he was leaving for Caprera on the following day. A number of generals, who had taken a dim view of his participation in the war in the first place, were glad to see him go. Gambetta, like many of his colleagues, was of the same mind, but he had more foresight than the others and he knew that the public reaction to Garibaldi's departure would be most unfavourable. The General was not to be discarded so easily; he might yet serve, as he had so often in the past, as a banner for people to rally round. So the minister sent two of his secretaries to implore Garibaldi not to leave without seeing him first. He was clearly not familiar with the General's temperament. 'If Monsieur Gambetta wishes to see me', replied the General, 'he may call tomorrow morning early. I intend to leave at eight.' Next morning at eight Gambetta was there to appoint him General of the Army of the Vosges.

On 13 October Garibaldi left Tours for Dôle, where he had been ordered to set up his headquarters.

He soon found out what the Army of the Vosges was all about. Except for one well-organized brigade of Mobile Guards, it was a gaudy mélange of sharpshooter units with an extravagant set of names: the *Franc-tireurs de la Mort*, the *Enfants Perdus*, the *Gentilhommes de Paris*, the *Guérillas d'Orient*, the *Volontaires de la Mort et de la Revanche*, and so on. As for their uniforms, they looked like a combination of opera singers, dandies, military men and bandits: the *Garibaldini* at their wildest had never looked so eccentric. In their

Stefano Canzio with his wife Teresita Garibaldi. The General's close, though not always faithful, collaborator, he received monies from the Italian government for information about Garibaldi's projects. Even today his role is not clear, although as a general and a Deputy his behaviour was always impeccable.

ranks were Frenchmen, Englishmen, Spaniards, Greeks, Italians, Montevideans, Algerians and even Egyptians.

Though France was to abandon them to their fate, these men were genuinely representative of the French people, and they found their natural leader in Garibaldi. And while we must not exaggerate the importance of their contribution, it is true nevertheless that they were responsible for the only French victories of 1870–1.

In addition to the above-mentioned groups of foreigners, about two thousand Italians hurried to the defence of the infant Republic. They were assembled and grouped at Chambéry and at Aix-les-Bains by two veterans of the expedition of the Thousand: Lieutenant Colonel Faustino Tanara and

Major Filippo Erba. As in the past, among the volunteers there was a unit of Genoese *Carabinieri* in their elegant grey uniforms. This time they had been organized by Stefano Canzio; as usual, they formed the élite corps of Garibaldi's army.

Canzio was to have a decisive rôle in this campaign. He had served under Garibaldi as a twenty-year-old youth with the *Cacciatori delle Alpi*, and later he followed him to Sicily. After the campaign of the Thousand he went to Caprera; he became a close collaborator of the General, and married his daughter Teresita.

Garibaldi divided the troops into three brigades. The first was commanded by General Bossack-Hauke, and was made up of a regiment of Mobile Guards, a battalion of *Franc-tireurs*, one English company, and one Spanish company led by Antonio Orense Milá de Aragón. The second brigade was placed under the command of Colonel Marie and later under that of Louis Delpèche, who had been Prefect of the Department of Bouches-du-Rhône and who, before the General's arrival, had organized a regiment of French volunteers. The third, under Menotti, comprised Mobile Guards, two battalions of Italian 'Chasseurs of the Argonne', and another from Nice.

Other groups joined the Army of the Vosges later. They included Gray's Explorers, Farlatti's Guides, a unit of mounted chasseurs, the Garibaldi Guides and others. Among the regular French formations were the *Chasseurs d'Afrique* and the *Garde Nationale*.

The French people got ready to make whatever sacrifices might be necessary, and they gave their full support to the *Garibaldini*. Not so the authorities. One of the chief difficulties of this campaign was that the Red-shirts had to take on not only the Germans, but also the local officials, who were mostly Bonapartist in their sympathies. The new government had not had time to replace the old mayors and prefects by tried and true republicans. The majority of these notables were still loyal to the old régime, and most were extremist Catholics who made no bones about their antipathy to the 'blasphemous' Red-shirts and to their chief, that well-known enemy of the Church.

In some cities the authorities manifested their hostility quite openly. At Autun, for instance, M. Reyras, a straight-laced magistrate of strict Bonapartist observance, declared that the Army of the Vosges was 'a gang of vandals, bandits and ruffians, miserable hyenas in search of carrion, who are paralysing the defence of Autun.' He accused them further of aspiring only to rank, of living in luxury, and of trafficking in contraband goods.

Exaggerations aside, there was probably some truth to what he said. As on other occasions, some rather dubious elements had no doubt infiltrated the *Garibaldini*. But the real reason for the magistrate's outburst was that the General had billeted his men in requisitioned convents and, with his usual tact, had remarked, in this clerical and Bonapartist city, that Napoleon III was 'the stupidest of tyrants'.

Relations with the central government were not much easier than with the local authorities. It was extremely nonchalant about providing arms and clothing; the lack of overcoats was especially grievous, as the temperature dropped to $18°$ centigrade below zero. Not until Christmas did they receive an adequate supply of clothing, some good Remingtons, and a battery of heavy-calibre, 27-barrelled machine-guns which the *Garibaldini*, for luck, christened Garibaldi, Menotti, Ricciotti, Canzio, Ouvrière and Délivrance.

Actually, the French themselves had to contend with short supplies. When Garibaldi requested some *chassepots*, General Alexis Cambriels replied, 'We haven't a single one in our magazines; furthermore, we have barely enough ammunition for ourselves.'

Matters were complicated by the fact that medical services in this campaign left a great deal to be desired, despite the valiant efforts of Timoteo Riboli, the head of the medical corps, and of his assistant, the ever-faithful Jessie White Mario. Riboli, who was sixty-one at the time, was a renowned surgeon, not only in liberal-revolutionary circles, but also in theatrical ones: he was known, in fact, as 'the Actresses' Physician'.

An even greater difficulty was the fact that the French command, either out of spite or disregard for the Red-shirts, kept Garibaldi's General Staff in the dark about the general situation at the front.

↲ Thus the *Garibaldini* had the distinct sensation of being used, but neither wanted nor loved, and this caused a great deal of tension. Menotti, who was always cool and calm, had a clash with a subordinate which almost led to a duel. At one point all the officers of the General Staff submitted their resignations on account of allegations of administrative irregularities which later turned out to be groundless. Poor Bourdon, Chief of General Staff, did the best he could for the troops, but since it was his duty to serve as go-between for the Army and the government, he was habitually made the scapegoat of the commanders' indignation.

Meanwhile, in spite of all the difficulties, the training of the volunteers continued, mostly under the supervision of Canzio, Menotti and Colonel Cristiano Lobbia. On 1 November Ricciotti arrived: he had been held up until now by the Italian police. He took charge of a fourth brigade made up exclusively of *Franc-tireurs*.

Early in November the French troops who were defending Dijon, to Garibaldi's left, were worsted by the advancing Germans and obliged to abandon the city to them. The loss of Dijon seriously disrupted the defence of the entire sector: the road to Lyons now lay open to the Germans, and if they were not stopped they could hope within a few days to break through the line of the Loire, behind which General Charles Bourbaky, who was now virtually the republican government's last hope, was in the process of organizing an army.

Garibaldi was ordered to fall back on Autun and to defend, at any cost, the Morvan massif and the steel-mills of Le Creusot, which were essential to the French economy. He fell back as ordered, but he did not limit himself to defensive actions. All along the front, day and night, he assaulted the German patrols which were occupying the villages, or lured them into ambushes with incursions and feints all along the front. It was the sort of guerrilla warfare which the *Garibaldini* found most congenial; for the forty thousand soldiers under General August Werder who had driven back the French along the Dijon-Dôle-Besançon front, on

the other hand, it represented a serious threat.

On 20 November at Châtillon-sur-Seine, Ricciotti's Fourth Brigade took a large Prussian infantry corps by surprise and put it out of action, taking 213 prisoners. Then General Werder, overestimating the size of Ricciotti's unit, sent out twenty thousand men against him. These troops were part of the force which was holding Dijon. This fact, plus the mood of optimism which Ricciotti's success had induced, gave Garibaldi the idea of launching a surprise attack on Dijon: to his troops, who were crying for action, he said, '*Eh bien*! *A Dijon!*' This was an error; the Germans still outnumbered the *Garibaldini* four to one.

They attacked on the night of 25 November. The fighting continued all the next day, but the Germans held out, and in the end Garibaldi had to order a retreat to Autun. The Prussians pursued them, and attacked the town on 1 December.

Garibaldi went (in a carriage, because of his bad foot and his rheumatism) to encourage the artillery with his presence: of all his troops they were the most exposed to the

Menotti with his General Staff. From the left: Achille Bizzoni, Menotti Garibaldi, Captain Droun and, sitting, Emile Seguin.

The uniforms of 1870–1. Rostaing, an officer in Ricciotti's Division. (Above) Ambrogio Curdi, a Mounted Guide. (Below)

enemy fire. Two Prussian columns occupied Bligny and then moved on Autun. They met more resistance from the *Franc-tireurs* than they had expected. After a dense exchange of artillery fire, a charge by the Genoese *Carabinieri*, Tanara's Legion and the Mobile Guards decided the outcome of the day's action: by six the Prussians were retreating. The *Garibaldini*, who had no desire to repeat the scene at Dijon in reverse, did not pursue them. Both sides suffered heavy losses, on account of the violence of the bayonet attacks and the precision of the artillery. But the *Garibaldini* had won their first significant victory of the campaign.

Meanwhile, to the right of Garibaldi's lines, not far from Autun, General Camille Cremer had put together an army of fifteen thousand men from the remains of the regular troops and the Mobile Guards. This army, however, was not co-ordinated with the Army of the Vosges; it took no part in the attack on Dijon or in the defence of Autun. Only the day after the German retreat did it move to occupy Bligny, which had now been abandoned. This belated and useless move incensed and infuriated Garibaldi's General Staff, but the General welcomed the opportunity for rest and a change of clothes. It was rare to have a break in those days.

But now the Franco-Prussian War was drawing to a close.

The army which General Bourbaky had hastily thrown together on the Loire now marched on Belfort. The Prussians, so as not to be encircled, withdrew from Dijon. On 28 December Garibaldi was ordered to occupy the city and to defend it at all costs. Meanwhile Bourbaky was defeated several times over, and he fled into Switzerland. Now the *Garibaldini*, all alone, found themselves facing an army of 250,000 men led by Prince Friedrich Karl von Hohenzollern. The Prussians were returning to Dijon, and from here they intended to invade the region of Lyons.

Garibaldi was aware of the strategic importance of Dijon, and he got ready to defend it tenaciously. He re-called all the units which were scattered about the area into the city. He sent for all the volunteers who had recently enlisted and who were now at Lyons. He reorganized his own troops so that the new arrivals could be inserted into a fifth brigade commanded by Canzio. He also reorganized the troops of General Philippe X. Pélissier, who were now assigned to him. In the end he had a force of forty thousand men. He made ready for the battle, which was to last three days and prove to be the final battle of his life.

At the crack of dawn on 21 January 1871, in the midst of a heavy fog which was to hamper the combatants for the next three days, the Prussian general Edwin H. K. von Manteuffel attacked the First Brigade, which constituted the first line of defence. The unit, without its commander, Bossack-Hauke, who had died in an ambush not long before, gave up and retreated to Daix.

The Prussians then attacked the second line, between Daix and Messigny (defended by Canzio's brigade and, in part, by Ricciotti's), and the heights of Mont-Talant and Fontaine, where the Garibaldian artillery under Delpèche and Menotti was installed.

The battle was mainly fought between Daix and Messigny, in thick fog and under heavy artillery fire from both sides. The officers of the General Staff were kept busy running from one end of the battlefield to the other, and to Garibaldi's headquarters on the heights of Mont-Talant, where they tried to keep the General abreast of the development of this blind struggle.

Around 3 p.m. everything was going in favour of the Prussians. They had occupied Daix and Messigny and were about to attack Tanara's legion, which was near to exhaustion as a result of the bombardment it had withstood all day defending the slopes of Mont-Talant.

But at that moment Canzio attacked Daix with his entire brigade. The first to break through were Orense's Spaniards; they were followed by the Genoese *Carabinieri*, while the squadron of *Chasseurs d'Afrique* charged the Prussian line from the rear. The attack was as violent as it was unexpected. The Prussians were not able to defend themselves adequately, and they were forced to abandon the

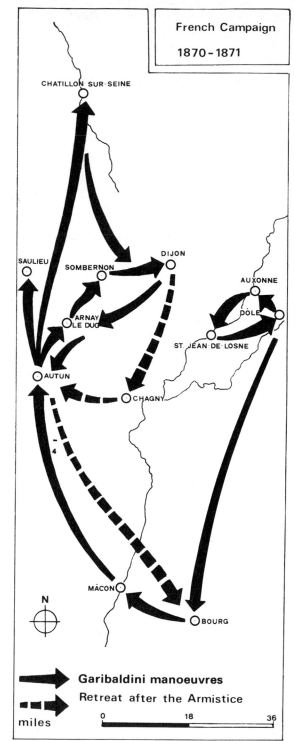

French Campaign 1870-1871

Garibaldini manoeuvres

Retreat after the Armistice

miles

village. At the same time, Ricciotti re-occupied Messigny.

The counter-attack threw the entire Prussian line off balance, and by 4.30 p.m. the tide of the battle had turned. The Prussians fell back, and that first day's fighting was concluded in favour of the Army of the Vosges.

Next morning the Germans renewed their attack. Their principal objective was the artillery installation of Mont-Talant. They moved slowly and cautiously: the fog was still very thick, and they were afraid of ambushes.

The offensive grew more and more savage. At noon the Prussian cannon were shelling the artillery positions of Mont-Talant and Fontaine, which reciprocated. Both sides were firing more or less at random, because the visibility was a mere fifty yards. But then the fog began to thin; now that they could aim with greater precision, the two artilleries became engaged in a kind of private duel. The shelling grew more intense.

The Prussian artillery was installed on a ridge opposite the *Garibaldini*. Several infantry regiments were concentrated around it. Garibaldi ordered his front line to begin a bayonet attack. The Prussians advanced to meet them, but were forced back again by the cannons of Mont-Talant. The *Garibaldini* were thus enabled to take the ridge without encountering direct resistance.

Aroldi, an eye-witness, has described the charge up this ridge:

'A Zouave in high boots was at the head of the whole column. With words and gestures he instilled courage in the hesitant *Moblots*. Virtually alone, he climbed until he reached a bush behind which a group of Prussians were lying low. They fought hand to hand; some of the Prussians fell. Other *Moblots* arrived on the scene, and put the remaining Prussians to flight. The Zouave and his handful of comrades chased them all the way to the top of the ridge.'

The Germans abandoned the ridge and the *Garibaldini* occupied it. The second day's fighting had only lasted two hours; it too had gone in favour of the Army of the Vosges.

On the night of 22 January the Prussians concentrated their forces in the vicinity of

Garibaldini *volunteers.*

Norges-la-Ville and Pouilly, on the road to Langres outside Porte Saint-Nicolas. This was the weakest point in Dijon's defence system. The Germans had already failed twice to enter the city at Porte Guillaume; they were now preparing a surprise attack on the opposite side of town.

But Garibaldi was prepared for this move. Leaving Menotti in charge of both the Mont-Talant and the Fontaine installations, he moved Delpèche's brigade to a point between Saint-Apollinaire and Mirande, two positions to the southeast of the city. He kept Ricciotti and Canzio in reserve inside the city itself.

However, the Germans attacked first in the

sector of Mont-Talant. Eight battalions of Mobile Guards had to bear the initial brunt; they held out alone for about an hour, until Menotti came to relieve them with fresh troops. The Prussians did not succeed in breaking through their lines.

But things were a bit more complicated on the left flank. Here too it was the Mobile Guards who had to withstand the first phase of the attack. But the pressure was too much for them, and they fell back. By 2.30 p.m. there were no further obstacles to the German advance outside Porte Saint-Nicolas.

Garibaldi then sent Ricciotti to occupy the Usine Bargy, a small factory a few miles from the city. He ordered him to hold on to it at all costs: 'If we lose it, we'll also lose Dijon', he said to his son. At the same time he ordered Canzio to create a second line of defence behind and to the left of the Usine Bargy.

Canzio, with the Isère battalion and the Spanish company, thwarted a German attempt to surround them.

The Prussians assaulted the factory boldly and repeatedly, but to no avail. Ricciotti's *Franc-tireurs* shot at them from the windows. Canzio prevented them from advancing any further; at the same time he reassembled and reorganized the dispersed Mobile Guards.

At sunset the battle was still undecided. Once again it was up to Canzio to resolve matters. He received an order to launch a bayonet charge against the Prussians, who were still pursuing some Mobile Guard units on his right. But Canzio went further, and attacked the village of Pouilly, which the Germans were holding. He took the village; the enemy's defences were once again thrown off balance. Ricciotti now moved in with the reorganized First and Second Brigades. In a last, supreme effort they routed the Germans, who abandoned Dijon definitively, leaving on the field – in what must be a unique instance of this – their dead, their wounded and the standard of the Sixty-first Pomeranian Regiment, which had been Ricciotti's direct adversary.

On 30 January word reached Dijon that an armistice with the Germans had been signed. But when, on the following morning, a delegation headed by Bourdon went to the German camp to discuss the placement of

General Maunteuffel.

outposts, they were told that the Departments of Côte-d'Or, Jura and Doubs – all the territory controlled by the *Garibaldini*, that is – were not included in the armistice.

Back in Dijon, nobody could believe Bourdon; it seemed impossible that the government should have signed an armistice which did not apply to the front held by the Army of the Vosges and without even consulting Garibaldi. The General sent a telegram to the government; only in the evening did he receive a reply, explaining that his army had been left out 'by mistake'.

What had really happened remains a mystery. It is just possible that the Berlin government was eager to conclude the campaign by defeating the Army of the Vosges. Bismarck had said, 'I want to get my hands on Garibaldi! I want to parade him through the streets of Berlin, with a sign round his neck saying "This is Italian gratitude!" '. It is also possible that the Prussian generals wanted to satisfy their Chancellor, and that the French government, unable to overrule them, accepted the clause. But as Aroldi wrote, 'No matter how one racks one's brain to find an excuse for the French government, one cannot avoid the conclusion that they deceived Garibaldi and his poor army in a most contemptible way.'

By way of confirming this lamentable state of affairs, the Germans attacked Mirande, to the east of Dijon, and began to concentrate their troops near the city in preparation for a punitive battle.

But Garibaldi had already decided to retreat. He left Dijon at 7 a.m. on 31 January and headed for Chagny. It was a long, tense march; they knew that if the Germans attacked them in force they would surely be annihilated. Garibaldi walked in absolute silence at the head of his troops; not a word of recrimination did he utter as they passed through the web of the Prussian lines. But he managed to bring them to safety. He was sixty-four now, and a physical wreck, but during the retreat he did not lose a single man.

'On 13 February we were at dinner', Aroldi tells us, 'Canzio, Bayard, Orense, Canessa and I. Six young men from the

Garibaldi gives his orders for the battle of Dijon.

Mobilisés came into the dining-room and sat at the table opposite us. It seems that one of them pronounced some ironic words at our expense, on account of the uniforms we were wearing. None of us noticed, except for Major Bayard who, as a Frenchman, had understood their whole conversation. It almost came to a duel, but fortunately the quarrel was smoothed over.'

This was not an isolated incident. Despite the affection of the population, hatred and contempt of the *Garibaldini* began to develop among the French troops; scuffles were frequent, and the contenders were lucky if they came away with no worse than a black eye. The only explanation for this phenomenon that comes to mind is that a great many ex-Bonapartists had put on republican colours without any real change of heart.

Garibaldi was elected deputy by six different Departments; leaving his troops in Menotti's charge, he went to Bordeaux, which was now the provisional seat of the government. Here he was greeted by popular demonstrations of enthusiasm.

At 2 p.m. on 13 February Garibaldi

entered Parliament, which was sitting in the Grand Théâtre of the city. He had already resigned as General and now, before the end of the sitting, the President read his letter of resignation as Deputy: '... As my last duty to the Republic I have come to Bordeaux, where the representatives of the nation have convened. But I must renounce the honour to which I have been elected.' However when the sitting was adjourned, Garibaldi rose and asked to say a word. He was got up, as usual in a red shirt and slouch hat, with the inevitable poncho over his shoulders. 'Take off your hat!' yelled a deputy of the Right. With that, pandemonium broke out. The Left rose to the General's defence; the Right, considering his asking for the floor and his manner of dress to be provocations, hurled insults and accusations. The President of the Assembly, Count Benoît d'Azy, was irritated by the furore. He asked Garibaldi what he could possibly have to say, considering that the sitting had been adjourned. He failed to understand that the General was asking for official permission to speak.

Adolphe Thiers cried, 'What is all this rubbish!'. 'This "rubbish" is Garibaldi, and he's worth more than the lot of you together', shouted someone in the balcony. This only

increased the confusion; Garibaldi never managed to make his speech. His mere presence in public was enough, as usual, to open a gulf between the politicians and the people: citizens would suddenly find the courage to speak their own minds, something which otherwise seldom happened. When he left the theatre he was surrounded by an enormous crowd, imploring him not to go. Garibaldi kept silent. He left for Marseilles, and from there he sailed to Caprera.

An authoritative voice spoke out in his favour – Victor Hugo's: 'Three weeks ago you refused to listen to Garibaldi. Today you refuse to listen to me. I shall go and speak far away from here.' And he left France to go into voluntary exile.

All the volunteers were demobilized by 1 March; they were free to return home.

It is certainly not true, as certain biased historians have claimed, that the *Garibaldini* saved France or that Garibaldi was a better strategist than Von Moltke. But there is no doubt that without the Army of the Vosges France would have suffered an even worse defeat than she actually did.

'The National Defence Government failed Garibaldi, and its own interests as well. But one must not forget the situation in which it found itself and the enemies it had to face. Of the latter, perhaps the Prussians were the least to be feared.' It was true. France was soon to live through an even greater tragedy, which at the same time would find her once again at the forefront of human history.

Victor Hugo. A fervid republican, he was often exiled from France because of his opposition to the anti-democratic government of Napoleon III and to the French military interventions in Italy in 1849 and in 1867.

DEATH OF A LEADER

Garibaldi returned to Caprera on 16 February 1871. The French campaign – the last he was to take part in – had lasted 130 days.

In the years that remained to him, political conflicts were to give way to the daily, increasingly urgent struggle against the miseries of human existence. His leg grew more and more painful, and now he was obliged to get about on crutches. But this barely disturbed him; what tormented him was the letter sent him while he was still in France by Francesca Armosino, the woman he had lived with for five years, announcing the death of their youngest daughter Rosa.

After Anita's death there had been a long series of women in the General's life. Women fell at his feet – not so much because of his fame as on account of his tenor voice, his masculine bearing, gentle manners, blue eyes and fair hair.

In 1855 Battistina Ravello went to work for him as a domestic at Caprera. She was a clumsy girl, the daughter of a sailor, who had one point in her favour – she was only eighteen. Garibaldi seduced her. He would have liked to marry her, but his family strenuously opposed the idea. A daughter was born of the union, a poor wild thing, abandoned by her mother (who was sent away from the island) and neglected by her father. Speranza, Garibaldi's next mistress, was put in charge of her upbringing, but the child died at an early age.

Battistina was soon forgotten when Garibaldi fell in love with Speranza, who was wise enough to refuse his hand: she was well aware that his amorous transports never lasted long. In marriage they would surely have been miserable, but their liaison grew into a sincere and lasting friendship.

During the 1859 campaign Garibaldi met the Countess Raimondi. Like Battistina she was only eighteen. But she already had a considerable past, including an affair with Luigi Caroli – who was to follow Nullo to Poland and die in a Siberian prison – by whom she was pregnant when Garibaldi married her. On their wedding day somebody passed Garibaldi an anonymous note just as they were leaving the church. It informed him of his wife's condition, and the marriage was over after five minutes' duration. The story was to drag on for years, to everyone's distress – especially when Garibaldi sued for a divorce: the press, naturally, published all the scandalous details it could get hold of, and it was a bitter and humiliating ordeal for both of them.

Francesca Armosino, a peasant girl from Asti, arrived at Caprera early in 1866 to act as a wet-nurse for his daughter Teresita's third child (Teresita was to have fourteen in all). She was plain, and was an illegitimate daughter of uncertain paternity. Nevertheless, she awakened the General's appetites, and a daughter Clelia was born to them on 16 February 1867; later there came Rosa, and Manlio, born on 23 April 1873. When Manlio was born Garibaldi was sixty-six years old, and on that occasion he wrote to Speranza, 'It's time to stop, don't you think? I'm getting older and older every day.'

And this was cruelly obvious: there were days when he couldn't get out of bed for the shooting pains in his bones. But he never gave up his bath. The ritual consisted of working up a healthy sweat by sitting in a large sealed box heated by a fire. After this Francesca would throw a bucket of cold water over him, give him a vigorous rub-down, and get him back into bed. This treatment was not prescribed by doctors – he never consulted them: it was his own conviction that cold water had therapeutic powers. He advised the same regimen for Teresita's children: 'Get them used to a cold bath every morning. They'll be prettier for it, and much healthier and stronger.'

When he had to stay in bed, he passed his time writing. He had been made a present of an adjustable writing-board, with a clip to hold the papers in place.

On the days when his rheumatism was less painful he rose early and, if the weather was fine, saddled his mare Marsala (who was also old and decrepit) and made the rounds of the island. When the mare died – possibly on account of the remedies, concocted from Marsala wine, with which the General tried to treat her – he mourned her deeply, and resigned himself thereafter to going about on foot.

He always wore his red shirt and poncho. He made his trousers himself, as long as his arthritic fingers allowed him to do so; they had no buttons, because he had never learned to sew button-holes, and were fastened by laces instead.

His diet was unchanged, despite his age and his ailments: he liked salted olives, a sliced tomato with olive oil, basil and anchovies, and half a glass of watered-down wine. He only really indulged himself to excess when broad-beans were in season. He ate little meat, but when he felt like it he cooked it in the South American manner, placing it on bare coals and eating it shred by shred as it roasted.

In his old age Garibaldi began to show signs of avarice. He went so far as to supervise the making of salad, lest precious oil be wasted. He stopped using sugar in the house, which he substituted with honey from his own bees. No doubt he learned these precautions from Francesca Armosino, who was always telling him that hunger was just around the corner (hoping thus to persuade him to accept the 'National Gift' which had been offered him and which he had always disdainfully refused). Of course it wasn't true. Francesca did a thriving business selling cattle and wine produced on the island, and she invested the proceeds in real estate in her home province.

Francesca was not the shrew that some historians have made her out to be. She looked after Garibaldi lovingly, and filled the last years of his life with a homely warmth which he might have lacked completely without her. She bathed him, coddled him, cut his hair. On the other hand, she kept an eagle eye on all his belongings and even, it seems, trafficked in them – certainly she knew the market value of a lock of Garibaldi's hair. Her avidity can no doubt be explained by her peasant upbringing: she was a woman who had known hunger first-hand.

Her mentality, in any case, was far removed from that of the *Garibaldini*. When she became mistress of Caprera, she gradually got rid of everyone she didn't like – especially those who reminded her of the cultural differences between herself and the General.

Soon Garibaldi's children and grandchildren began to move away, and their place was taken by Francesca's relatives. Where once the house on Carpera had been open to everyone; where languages and dialects of all nations were to be heard; and where time was passed in target practice and political argument, now only the heavy Piedmont dialect was spoken, and the only subjects of conversation were money and the wretched National Gift.

These changes were a source of suffering for Garibaldi, but he did nothing to stop them. That fearless warrior had such need of domestic peace that he was prepared to make any sacrifice in order to preserve it.

The National Gift – thus styled so as not to offend the General's sensibilities – was simply an annuity of 50,000 lire a year which the State had decided to award him after the press had made heavy weather of Garibaldi's poverty. He had always declined it, saying that he didn't want to be a prisoner of the Government. Francesca persuaded him to sell the yacht which some English admirers had given him. He made 80,000 lire on the sale but, ingenuous as ever, he entrusted the money to a former comrade, Antonio Bo, who ran off with it to America. He then took out a mortgage on the island from the Bank of Naples, and it was at this point that the press began to speculate about his finances.

Eventually Francesca had her way about the annuity. Garibaldi felt humiliated and in any case very little of the money found its way into his pockets. Twenty thousand lire went to Menotti to save him from bankruptcy, 5,000 to Ricciotti, 4,000 to Teresita, 2,000 to Francesca, 2,000 to Clelia, 2,000 to Manlio, 10,000 for an insurance policy of which the two youngest children were the beneficiaries, and the remaining 5,000 to pay off Ricciotti's debts.

Considering the way the money was used, one cannot but suspect that it was his children as well as Francesca who prevailed upon him to accept the 'humiliation'. Menotti, in fact, had gone into the construction business, but had made a muddle of things for want of experience. Ricciotti hit the high spots: he lived in London, far beyond his means, and scandalized his father's comrades-in-arms by selling the 'Star of Arthur', a decoration awarded

Garibaldi with his third wife Francesca Armosino.

Garibaldi in the last years of his life.

his father after the expedition of the Thousand. His father's sword and other relics met the same fate, and he got so involved in shady commercial affairs that he was arrested, though officially this was on political charges.

Garibaldi sought consolation from all these woes in his writing. It was an old mania of his, but he liked to say that he did it 'to earn his bread honestly'. His first work was *Clelia*, a historical novel of seventy-six chapters complete with appendix and epilogue. It was based on the events of Monterotondo and Mentana and was full of historical personages, good and bad, portrayed in black and white with very little grey. His anticlericalism was by now paroxysmal, and naturally all the bad characters were connected with the Church in one way or another. The novel was an absurd mélange of real and fictitious episodes, but it was a handy medium for hurling invective at all those whom the General held responsible for the defeat of Mentana: the French, the Mazzinians, the moderates and, of course, the clergy.

Getting it into print was not easy. Even those publishers who were eager to exploit the name of Garibaldi turned it down as soon as they had read the manuscript. In the end an English house published it in translation as *The Rule of Monk*. An Italian publisher then followed suit, but the book was disastrously received in both countries.

The aspiring writer was not so easily discouraged, however; he soon produced two more volumes: *The Volunteer Cantoni* and *The Thousand*. This time his friends mounted a big publicity campaign, and underwrote the publication of *The Thousand* with a public subscription. Garibaldi pocketed the tidy sum of 10,380 lire in author's rights; he never knew that of the 12,640 people who had been approached as potential subscribers more than 8,000 had not replied to the offer. Like *Clelia*, *The Thousand* was a historical novel which had little to do with the real events it was supposed to be recounting. In short, Garibaldi would have done better not to publish these books; they only tarnished his reputation.

On 14 January 1880 his divorce from Countess Raimondi was made final and he was able to regularize the position of Francesca and their children. On the 26th Giuseppe Garibaldi, farmer, and Francesca Armosino, housewife, were married by the mayor of La Maddalena. Everyone was there: Menotti with his wife Italia, Teresita with her husband Canzio, and a great brood of grand-children. Only Ricciotti was missing. Sitting in the carriage afterwards, Garibaldi was overcome by emotion, and wept.

The press made a great fuss of the occasion, and of course did not lose the opportunity of unearthing all the old stories about Countess Raimondi. But the Countess herself had remarried; the drama was over, and that anonymous note, with all the truth or false-hood it contained, had finally ceased to cause pain.

That year the General's health declined. Soon he was more or less permanently con-fined to his bed, in the room where he was to die. Today the room has been transformed into a kind of shrine. An episode which Signora Garibaldi recounted years later to the journalist Ugo Ojetti is worth reproducing here for its human interest.

'When did I move him into the room where he died? It was in 1880, for his birthday, 4 July. In April my husband had had a bad attack of rheumatism. Two doctors told me that he'd have trouble for three months, until the hot weather came. He complained that he couldn't see the sea from our bed. Without the sea he felt suffocated. So I thought I'd have the room at the end prepared for him, the room you've just seen. . . . But I wanted to surprise him. The rock had to be levelled outside, and all in three months' time. Fortunately I found two stone-cutters who were working the other side of La Maddalena, at Cala Francese. And I brought two masons, Agostino and Riccardo, over from Leghorn. I put it to them straight: "I'll pay you whatever you ask", I said, "if you finish the job by 4 July; otherwise you won't get a penny." I had the agreement put in writing. I kept the whole thing from my husband; I only told him that I was having the door enlarged back there, in case we ever wanted to move his bed out-doors. "That'll cost a lot", he said. "Oh no", I said. "Do as you like, Francesca", he said,

"only see to it they do a good job." He could hear the hammer-blows on the stone from his bed. "They're only enlarging the door? They're taking a long time – watch out, that's going to cost a lot of money."

'I had an iron bed brought from Leghorn, you've seen it, with a mosquito net and a nice chandelier and new chairs and an armchair. I also ordered some pots of gardenias – they were his favourite flower, and they didn't grow here. And some fishermen at La Maddalena had formed a musical band: they came to ask me if they could make Manlio their president and if I could give them a flag. I could make them a tricolour, but not one with the coat-of-arms: that was too difficult. Together with the tricolour for the band I sewed a lot of other flags to decorate the new room. Then 4 July came. "Now just leave things to me", I said to my husband. I got him dressed and tidy and put him in his bath-chair. I managed it all alone, of course. I was strong, you know, and from the moment we met nobody else ever touched my husband. I got him up all by myself, I changed him, I put him in his bath, I put him to bed, I pushed his bath-chair.

'I walked backwards, pulling the chair; I could see how happy he was. We went through the dining-room, where the visitors' book is, and then through the other room, the salon. I opened the door of the new room with my shoulder; it was full of sunlight – you can imagine, it was July and the windows were wide open; now they're always shut on account of the wreaths. For a minute he held his breath. He looked at the bed, the win-dows, the door, the chandelier, the flags, the gardenias in bloom. Then at a signal from Manlio the band from La Maddalena struck up the anthem. And my husband burst into tears, and he kissed my hands, and he pulled me down to kiss my face, and then he kissed the children and cried again. He kept saying "Thank your mama, thank your mama." It took me a quarter of an hour to calm him down.'

On 1 July 1882 Dr Cappelletti, the ship's doctor of the *Cariddi*, which was anchored off La Maddalena, received an urgent message to come to Caprera. The General was having trouble breathing on account of a bad bronchial congestion.

Menotti and Francesca were at his bedside. Soon his throat became paralysed. The death-rattle had begun, though he was fully conscious. He passed the night, and the following day, looking out the window which Francesca had had made for him. In the afternoon two blackbirds came and perched on the sill of his window – 'Perhaps they're the souls of my little girls', he murmured. Then he asked where Manlio was, and what time it was. But he didn't hear the reply. It was half-past six in the evening on 2 June 1882. The charismatic chief was dead. The official historians began to tamper with the facts at once, and Garibaldi's world was buried beneath monuments, bronze wreaths and marble plaques. Only two really human relics remain: the calendar, now yellowed with age, open at June, and the preface he wrote to the last version of his memoirs:

'Mine has been a tempestuous life, made up – like most people's, I believe – of both good and evil. I may say that I have always sought the good, for myself and for my fellow men. If on any occasion I have done evil, I have done so involuntarily.'

Garibaldi at Caprera.

237

Garibaldini *volunteers during the first Greek campaign.*

The Third Generation

The General's absence and his forced idleness on Caprera neither dampened his followers' enthusiasm nor lessened their desire to participate in the struggles for independence, even though it would be many years before the *Garibaldini* could once again be considered a great force.

At the end of the French campaign some of the *Garibaldini* went on to Paris, where the Commune was a cause to fight for. Others returned to their own countries and threw themselves into the political strife for working-class rights.

In 1874 we find them in Spain, where they had rallied to the defence of the infant Republic. They had formed a legion of about a hundred men, under the command of Antonio Orense Milá de Aragón, a Spanish officer who had been with the Garibaldian General Staff during the French campaign of 1870. Their contribution was limited, partly because of their reduced numbers, but also because the campaign itself was very brief: in this struggle between republicans, Carlists and cantonalists, the Bourbon monarchy, to everyone's surprise, came out on top. Or, as they said at the time in Madrid, 'The republicans killed the Republic!'

When Garibaldi died, most people thought that the Red-shirt movement would die with him. But the younger *Garibaldini*, who had seen action only in 1867 and 1870, wanted to emulate their predecessors. And they felt that the world still needed them.

These were the 'third-generation' *Garibaldini*. The press considered them less newsworthy than their forebears, and certainly their rôle in history was less crucial. But their idealism was in the old tradition, and it was not less genuine for the lack of publicity.

The leader of this third generation was a man whose aspirations were similar to theirs: Ricciotti Garibaldi, the third and the most bellicose of the General's chidren, born at Montevideo on 4 February 1847. He was not a great strategist like his father; he won no great battles, nor did he change the fate of nations – history never offered him the opportunity. But he was a good commander; whenever he undertook a campaign he coped effectively with whatever problems presented themselves. And his political tact was certainly superior to his father's.

Ricciotti acquired his first military experience at Bezzecca in 1866 as one of Missori's Mounted Guides, where he gave immediate proof of his leadership ability and sound military intuition. His father had sent him with a message to another commander; as he was returning, he saw the standard-bearer of the Ninth Regiment fall in action. The troops were momentarily confused. Realizing the importance of the flag for their orientation as well as for their morale, Ricciotti dashed to retrieve it and led the men in a counter-charge.

The following year he was in Greece, but his presence there was purely symbolic; peace came before he saw action. He returned to Italy just in time to assist his father in the disastrous Roman campaign of 1867. In 1870, after an abortive attempt at rebellion in southern Italy, he went to France and distinguished himself as commander of the Fourth Brigade.

Ricciotti was always generous towards his enemies: he respected their ability and their good faith. During the 1867 campaign he arranged for a priest to attend the wounded Pontifical prisoners, offering his personal guarantee that the priest would not be molested. This was no mean feat, considering the rabid anticlericalism of the *Garibaldini* at the time.

It was in the Balkans, and especially in Greece, that Ricciotti's leadership was principally put to the test. The Balkan peninsula, almost totally under Turkish domination, had long represented a 'problem' for the European liberals. The Ottoman Empire was known as the 'sick man of Europe', but it was actually in better health than most people supposed: it was certainly capable of speedily suppressing rebellions within its borders.

The Russians and the Austrians had their eyes on the Balkan peninsula as did the liberals, but their aim was to replace Turkey as the dominant power in the area. During the second half of the 19th century they actively interfered in the political affairs of the various new Balkan states and also physically occupied certain small territories.

But the revolutionaries did not give up, and the 'independence of the Balkans' became one of the great causes. In July 1862

Garibaldi had written a message to the Slavs: 'Unite, and forge a single people. Forget your hatreds, discords, religious and racial prejudices. Let the thought of revenge and liberty bring you together.'

But the desire for liberty never seemed to take root among the masses, and all attempts at revolt were reduced to sterile guerrilla conflicts. The *Garibaldini*, nevertheless, did not fail to offer their support.

When in 1875 Bosnia-Herzegovina rebelled against the Turks, and the rebellion spread quickly to the adjacent provinces, a band of Red-shirts led by the veteran Celso Cerretti placed themselves at the disposal of the rebel chief Mičo Liubibratič. But the revolt was a failure. In 1878, with the blessing of the Congress of Berlin, Austria wrested the area from Turkey, and the independence movement had to start all over again.

When he heard of the invasion, Garibaldi launched an appeal to the Austrian soldiers: 'Take to the hills! Do not be led against your heroic brethren of Herzegovina, who freed Europe from a horrible Empire.' But the appeal fell upon deaf ears; a few Austrians deserted, but not enough to alter the outcome of the invasion.

After this the cause of Balkan independence was promoted only by a few pamphleteers, and they could not hope to prevail against the vested interests and the fears of the other European nations. Nothing at all was done, despite prophetic warnings that if the Balkans were not given their independence, an explosive situation with serious implications for the whole continent might arise. And, in fact, the unsolved problems of the 'Balkan powder-keg' were to have tragic consequences, years later, for the entire world.

The involvement of the *Garibaldini* in Greece was far more substantial and significant. It began shortly after the expedition of the Thousand, when a man called Zuccoli, at the head of the Greek and Albanian volunteers who had fought with Garibaldi in Sicily, went off to fight in Crete, which was rebelling against Turkish rule.

In 1821 Greece had risen to overthrow the centuries-long Ottoman occupation. The spokesmen for the rebels and their aspirations were Pierre-Jean Béranger and George

Ricciotti Garibaldi at the time of the 1897 expedition in Greece.

Gordon, Lord Byron (who was to die during the siege of Missolónghi in April 1824). Thanks to the influence of these two poets, Philhellenic Committees sprang up all over Europe, their purpose to promote the Greek cause in every possible way. Many liberal exiles also went to Greece after the failure of the Constitutionalist uprisings of 1821.

But the support of these volunteers was not in itself sufficient. International opinion was so shocked by the cruelty with which the Turks repressed the revolt that the great powers had to intervene. The British, French and Russian fleets defeated the Turks at Navarino in 1827; the Sultan sued for peace, and a treaty was signed at Adrianople in 1828.

Greece was recognized as an independent nation in the Protocol of London (1830). But much Greek territory, including Epirus, Macedonia, Crete and most of the Aegean islands, remained in Turkish hands. The inhabitants of these areas, Greek in language and culture, naturally aspired to independence, and for decades a state of undeclared war existed between Greece and Turkey.

In 1866 a revolt broke out in Crete. About two thousand *Garibaldini*, veterans of the recently terminated Third War of Independence, rushed to Athens. They left the various Adriatic ports in small groups and assembled in Syra. Part of their number was sent to Crete at once, aboard two steamers: the *Panhellenion*, commanded by a certain Orlof, and the *Idra*, commanded by Captain Correntini, an Italian who lived at Galaxidhion.

Contrary to expectations, this first nucleus was merged with various Cretan formations commanded by Lambrakakis Bisanzios and by Colonel Coroneos. Only one fairly large group remained intact; its leader, Major Luciano Mereu, was a brilliant Garibaldian officer who had already distinguished himself in the wars of the Italian *Risorgimento*.

The Cretan campaign was a total disaster, partly because of the rivalry between the Greek leaders and their inefficiency, and partly because the Turks were superior in numbers and armaments. And lastly, as Garibaldi justly pointed out, because the Greek–Turkish conflict could hardly be resolved on an island which was too small for major manoeuvres; it would have to be worked out on the mainland, and when that happened all of the Balkans would surely take up arms against Turkey.

The *Garibaldini* did not succeed in winning the Greeks over to this point of view. In any case, they were too few to guarantee adequate support in the event of a full-scale war with Turkey. The uncertainty of the situation, however, was itself one of the reasons for the scarcity of volunteers. War had not been officially declared; the Greeks, understandably, were unwilling to do so because they were decidedly inferior in strength. But by not declaring war they kept away many prospective volunteers, who had no wish to make a wasted trip.

The *Garibaldini*, in fact, were received with hostility by many of the Cretan partisans: the red shirts reminded them of the red lapels and trousers worn by many Turkish units. It took a lot of arguing to convince them that the *Garibaldini* were not Turks!

The encounters in Crete consisted of futile attacks on fortresses and of mountain ambushes which today are euphemistically called battles. We list them here for the sake of completeness: Alikambo (28 October), Promezo (1 November), Spekia (21 November), Kipamosi and Malevis, where the *Garibaldini* fought Egyptian units who had come to aid the Turks (15 December), and Gerakari (22 February 1867), which was the last victory of the campaign.

After that, the pressure on the *Garibaldini* was overpowering. Those who did not die in battle or of gangrene – medical aid was non-existent – were taken to safety on a Russian frigate.

Early in 1867 another band of volunteers set out for Greece. They were forty men from Leghorn, led by the old Red-shirt Andrea Sgarallino. At Caprera they were joined by Ricciotti Garibaldi. He bore a message from the General to the Greek authorities, urging them to transfer the conflict to the mainland and assuring them that once a revolt of some

A Garibaldino *sergeant with two Greek priests who had joined the Red-shirts.*

Garibaldini *in 1897. Note how the red shirt has become a double-breasted blouson.*

importance broke out in Epirus (the theatre of operations which he recommended) he himself would intervene with a sizeable force.

On arrival at Syra, the group was sent to Athens, where all the volunteers were now being assembled. They were quartered at Piraeus in the same building as a contingent of Cretan refugees. The *Garibaldini* flirted so outrageously with the girls that it provoked a violent reaction in the mothers, who 'invaded the volunteers' part of the building and in a flash chased out all our young men!' Appeasing them was not an easy task.

Meanwhile, the situation between Greece and Turkey seemed to have reached a crucial point: war.

Some of the volunteers had already begun to march towards the Turkish-held province of Epirus. The regular army was all set to join them as soon as they crossed the border. But then the European powers intervened: they informed the Greeks that unless they disbanded the volunteer formations and sent them home, they would not prevent Turkish

frigates from bombarding Athens. The government had no choice but to make the best of a bad job and to postpone once again the realization of the aspirations of the Greek people.

Greece was forgotten for the next thirty years. People still sympathized, but its failure to take advantage of the situation created by the Russo-Turkish War in 1872 together with the deep political lethargy into which it seemed to have fallen encouraged those interested to turn their attention elsewhere.

The new disturbances in Crete in 1886 reawakened Europe's interest in the area. Many Greek officers and soldiers hastened to the island to give a hand to the rebels, while the nation prepared for war. But once again European diplomacy nipped the conflict in the bud, and yet again the Greeks had to renounce – temporarily – their hopes.

Again in 1897 Crete rose up against Turkey, this time under the leadership of the patriot Venizelos. The European press at once espoused the Cretan cause, but not the European governments: they sent an international fleet with the alleged aim of restoring order and putting a stop to Turkish atrocities. But instead it committed atrocities of its own, shelling the defenceless Cretan partisans at Ierápetra and Akrotiri.

News of the revolt rekindled the passions of the *Garibaldini*. On 20 March 1897 Ricciotti received a letter from Crete which outlined the state of affairs on the island and hinted that steamships might be obtained from the Greeks for the transport of large numbers of volunteers.

The Greeks never produced the ships, however, and many other obstacles stood in the way of the *Garibaldini*'s participation in the struggle for the freedom of Crete and for the national unity of Greece.

The first obstacle was the Italian government, which had been one of the first to send a 'peace-keeping' force to Crete. It did all it could to dampen the enthusiasm of the public and to forestall an intervention of the *Garibaldini*. When it saw that its efforts at persuasion were ineffectual, and that the volunteers were preparing to set out, it imposed a blockade on the ports, so that no troop-ship could sail. In the ensuing struggle between the *Garibaldini* and the authorities there was more than one skirmish with the *carabinieri*. Shots were fired; no one was killed, fortunately, but there were a great many arrests.

Transportation also became a major problem. The proprietors of phantom ships took money on account and then disappeared; other shipowners continued to increase their fee for the hire of their vessels even after a supposedly final price had been agreed upon.

Canzio and Menotti were opposed to the undertaking – not that they did not share the ideals which inspired it, but they felt that the lack of organization was bound to doom it to failure. In the end, though, their enthusiasm caught fire; they set about organizing relief expeditions, and both of them landed in jail, charged with 'provocative actions with regard to a public official in the discharge of his duty'.

There were still other difficulties. Units of self-styled *Garibaldini* refused to recognize Ricciotti's authority. The Greek government stated publicly that it would negotiate the formation of an irregular military force only with General Ricciotti Garibaldi. But it too was apprehensive about these republicans and socialists – there were even a few avowed anarchists in their midst – and in practice it did everything it could to prevent the constitution of too large a Garibaldian force. In short, it was the same old story.

But none of these hindrances could put a stop to the public's enthusiasm. Ettore Socci, an old-time *Garibaldino* and member of parliament, has left a description of the state of affairs in Italy:

'As news of the insurrection in Crete spread, and the newspapers reported that the Athens government, eager to defend the cause of liberty as personified in these heroic rebels, was sending arms and recruiting volunteers, in Italy a great ferment took place. From the Alps to farthest Sicily the most zealous of youths, the boldest of university students, the oldest and most tried of patriots felt it their duty to proclaim to the world that the Greek cause was the cause of civilization. Assemblies, public meetings and demonstrations were held in every part of the peninsula. People applauded beneath the windows of the Greek consulates. In parliament Imbriani inveighed against the Turks and the Sultan; Cavallotti, a devotee of ancient Greece, saluted its rebirth in winged verse. A number of youths, too impatient to await developments and convinced only of the sacredness of the cause, set out for Greece without further advice or encouragement.

'The urge to go became a burning desire: it was a sacrosanct duty to perpetuate the glorious tradition of the red shirt, symbol of liberty for the oppressed and of justice for all. To see a brother in every suffering human being, and one's own fatherland in every oppressed nation: this was the mission to which Giuseppe Garibaldi had remained faithful until the very end of his days . . .'

Antonio Fratti and Federico Gattorno now joined Ricciotti in making some sort of order out of total chaos. Both were old *Garibaldini* – Gattorno had even taken part in the defence of the Roman Republic – and both were now members of parliament. Thanks to their assistance, a sizeable number of volunteers, singly or in groups, were able to elude the surveillance of the police, and set out for Greece.

Amilcare Cipriani (on the left) with Daily Telegraph *correspondent Burleigh (centre) and Mr Noel, head of the Red Cross.*

However no one was in Athens to meet them and organize them, so most of them joined the International Philhellenic Legion. This was made up of units from various countries, including dubious 'Garibaldian' units such as the Bertet Legion and the group led by Amilcare Cipriani. The latter had taken the pretentious name of 'Death Company', but its courage and its ability were quite genuine. The Bertet Legion was kept separate, as it was feared that friction might develop between it and the Red-shirts – in fact it was sent to fight in an entirely different sector. And a unit led by Nicola Barbato was too impatient to wait any longer: it left for Crete immediately and was absorbed by the partisan formations there. But the other groups were all united in the 'Garibaldi Corps', as it was officially called in 1897.

Cipriani's Death Company had been the principal volunteer formation prior to Ricciotti's arrival. It was a legion of 78 men armed and equipped by the Etniki Ektaria, the Greek 'National Society'. Cipriani was a typical old-fashioned 19th century revolutionary, a republican and a socialist. As a fifteen-year-old he had fought with the Piedmont regular army in the campaign of 1859. The following year he deserted to join the Thousand, and from then on he remained a Red-shirt, taking part in all of Garibaldi's later campaigns. In 1871, after the French campaign, he became a colonel of the Communards. When the Commune fell he was sentenced to ten years as a deportee in New Caledonia. After his return to Italy he was elected Deputy several times – but he never sat in parliament, because he refused to take the oath of allegiance to the King.

On 19 March the Death Company, in conjunction with a Greek unit of about three thousand men led by two former officers of the regular Greek Army, Melonas and Kapsalapoulos, set out on a raid. Their plan was to invade Turkish-held territory in order to spark a revolt among the populations of Epirus and Albania.

At 7 a.m. on 9 April a vanguard commanded by Daveli (nicknamed the 'Terror of the Turks') and including the Death Company crossed the border, attacking and destroying the Turkish installations there. They soon occupied the passes of Métsovon and Samovini, between Grevena and Dheskáti, and the battle then centred on the fortress of Baltinon which the rebels besieged. On the following day a Turkish regiment came to relieve the fort, but it was defeated and forced to retreat. The garrison within the fortress attempted two sorties on the 10th, to no avail. A third, at dawn on the 11th, was successful, but the field was strewn with Greek and Turkish corpses; the Death Company was now reduced to thirty-two men.

That afternoon the rebels marched twelve kilometres into Macedonia, heading for Kraniá. Three of their leaders perished in a skirmish at Kipria. By evening they reached the vicinity of Kraniá, set up their outposts, and encamped on the hills surrounding the town. At dawn on the morning of 12 April they were attacked by a thousand or so Turks, who placed them in serious difficulty without, however, beating them definitively. But at 3 p.m. word came that three thousand more Turks were on their way. The Greeks, fearing they would be surrounded, and in full panic, fled in disarray. The Death Company remained at its post, despite entreaties to withdraw. Then about fifty Greeks, led by a priest, were taken prisoner by the Turks. Cipriani led a daredevil charge, into which he dragged the demoralized Greeks, and freed the prisoners.

But the Turks had almost encircled them and their only way out was to cross a narrow mountain pass that led back into Greek territory. The Turks pursued them, subjecting them to relentless rifle-fire, and the Greek retreat, although covered by the Death Company, was a disaster.

Back in Greece, the volunteers assembled the next day at Koutzofliani. They had to admit that the raid had proved a failure, especially as the population of the Turkish-occupied territories had not shown any inclination to rise in revolt. The general consensus of opinion was that there would be no war after all. And so, on 13 April 1897 Cipriani disbanded his legion. Four days later, on 17 April, war between Greece and Turkey was declared.

Meanwhile Luciano Mereu, the veteran Red-shirt who had taken part in previous Garibaldian efforts in Greece, arrived in Athens. He was promptly joined by Gattorno, and the two of them set about organizing the *Garibaldini*, whose number was now increasing. Three battalions were formed, two made up of Italians, and one of Greeks (Gattorno later formed a fourth battalion, of mixed composition, but it was not effective in time to take part in the campaign). There was also an English section at the command of Major Enric Short, and a French under Captain Paul de Barre. The entire force, including General Staff, engineers and the three hundred troops of the Fourth Battalion (never to see action), consisted of 1,323 men.

As usual the volunteers came from every conceivable background. There were students, labourers, professional men and a great many journalists who thought they could best cover the campaign by enlisting. The most singular of these was Palmer T. Newbold, the correspondent of the *Star*: he fought the Turks ferociously, but the minute an armistice was declared he rushed to the enemy camp to gather news of the other side.

Another key figure of the campaign was Count Alexander K. Romas, a member of the Greek parliament and a former minister of education. A French deputy, Antide Boyer, served as second-lieutenant with the General Staff. So many parliamentarians enlisted, in fact, that Ricciotti declared he had never seen 'such a political General Staff'. Their strictly military contribution was perhaps not memorable, but they proved invaluable in smoothing over differences with the Greek authorities. In this campaign, in fact, the *Garibaldini* were anxious as never before to be considered 'good boys'.

The red shirt made its appearance in Greece with a different cut: it was now a sort of double-breasted blouson-type jacket which came down to just below the waist. *Garibaldini* headgear was the familiar soft peaked cap, and they wore the trousers of the Greek cavalry. The government supplied everyone with Gras rifles.

In this campaign the medical service was first-rate. The Red Cross of many countries sent volunteers; the Germans were especially

Edhem Pasha, victor of the battle of Dhomokós.

effective, thanks to their organization and to the means at their disposal. But the medical officer who stood out among all the others was a Dane, Dr Niewenhuis, who was serving with the English section.

The *Garibaldini* were ready for battle. But towards the end of April the Greek government began to vacillate. It now appeared they were no longer inclined to carry on with the war or to send the Red-shirts into action. The regular army suffered a defeat in Thessalia, and the government immediately asked for a truce: this was interpreted as a prelude to peace negotiations. Once again international diplomacy was manipulating events behind the scenes. But if a peace were to be signed at that particular moment, it would certainly be more favourable to Turkey than to Greece.

At this point a group of Greek patriots forced the government's hand. Three thousand volunteers led by Markos Botzaris (grandson of one of the heroes of the 1821 rebellion) formed a unit which they called the 'Epirote Phalanx'. They carried out an audacious raid on Turkish territory, thus breaking the truce. And they accomplished their purpose: hostilities were resumed.

But the government did not back up Botzaris' initiative by sending troops and supplies; more than ever it seemed that its real aim was to bring the war to an end. It has been suggested that the military actions which came later, the battle of Dhomokós and the defence of the Phourka pass, were deliberately designed to dampen the ardour and quell the aspirations of Greek patriots. If this was indeed the case, no words are strong enough to condemn such a cruel waste of human lives.

Ricciotti arrived in Athens from Italy on 24 April. Too much time had been lost. The *Garibaldini* in Greece were not yet properly organized, and the political situation was already beginning to deteriorate. If the Red-shirts were to uphold their prestige, they would have to find an opportunity to fight. The occasion soon presented itself in the form of the first and last real battle of that curious war.

On 8 May Ricciotti and the Second and Third Battalions left Athens to join forces with the Greek Army; the First, led by Mereu, had already set out on 26 April.

General Edhem Pasha, the commander of the Turkish forces in Greece, had resumed operations on 5 May after the breaking of the truce by the Greeks. He assembled five divisions at Fársala; they were led by General Hairi Pasha, Neschat Pasha, Mendouk Pasha, Haidar Pasha and Hamdi Pasha. On the 15th he set out from Fársala and headed for Dhomokós, where the Greek army concentrated; he arrived on 17 May, ready for battle.

The Turkish offensive was to be conducted as follows: Mendouk's division was to attack the right flank of the Greek army, while Hamdi, by crossing the hills in the direction of the village of Karatzali, was to tackle the Greeks from the rear, thereby impeding their retreat; Neschat's division was to confront the Greek army head on and occupy the village of Dhomokós, while Hairi attacked their left flank, where Ricciotti and the *Garibaldini* were located; Haidar's troops were to be held in reserve, five miles or so behind the Turkish lines.

Hamdi Pasha began the attack with an attempt to encircle the Greek positions. But he met with particularly stubborn resistance, and it was 6 p.m. before he had reached his

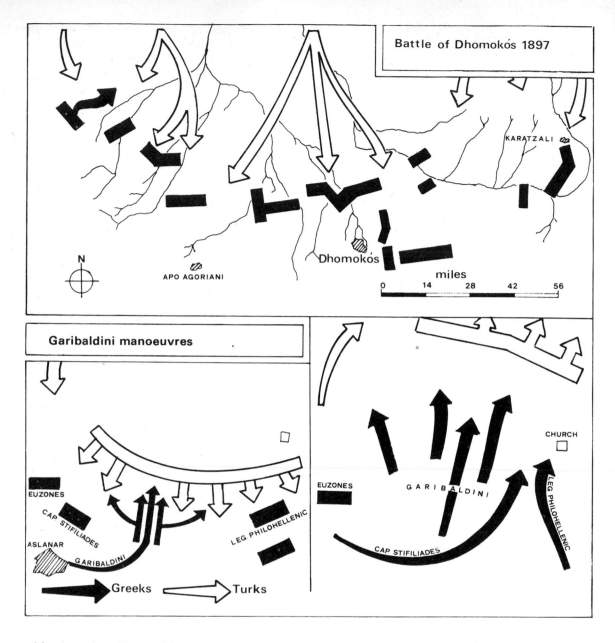

Battle of Dhomokós 1897

KARATZALI

N

APO AGORIANI

Dhomokós

miles

0   14   28   42   56

Garibaldini manoeuvres

EUZONES

CAP. STIFILIADES

ASLANAR

GARIBALDINI

LEG. PHILOHELLENIC

➤ Greeks   ⇨ Turks

CHURCH

EUZONES

GARIBALDINI

LEG. PHILOHELLENIC

CAP. STIFILIADES

objective, the village of Karatzali, to the east of Dhomokós.

By midday the entire Greek line was under attack. Neschat's division, backed up by the artillery, thrust at the centre. It was the best, most up-to-date of the Turkish line divisions and the entire infantry was armed with Mausers. Nevertheless, it met with strong opposition from the Greeks and at 3.30 p.m. it was obliged to call in the reserve division, and even so it was unable to break through the Greek lines until 5 p.m. Then, at 6.15, Hamdi, who had at last taken Karatzali, began

to shell the Greek trenches from the right. The Greeks had no choice but to abandon their positions and fall back.

By 7.30 the Turks had virtually won the battle. The Greeks were fleeing towards the Phourka pass.

But the Turks failed to follow up their advantage, or possibly they had been unable to complete their encircling manoeuvre on account of the unexpectedly strong resistance they had encountered from the 5,000 men of the Tertipis division on the Greek left flank. At the far end of this flank was the Philhellenic

Legion, an exiguous Greek company called the Euzones, and a small battery, and to the rear of these units was Ricciotti with the Second and Third Battalions.

Hairi Pasha kept Terpitis' division engaged with the main body of his troops; then, around 4 p.m., he sent an infantry brigade and a strong cavalry detachment to attack the Philhellenic Legion.

The Gheghides, an irregular Turkish formation, sprang to the assault crying, 'You want Crete? All right, we'll give you Crete!'

The Turks were winning. The Philhellenic troops, in fact, were about to succumb – when 'suddenly a blaze of red appeared in the cornfield to the left of the hill; then it became a line'.

Ricciotti had seen the danger the Greeks were in from the heights of Amaslar. Without hesitating, he and his men entered the battle, attacking the centre of the Turkish lines, and breaking through. A furious conflict ensued; it raged all about a ruined building – perhaps a church – on which was painted the image of the Virgin. The Turkish cavalry moved in to relieve the Gheghides. They tried an enveloping movement, and almost cut off the *Garibaldini*, who in their exuberance had advanced too far. But then the Euzones counter-attacked, backed up by the Greek battery, and put a stop to the Turkish manoeuvre.

The verve of the *Garibaldini* was contagious, and now the Euzones, the Philhellenic troops and the company under Captain Stifiliades joined Ricciotti's men in the attack. Their battle-cry was 'By order of the General – *Embròs*!' (*Embròs*! is Greek for 'Forward!').

The other Greek divisions were now retreating, but at 7 o'clock Ricciotti ordered the men under his command to attach their bayonets for a final charge. This was not necessary. The Turks abandoned their positions and fell back. It was an error on their part; had they counter-charged they would certainly have had the best of the debilitated *Garibaldini*. Ricciotti himself later admitted as much.

The battle had been a terrible three hours, especially ferocious in the hand-to-hand combat as neither side was interested in taking prisoners. Only two of the Gheghides were captured; they owed their lives to the vigorous personal intervention of Romas and Mereu.

Ricciotti deplored this futile slaughter, the more so since he admired the bravery and tenacity of the enemy, who despite their losses had only fallen back about a mile until they received orders that they should retreat further.

Turkish artillery of the time.

Battle of Dhomokós. The Garibaldini *charge the Gheghides.*

At one in the morning Ricciotti, who had remained on the positions he had taken, received the order to retreat. But he was reluctant to do so before he had time to bury the hundred men he had lost – Fratti, his closest collaborator, among them – and to round up other troops who were dispersed in the vicinity. The Greek commander, on the other hand, was unwilling to wait. The *Garibaldini* soon found themselves alone on the battlefield.

When the dead had been buried Ricciotti wanted the French and English sections, who were some distance away, to join up with him as he began the retreat. He gave the order to Major Short, who was to pass it on to Captain de Barre. This gave rise to an amusing episode. Short, in fact, spoke no French and De Barre understood no English. The order was misunderstood completely, and the French section arched off in the direction of the Turkish lines.

'De Barre had been on the march for some time when from the top of a hill he espied the Turkish camp a mile or so to his left; to his right was a hamlet, from which came the sound of the crowing of fowls. Excellent strategist that he was, he sent a detachment of eight men, at some distance one from the other, against the encampment – where thousands of Turks must have been gathered; he sent the remaining eight men into the hamlet to requisition the fowls. The Turks were astonished to find themselves under attack from this miniature force; they swarmed from their tents and stood about staring. But the eight Frenchmen continued to shoot, and eventually the Turks decided to send a squadron or two to deal with them. But the other eight by this time had succeeded in capturing the birds, and De Barre was able to order a dignified retreat, with his dinner assured for that day at least.'

But the retreat was not always so jovial. Food was scarce, except for salty cheese and Mastica, a local liquor which caused severe intestinal inflammations. The Turkish army did not attack them, but it stuck close to their heels, which kept them in a constant state of psychological tension.

When the *Garibaldini* arrived at the Phourka pass, where they had expected to rejoin the Greeks, they found it occupied by the Turks. The Greeks had retreated to

Thermopylae, and Ricciotti's troops caught up with them on 21 May. Here they also found what remained of the First Battalion.

This unit had been operating independently: on 25 April it had left Athens for Epirus, under Mereu's command. On the way back it fell in with the Greek army at Dhomokós. Ricciotti sent word for them to join up with him at Dranitza, a few miles to the west. But circumstances prevented them from making the move: first there was difficulty in the distribution of matériel; then the Greek commander at Dhomokós forbade their departure, because he believed the road to Dranitza to be held by the Turks; finally, the Turkish attack commenced.

They were sent to the front line below Dhomokós at 10 a.m. All day they bore the brunt of the Turkish assault. Mereu had gone on ahead to join Ricciotti, so they were now under the command of the lieutenant-adjutant Major Antonio Mosca, and Amilcare Cipriani, who was badly wounded.

The First Battalion at the Battle of Dhomokós.

The battalion did not suffer excessively heavy losses during the battle, but once the retreat began and the troops came out into the open their red shirts made an easy target for the Turks. Their leaders, carried away by the desire to be heroic, set a bad example for the men by neglecting the most fundamental rules of prudence. There were 148 of them left after the battle of Dhomokós; during the retreat they lost another fifty.

Many of the troops left the retreating battalion to join Ricciotti. They made their way through the hills, and were extraordinarily lucky: they managed to reach him without encountering any Turks.

At Thermopylae Ricciotti received news of another armistice. And he was assured that this time it was the prelude to a permanent peace. His task was therefore over, and he asked to be sent home with his men.

The series of incidents which marked the homeward voyage were to be the source of much ill feeling and controversy.

They were put aboard a ship called the *Urania*, but since she was carrying a cargo of flour the *Garibaldini* were packed on to the

The long march from Dhomokós to the Thermopylae.

bridge. When they stopped at Athens, the authorities tried to prevent them from coming ashore, despite the fact that their personal effects had been left in the Illissia barracks there. The men were ready to mutiny, and Ricciotti had to act quickly to prevent a tragedy. In the end he obtained permission for them to disembark, but only on condition that they be back aboard the ship by 8 p.m.

The Greek *Garibaldini*, on the other hand, were transferred to another ship and sent to the island of Póros, where they were kept virtually in quarantine. Eventually they were brought back to Athens, but the government took no interest in their fate and many were obliged to beg for a living.

The British stayed in Athens to wait for a ship which would take them directly home. The French and the Italians were taken on a government ship to Brindisi. It stopped at Corfu, but again they were forbidden to go ashore. Some of them jumped into the sea and

swam to the port. The Greek gunboat which was 'escorting' them was on the point of firing on these Red-shirts, but once again Ricciotti managed to ward off tragedy.

There were two reasons behind the Greek government's strange conduct. On the one hand, it feared that if the *Garibaldini* were allowed to land at Athens they might stir up the opposition of the people to a peace treaty which contradicted the aims of the war. On the other, it was under pressure from both Italy and Austria to see to it that they were not given a chance to land in Dalmatia and cause trouble there. It was even proposed that an Italian warship be sent to Corfu to make quite sure that they continued their voyage to Brindisi.

But this did not prove necessary. After a brief rest at Corfu the *Garibaldini* left for Brindisi with perfect docility. Another campaign was over, and they were anxious to return to civilian life. But, as Giuseppe Garibaldi had been fond of saying, 'Just as one thinks that everything is over, it turns out that something remains to be done.'

Garibaldino volunteers in the Greek-Turkish war of 1911 when, under the symbolic command of Ricciotti, but in truth under Peppino Garibaldi, they returned to fight for Greece and defeated the Turks at Drisko.

The surviving Garibaldi brothers photographed in 1915 on their return to Italy wearing the grey-green uniform of the regular army. They are wearing a black band on their arms in mourning for their brothers who died in France.

The Last of Them All

On 28 June 1914 Archduke Franz Ferdinand von Habsburg, heir to the imperial throne of Austria–Hungary, and his wife Sophia, were shot dead at Sarajevo by the revolutionary Gavrilo Princip.

It was said later that a gypsy had predicted the event. But even Bismarck had realized that sooner or later 'war would break out over some foolishness in the Balkans'. The foolishness, unfortunately, involved two enemy states: Austria and Serbia.

The Austro-Hungarian Empire had lost rich provinces in Italy and Germany, but for years it had been trying to supplant Turkish hegemony in the Balkans. At the same time the Russians, with their pan-Slavistic ideology, had been pursuing the same objective.

Serbia, officially an independent kingdom, had in fact been completely dependent upon Austria. But in 1901 the ruling Obreanovich dynasty was replaced by that of the Karageorgevich. The country allied itself with Russia and, in a series of successful military campaigns, virtually doubled its national territory. And now it aspired to liberate other Slavic lands from Austrian rule.

The Emperor of Austria was Franz Josef. He had been reigning since 1848, and his ideas were still those of the first half of the 19th century. His foreign minister, the elegant and sophisticated Count Leopold Berthold, was hardly more enlightened. In their blindness, in fact, Emperor and minister together paved the way for World War I by using the assassination as a pretext for extirpating, as Franz Josef put it in a letter to Kaiser Wilhelm, 'Russian and Serbian pan-Slavism' and for 'isolating Serbia and reducing its territory.'

Germany had been allied with Austria since 1882, and the treaty had been renewed several times. The Germans felt threatened by nations which resented their economic and military growth or which were anxious to cancel 'the dishonour of defeat'. They had counselled moderation during a similar crisis two years before, but now Berlin's reply to Franz Josef's letter was 'Immediate action against Serbia is the best solution.'

The war was the result of the fears and suspicions which, towards the end of the 19th century and the beginning of the 20th, had led to an insane armaments race and to military alliances which provided for 'relentless interventions'.

A European conflagration of unprecedented scale had been predicted by all the professionals of international politics; they had done nothing to prevent it, however. When a high-ranking personage in the British Admiralty heard the news from Sarajevo, he observed, 'If war comes now, it will inevitably be a general one', and today the message which the British squadron that took part in 'Kiel Week', a naval festivity, sent its German counterpart at the moment of weighing anchor seems a bad joke: 'Friends in the past, friends forever.'

On 28 July Austria declared war on Serbia. On the 31st Russia announced a general mobilization. Germany declared war on Russia on 1 August, and France and England immediately entered the conflict on the Russian side. Thus began World War I. France had been preparing for it patiently for forty years, in the hopes of regaining the territories she had lost in 1870; Russia was eager (most foolishly, as it turned out) to put her enormous military machine to some use; England wanted to check German expansion; Germany needed an outlet for her prosperous industries.

The war lasted four years and cost eight million lives. And it solved nothing. The same problems would again come to a head twenty

The arrest of Gavrilo Princip.

Enrolment of Garibaldini *at Montélimar.*

years later, this time resulting in even greater slaughter.

During the first year of the war, Italy's policy remained uncertain. As a member, with Germany and Austria, of the triple alliance, she might be expected to side with those two countries. But the treaty called for an automatic intervention only if a member-nation was attacked by a non-member, whereas now Germany and Austria were the aggressors. The government seized upon this clause: it could see no benefit accruing to Italy from the war, and it was opposed to further Austrian expansion in the Balkans. The socialists and the trade unions were convinced that the war was contrary to the interests of the proletariat, and public opinion in general was against siding with the central powers. Anti-Austrian feeling ran high, as Austria still held on to two Italian provinces; the Trentino and Venezia Giulia. Despite the alliance, there had recently been friction between Vienna and Rome.

On the other hand, Italy seemed destined to enter the war, because of her geographical position and because a large portion of the population saw in it a good opportunity to complete the process of national unification once and for all, by annexing the territories which were still in Austrian hands.

For opposite reasons, Italian entry was hoped for and feared by both sides. The Italians could blockade the Austrian navy in the Adriatic, preventing its use in the Mediterranean. Or it could join forces with Austria and pose a serious problem for the British navy, while simultaneously aiding the Turks, who were allies of the central powers. The Italian army, furthermore, could interfere with the allied defence system, not only on the European continent, but also in Africa, by tying up colonial troops and preventing them from coming to the aid of the mother country. Or it could attack Austria–Hungary and divert a sizeable number of her troops from the Russian front, while at the same time threatening the allies of the central powers in the Balkans.

Both sides, therefore, sought to convince the Italians to join them. At home, the debate between interventionists and anti-interventionists waxed passionate. Meanwhile, a small

*English ex-*Garibaldini *parade through London recruiting for World War I.*

group of men, unmotivated by utilitarian considerations, were preparing to fight for France and for her liberty. They were the *Garibaldini* of 1914: the last *Garibaldini*.

Between 1897 and 1914 the Red-shirts had continued a struggle for national independence, and its maintenance, throughout the world. Thus, in 1900, 361 of them under Colonel Ricciardi had gone to South Africa to fight with the Boers. They were assigned to the Foreign Legion, under Emile Arie van Ameringen.

They were all staunch republicans, and some of them were anarchists. When they returned to Europe they landed at Trieste, and here they were arrested by the Austrian authorities because of their subversive views. Later they were arrested by the Italians, on account of the diplomatic embarrassment they had caused: Rome officially agreed with London about the Boer question.

Between 1903 and 1911 Ricciotti Garibaldi, who had founded a committee for the freedom and independence of Albania, tried several times to organize an expedition to fight for the liberation of that country. But he was thwarted each time by the Italian government, which wanted to avoid the trouble with

Austria which this might cause.

In 1912 the First Balkan War broke out: Serbia, Montenegro, Bulgaria and Greece sided against the Turkish Empire. Ricciotti's *Garibaldini* hastened to fight with the Greeks. Once again, and for the last time, the old red shirt could be seen on a battlefield. The whole Garibaldi family was there, including Ricciotti's wife Costanza, and his daughters Anita and Rosa, who had volunteered as nurses.

The corps was made up of two thousand men in all, including Italians and Greeks: a marginal group in itself. But despite their small number, and Ricciotti's advanced age (to which some observers attributed the meagre results of the expedition), they managed to overcome ten thousand Turks at Drisko, affirming once again their invincibility.

Their presence could hardly affect the outcome of the war; it served more than anything else to keep alive a name and a legend which still aroused the world's curiosity and commanded its respect. But volunteers no longer came flocking as they once had. Furthermore, the very image of the *Garibaldino* as unpaid 'soldier of fortune' who went to fight in other countries for the cause of liberty had lost much of its meaning. In this new age of unprecedented nationalistic rivalries, combattants who went to fight in other countries were not usually to be thought of as standard-bearers of liberty.

Nevertheless, it was against this *mal du siècle* that the *Garibaldini* now took up arms, for the last time in their history. Time had passed them by: their ideals seemed as faded as the colour of their shirts. This time the General's grandchildren led the volunteers. They were all Ricciotti's sons: Giuseppe II (known as Peppino), Ricciotti Junior, Sante, Bruno, Costante and Ezio. They had all acquired a good military training on various battlefields. The most experienced, and therefore the leader of the brothers, was Peppino. He was then thirty-five, and he had fought in Greece in 1897, with the Boers in 1900, in Mexico with Pancho Villa against Porfirio Diaz, and again in Greece in 1912–13. He was officially Chief of Staff of the *Garibaldini*, but he was in effect commander of the Legion.

When World War I broke out, Peppino and Ricciotti Junior, following their grandfather's footsteps, offered their swords to France; their brothers soon followed suit. Volunteers immediately began to offer their services, in Italy as well as in France. But things were not easy for them in either country. The Italian government was observing a policy of strict neutrality, and wanted to avoid diplomatic incidents; it therefore did all it could to sabotage their efforts. And in France the regular army took a dim view of the constitution of an independent military corps: the volunteers were more than welcome, of course, but the authorities wanted them to enroll in the Foreign Legion, which for the first time in its history was fighting on French soil.

At the outset, the French war minister sought to organize a vast volunteer legion which would also include the *Garibaldini*. But he was prevented from doing so by the military, who insisted on keeping the *Garibaldini* separate from the other volunteers. In fact, of the 17,000 volunteers who came to France, 14,000 joined the battalions of the Foreign Legion (though some later formed independent legions because of political developments in their homelands); only 3,000 were assigned to the Garibaldi Legion. The attitude of the French army was understandable enough, for two reasons: though Italy was neutral at the moment, it might enter the war in the future, and one could not be sure on which side; and

The elderly Ricciotti inspects the Garibaldini in the Avenue des Champs Elysées. Behind him, on the left, his son Peppino.

'free corps' had no place in modern warfare, which depended on the organized interaction of disciplined units.

On 24 August 1914, accompanied by the French senator Rivet, Peppino, Ricciotti Junior and Bruno presented the premier, Viviani, with a memorandum in which they proposed the constitution of a Garibaldi Brigade of 7,500 men, to be made up of volunteers from all nations, who were now beginning to arrive in France. But Viviani had other problems on his mind: the army had suffered a series of defeats and the German offensive was threatening Paris; the government had to be transferred to Bordeaux. For the moment it had no time to consider the Garibaldi brothers' proposal.

Meanwhile, despite all the obstacles, the first wave of Garibaldian volunteers was arriving in France. The government had issued no instructions, so they were lodged provisionally in the barracks of Nîmes and Montélimar. In line with Garibaldian tradition, every age, social condition and political faith was represented. Many were veterans of earlier campaigns; their commander at Montélimar, Major Orlando Carini, had been wearing the red shirt since the battle of Mentana.

On 7 September the government requested Peppino to send an emissary to Bordeaux to discuss his proposal for a Garibaldi legion. Ricciotti Junior was sent; only with difficulty did he come to an agreement with his interlocutor, Colonel Martin, the head of the infantry department of the war ministry. In the end Ricciotti was authorized to constitute the legion, but on condition that it be incorporated into the Foreign Legion. Ricciotti agreed and thus the 'Fourth Regiment of the First Foreign Legion' came into existence.

Peppino was placed in command of the Legion with the rank of Lieutenant Colonel. Second in command was Major Peat de Garat, as a sizeable number of legionaires were French. The choice of Peppino posed no problem, but the same was not true of the choice of a uniform. The *Garibaldini* wanted to wear the legendary red shirts of their pre-

Bruno Garibaldi in French uniform. (Above)
Garibaldini *in the trenches.* (Below)

Bruno's body carried back through the lines.

decessors, but two practical considerations rendered this inadvisable. The red shirt was too visible in an age when battlefields were no longer shrouded in gunpowder smoke – most of the world's armies, in fact, had by now replaced their old ostentatious uniforms with those of a dull colour, giving them some protection. Secondly, it was feared that should any of the *Garibaldini* be taken prisoner, they might be shot as spies if they were not wearing French uniforms. In the end it was agreed that they might wear their red shirts under the blue greatcoat of the French army.

The Garibaldi brothers lost no time. On 14 September they were at Montélimar. With the aid of a few French officers, they undertook the organization and the training of the volunteers, who were divided into three battalions, with a total of twelve companies and two units of machine-gunners.

Setting up a military corps *ex novo* is always problematic, but the brothers were faced with special difficulties. The *Garibaldini*

were well known as republicans, and therefore the republican movement in Italy felt entitled not only to have its say in the constitution and the formation of the legion, but also to negotiate concerning it with the French government. This was against the wishes of the brothers, who did not want their corps to be identified with any political group; they feared that the meddling of the republicans might lead to the legion being dissolved. Peppino therefore informed the government that no one was authorized to speak for the legion, and he broke definitively with the movement by persuading the government to dissolve a 'Republican Company' which had been formed autonomously at Nice.

On 7 November, upon Peppino's insistence, the *Garibaldini* were at last sent to the war zone.

At the outset, the French government had wanted to use the *Garibaldini* in Dalmatia, but realizing that the Italian government would never consent to the presence of Italian volunteers in that territory, they abandoned the idea. On 20 November they were incorporated into General Gouraud's Tenth Division, and on 12 December they were sent to the front in the Argonne Forest, west of Verdun, where trench warfare of the most ferocious sort had been dragging on for months amid a sea of barbed wire.

On 26 December the Fourth Regiment of the First Foreign Legion received its baptism of fire. Orders were to attack the enemy at a place called Abri de l'Etoile, in concert with a few of Colonel Valdant's French infantry battalions and with the support of two units of engineers and one of machine-gunners. But the whole operation was a series of errors as gross as they were disastrous. The artillery not only gave inadequate support; as often as not it shelled the *Garibaldini* themselves. The commander of a French battalion, a certain Dugla, had a bugle sound the signal for a charge, thus giving the Germans plenty of time to get ready for him. When the *Garibaldini* broke through the barbed wire that separated them from the enemy trenches and were about to charge the Germans, they were met by a dense volley of fire which left many holes in their ranks. They managed to take two lines of German trenches, but they were unable to take the third and, after three hours of combat, they were obliged to retreat.

The day's losses were heavy. There were 111 wounded, 16 missing and 31 killed. Among the dead was Bruno Garibaldi. Bruno was not a member of a line battalion, but he had charged on ahead all the same. He was wounded early on, but ignored the fact; even when he was struck a second time he continued his charge, until a third bullet killed him. His body was left behind in 'no man's land', and only several days later did two courageous *Garibaldini* manage to recover it.

After six days behind the lines, on 5 January 1915, the *Garibaldini* returned to the trenches. Their objective was a strong enemy position on a low rise called Courtes Chausses. This time Peppino obtained authorization to lead his men personally; the attack was co-ordinated with an attack by French troops under Colonel Valdant.

Peppino, like his grandfather, was a great believer in bayonet charges. But he realized that times had changed and that the Germans, from the safety of their trenches, could massacre them if they advanced across open country. So he preceded his charge with a heavy bombardment of the German lines; then, as Colonel Valdant put it, 'before the remains of the enemy trenches came down to earth again, they attacked.' They easily overran the three enemy trenches; in a single charge they took 120 prisoners, three machine-guns and two mortars.

The action was swift, violent and successful, but again the *Garibaldini* suffered a tragic loss: Costante Garibaldi. Like Bruno, Costante had been with the reserve troops – and, like Bruno, he had wanted to take part in the attack personally, and was killed.

That day 47 of the *Garibaldini* were killed, 172 wounded and 77 missing. So serious were their losses that again they were sent back behind the lines to reorganize. But on 7 January they were recalled to the front.

The Germans had attacked in force at Abri de l'Etoile, virtually destroying the French Forty-sixth Infantry Regiment, occupying all the positions in that sector, and threatening the French heavy artillery installations.

The battle went on for two days, from the 7th till the 9th. It was tough going for both sides, but in the end the Germans had to retreat. The *Garibaldini* retook all the lost positions, and came to the rescue of those exhausted survivors of the Forty-sixth who were still holding out. This time their losses were relatively light: 15 killed, 54 wounded and 42 missing.

Meanwhile, Italy had made up its mind: on 24 May 1915 it declared war on the central powers. Thereupon the *Garibaldini* returned home; they enrolled in the *Alpi* Brigade, a unit which preserved the traditions of the *Cacciatori delle Alpi* which Giuseppe Garibaldi had commanded half a century before.

In a fortnight's fighting in France, 93 of them had been killed, 136 were missing in action, and 337 wounded. In recognition of their bravery, they received eleven crosses of

Clemenceau and Peppino Garibaldi. Though only a token group, the Garibaldini *returned to France in 1917, when the* Cacciatori delle Alpi *Brigade, at the orders of Brigadier General Peppino Garibaldi, were sent to France. All the surviving members of the Garibaldi family were in the corps, including the women, who had joined the Red Cross.*

Knights of the Legion of Honour, and four military medals.

Thus came to an end an epic which had begun seventy-two years before on the plains of South America.

For the record, the *Garibaldini* returned to France in 1917, led by Peppino, who was now a Brigadier General of the Italian army. But now they called themselves the *Alpi* Brigade and they wore grey-green uniforms.

The name of the *Garibaldini* did not die out, however; it lived on in the 'International Brigades' during the Spanish Civil War, for instance, and among the partisans in Yugoslavia and Italy during World War II. But these brigades were in the service of ideologies and regimes which had little to do with the spirit of the old Red-shirts. Ezio Garibaldi's *Garibaldini*, for instance, sided openly with Fascism.

The Garibaldi family, in fact, was now divided by political differences. Though Ezio became a fascist, the other surviving brothers were staunch opponents of the regime, and the price they paid was exile, or worse: Sante died as a result of the ill treatment to which he was subjected at Dachau. But all this insanity is recent history. The epic of the Red-shirts ended there in the Argonne. All that remains of them are a few old engravings, some souvenirs and relics, and an enormous quantity of opinions – most of them hopelessly contradictory – as to their achievement. Certainly, the *Garibaldini* are incomprehensible to our world of concrete and machinery; today we can only take note of how far removed we are from their dreams, their aspirations and their ideals.

Bearing all of them in mind, let us conclude with the judgment of the General on himself:

'Mine has been a tempestuous life, made up – like most people's, I believe – of both good and evil. I may say that I always have sought the good, for myself and for my fellow men. If on occasion I have done evil, I have done so involuntarily.'

Chronology

1807	July 4	Birth of Garibaldi at Nice
1826–1832		Various voyages on merchant ships.
1833	April	Encounter with Emile Barrault and meeting with Gian Battista Cuneo.
	December	He meets Mazzini in Marseilles and joins *Giovine Italia*.
	December 26	He enlists in the Piedmont Navy at Genoa.
1834	February 3	He embarks on the frigate *Des Geneys*.
	February 4	The insurrection at Genoa is a failure. Garibaldi flees to Marseilles.
	June 3	The Divisionary Council of War in Genoa condemns him to death in his absence.
1835	Winter	He leaves Marseilles for Rio de Janeiro.
1836	Spring	He arrives at Rio de Janeiro and meets Luigi Rossetti.
1837	May 4	Garibaldi and Luigi Rossetti are granted permission to fight for the Republic of the Rio Grande, as corsairs, against Brazil.
	May 7	Departure of the *Mazzini*.
	May 7–11	Capture of the *Maribondo*.
	May 11	Capture of the *Luisa* which is re-named *Farroupilha*.
	June 15	Naval battle against the Uruguayans at Punta de Jesús y María. Garibaldi is seriously injured. G. Fiorentino is the first man to die under the General's command.
	June 23	*Farroupilha* is captured and the prisoners are held at Gualeguay.
	November	Garibaldi attempts to escape and is tortured after his recapture.
1838	July	Garibaldi is released and re-joins Rossetti in Montevideo. They go back to the Rio Grande and continue the running war against Brazil.
	July 14	Shipwreck of the *Farroupilha II*.
	August	Garibaldi meets Anita.
	Sept–October	Naval battles.
	November 15	Naval battle of Laguna. Garibaldi sets fire to his ships and sinks them to avoid their capture by the enemy.
1840	September 16	Birth of Garibaldi's son Menotti at Saint Simon.
	Winter	Retreat of the Rio Grande troops.
1841	Spring	Garibaldi returns to Montevideo and works as a salesman.
1842	January	Garibaldi takes command of the Uruguayan navy in the war against Argentina.
	March 26	Garibaldi marries Anita in a religious ceremony.
	June 27	Departure of the suicidal mission to Paraná.
	August 15–17	Naval battle of Costa Brava. To avoid surrender Garibaldi burns his ships.
	November 21	Garibaldi is given command of another naval squadron.
	December	The Uruguayans are defeated and obliged to retreat by land; once again the ships are burned.
1843	February	Start of the siege of Montevideo.
	April 20	The Italian Legion is formed in Montevideo.
	June 10	Battle of El Cerro.
	July	Anzani arrives in Montevideo and reorganizes the Legion.
1844	March 28	Second battle of El Cerro.
1845	September 6	Occupation of the island of Martin García.

	November 3	Occupation of the town of Salto.
	December 6–23	Battle of Salto.
1846	February 8	Battle of San António del Salto.
1847	February 4	Garibaldi's second son Ricciotti is born in Montevideo.
1848	January 12	Uprising starts in Palermo and quickly spreads throughout Italy.
	March 23	Piedmont declares war on Austria.
	April 15	Garibaldi and his followers leave for Italy.
	June 23	They land at Nice.
	June 28	Arriving at Genoa, they are 150 legionaires.
	July 5	Garibaldi meets King Charles Albert at Roverbella and offers him his sword.
	July 14	The Provisional Government of Milan engages Garibaldi as a general.
	August 15	Battle of Luino.
	August 25	The Piedmontese are defeated at Custoza.
	August 26	Battle of Morazzone.
	August 27	Garibaldi's men take shelter in Switzerland.
	November 24	Flight of Pius IX from Rome to Gaeta.
	December 8	The *Garibaldini* are invited to Rome.
1849	January	March across the Appennines to Rieti.
	January 20	Garibaldi is elected Deputy to the Roman Parliament by the town of Rieti.
	February 5	He arrives in Rome and is present at the opening of Parliament.
	February 9	The Roman Republic is proclaimed.
	March 23	Definitive defeat of the Piedmontese. Charles Albert abdicates.
	April 24	The *Garibaldini* are called to Rome from Rieti. Garibaldi is nominated Brigadier General of the Roman Republic.
	April 25	The French land at Civitavecchia to attack Rome.
	April 27	The *Garibaldini* enter Rome.
	April 30	First victory against the French in Rome. Garibaldi is wounded in the abdomen.
	May 4–19	Neapolitan campaign (battles of Palestrina, Valmontone, Velletri).
	June 3	The French recommence the attack on Rome.
	June 30	Last battle and the fall of the Roman Republic.
	July 2	Garibaldi leaves Rome with Anita and his men, determined to continue the fight.
	July 31	On arrival at San Marino, Garibaldi disbands the Legion and departs with 250 of his most faithful followers.
	August 1	At Cesanatico, they embark on 13 fishing-boats and head for Venice. The Austrians fire on them; they land at Magnavacca and split up.
	August 4	Death of Anita.
	Aug 5–Sept 2	Garibaldi escapes across country through Romagna and Tuscany.
	September 7	Garibaldi arrives at Genoa and is arrested by the Piedmont police.
	September 16	Garibaldi leaves Genoa for his second exile.
1850	June 12	He embarks for New York.
	July 30	He arrives in New York and works as a candle-maker for Antonio Meucci.
1851–1852–1853		As a Merchant Captain Garibaldi travels round America, China and Australia.
1852	November 4	Cavour becomes Prime Minister of Piedmont.
1854	January 12	In command of a merchant vessel, Garibaldi leaves from New York for Europe.

	February	Garibaldi in London.
	May 7	He arrives at Genoa.
1855	December 29	With an inheritance he buys half of the island of Caprera.
1857	January	He moves to Caprera permanently.
1858		Garibaldi establishes contact with the 'Genoa Group'.
	August	Interview with Cavour.
	December 31	At his request a 'Garibaldi Anthem' is written by Mercantili, with music composed by Olivieri.
1859	January 24	Secret treaty between the French and the Piedmontese.
	March 1	Volunteers begin to arrive in Piedmont.
	March 2	Garibaldi meets the King and starts enlisting volunteers.
	March 17	Garibaldi is nominated a Piedmontese Major-General and commander of the *Cacciatori delle Alpi*.
	April 27	War breaks out between Austria and Piedmont. France takes the Piedmont side.
	May 14	The *Cacciatori delle Alpi* are joined at Casale Monferrato by the Mounted Guides and the *Carabinieri Genovesi* who remain a special corps.
	May 21	They cross the Ticino river.
	May 23	Occupation of Varese.
	May 26	Battle of Varese.
	May 27	Battle of San Fermo.
	May 31	Battle of Laveno.
	June 6	They take Lecco.
	June 8	They take Bergamo.
	June 14	Battle of Treponti.
	July 8	Armistice of Villafranca.
	July 23	End of the second campaign of Lombardy.
	August 1	Garibaldi resigns his commission as a Sardinian general.
	August 17	He is made a Major-General in the Army of Central Italy. Many of his men follow him.
	September	He launches the subscription for 'a million rifles' for the unity of Italy.
	November 16	He resigns from the Tuscan army.
1860	March 24	Nice and Savoy are assigned to France.
	April 4	Uprisings at Palermo, Messina and Catania. Crispi and Bixio start preparing an expedition to go to their aid.
	April 12	Garibaldi is elected Deputy to Parliament by Nice.
	April 23	He resigns as Deputy.
	May 6	The Thousand leave from Quarto.
	May 11	The landing at Marsala.
	May 13	Occupation of Salemi. Garibaldi proclaims general conscription and assumes the Dictatorship in the name of King Victor Emanuel II.
	May 15	Battle of Calatafimi.
	May 27	The *Garibaldini* enter Palermo.
	June 6	The Neapolitan Royalists in Palermo surrender and evacuate their troops.
	June–July	The *Garibaldini* assume the name of the Southern Army.
	July 20	Battle of Milazzo.
	August 1	By convention with the Bourbons, the whole of Sicily is liberated.
	August 19	Bixio's division lands at Melito.
	August 21	Battle of Reggio Calabria.
	August 22	They occupy Villa San Giovanni.

	August 30	The last Bourbon troops surrender: Calabria is liberated.
	August 31	The *Garibaldini* arrive at Cosenza.
	September 7	Garibaldi enters Naples.
	September 19	Battle of Caiazzo.
	October 1–2	Battle of the Volturno.
	October 26	Garibaldi meets Victor Emanuel II at Teano.
	November 8	He presents the King with the annexation of Southern Italy.
	November 9	Garibaldi sails for Caprera.
		The Southern Army is disbanded. Zuccoi leaves for Crete with a sizeable group of *Garibaldini*.
1861	March 17	Proclamation of the Kingdom of Italy.
	March 27	Garibaldi is elected Deputy from Naples to the new Italian Parliament.
	June 6	Death of Cavour.
	August	Garibaldi is offered a command in the Union Army by President Lincoln.
1862	January 27	Remnants of the Southern Army are incorporated in the Italian Army.
	June 27	Garibaldi leaves Caprera for Palermo.
	August 29	Skirmish at Aspromonte. Garibaldi is wounded in a leg.
	August 31	Garibaldi is imprisoned in the fortress of Varignano (La Spezia).
	October 5	General armistice.
1863	January 18	The Poles revolt against the Russians.
	April	Nullo leaves for Poland with 38 volunteers.
	May 2	600 Poles join Nullo and they cross the frontier.
	May 5	Battle of Krzykawka. Death of Nullo.
1864	Mar 26–Apr 28	Garibaldi's visit to England.
	June–July	Projects for *Garibaldino* interventions in the Balkans.
1865		English admirers purchase and make a gift of the other half of the island of Caprera to Garibaldi.
1866	April 8	Italo–Prussian alliance.
	June	Formation of the Italian Voluntary Corps.
	June 20	War breaks out between Austria and Italy, the ally of Prussia.
	July 3	Battle of Monte Suello.
	July 16	Battle of Caffaro.
	July 18–19	Battle of the Ampella Fortress.
	July 21	Battle of Bezzecca.
	August 9	Although victorious, the *Garibaldini* receive orders to retreat from the Tyrol.
	November	2,000 *Garibaldini* go to Greece. Luciano Mereu, with a small group, is in Crete and active in the revolt.
1867	January	Andrea Sgarallino leaves for Greece with 40 volunteers and Ricciotti.
	September 9	Garibaldi and some of his collaborators attend the International Peace Congress in Geneva.
	September 22	While preparing the invasion of the Papal State, Garibaldi is arrested at Sinalunga. Menotti continues to organize the men nevertheless.
	September 26	Garibaldi is confined to Caprera.
	September 28	The *Garibaldini* cross into Papal territory.
	October 14	Garibaldi escapes from Caprera.
	October 23	He re-joins his men at Passo Corese. The Cairoli brothers fight at Villa Glori.
	October 25	Battle of Monterotondo.
	November 3	Battle of Mentana (the Great Defeat). The volunteers are disbanded at Passo Corese.

	November 5	Once again Garibaldi is arrested and imprisoned in the Varignano.
	November 25	Released, he returns to Caprera.
1870	September 2	The French are defeated at Sedan.
	September 4	The Republic is proclaimed in Paris.
	September 7	Garibaldi offers his services to France against the Prussians.
	September 20	The Italians occupy Rome.
	October 10	Garibaldi is given command of the Army of the Vosges. Volunteers start arriving in France.
	November 20	Ricciotti takes the Prussians by surprise at Châtillon-sur-Seine.
	November 25–26	First battle of Dijon.
	December 1	Battle of Autun.
	December 28	Occupation of Dijon.
1871	January 21–23	Second battle of Dijon.
	January 29	Franco-German armistice.
	January 31	The *Garibaldini* start pulling back from Dijon.
	February 13	Having been elected Deputy to the French Assembly, Garibaldi resigns.
	March	The *Garibaldini* are disbanded, and some of them go to the Commune.
1874	November	Garibaldi is elected Deputy in Rome. Some 100 *Garibaldini* are in Spain with Antonio Orense.
1875		Celso Cerretti and a group of *Garibaldini* take part in the revolt in Bosnia and Herzegovina at the orders of Mićo Ljubibratić.
1880	January 14	The Court of Appeals in Rome annuls Garibaldi's marriage to Countess Raimondi.
	January 26	In a civil ceremony he marries Francesca Armosino, the mother of his children Clelia and Manlio.
1882	June 2	Garibaldi dies on Caprera.
1897	March 20	Ricciotti is invited to recruit volunteers to send to Crete where a revolt has broken out.
	March	The Death Company is formed in Athens by Amilcare Cipriani.
	April 9	They cross into Turkish territory with a large contingency of Greek volunteers.
	April 13	Returning from the raid, Cipriani disbands the Legion.
	April 17	Greece declares war on Turkey.
	April 24	Ricciotti arrives in Athens.
	April 26	Mereu leaves Athens for the front with the 1st Battalion.
	May 8	The other two battalions leave for the front.
	May 17	Battle of Dhomokós.
	May 21	After a long, independent retreat the *Garibaldini* reunite with the Greek army at Thermopylae. They receive orders to return to Athens and disband.
1900		A small number of *Garibaldini* go to South Africa to fight with the Boers.
1912		*Garibaldini* participate in the Greek-Turkish War.
1914	July 28	Austria declares war on Serbia. World War I begins.
	August 24	Ricciotti's sons propose the formation of a *Garibaldini* Legion to the French government.
	September 7	The proposal is accepted.
	November 7	The *Garibaldini* enter the war zone.
	December 12	They move to the Front in the forests of the Argonne.
	December 26	Bruno Garibaldi dies in the fighting at Abri de l'Etoile.

1915	January 5	Costante Garibaldi dies at Courtes Chausses.
	January 7–9	Third battle of Abri de l'Etoile.
	May 24	Italy enters the war. The Legion is disbanded and they return to Italy.

Bibliography

GENERAL WORKS

Campanella, Anthony P., *Giuseppe Garibaldi e la tradizione garibaldina biografia dal 1807 al 1970* (Geneva, 1971). (Extremely useful for research.)

Abba, Giuseppe Cesare, *Garibaldi nel 1° Centenario della sua gloriosa nascita* (Milan, 1907); *Cose garibaldine* (Turin, 1907).

Balbiani, Antonio, *Storia illustrata della vita di Garibaldi* (Milan, 1860).

Bizzoni, Achille, *Garibaldi nella sua epopea* (Milan, 1932).

Boggio, Pier Carlo, *Da Montevideo a Palermo: Vita di Giuseppe Garibaldi* (Turin, 1860).

Bordone, Joseph-Philippe, *Garibaldi, La République Romaine, Les Mille, Armée des Vosges* (Paris, 1891).

Brambilla, Ettore, *Garibaldi e i Garibaldini* (Como, 1910).

Candeloro, Giorgio, *Storia dell'Italia moderna* (Milan, 1964).

Cesari, Cesare, *Corpi Volontari Italiani dal '48 al '70* (Rome, 1921).

Comandini, Alfredo, *L'Italia nei cento anni del secolo XIX giorno per giorno illustrata* (Milan, 1900).

Comes, Salvatore, *Chiaroscuro di un mito* (Rome, 1972).

Corselli, Rodolfo, *Garibaldi – La vita, l'opera, attorno al grande astro* (Palermo, 1933).

Croce, Benedetto, *Storia d'Europa nel secolo XIX* (Bari, 1957).

De Luca, Pasquale, *I liberatori: visioni e figure del Risorgimento* (Milan, 1907).

Garibaldi, Giuseppe, *Scritti politici e militari* (Rome, 1907); *Memorie autobiografiche* (Florence, 1888); *Scritti di—, Edizione nazionale degli Scritti di Giuseppe Garibaldi a cura della Reale Commissione* (Bologna, 1932–7).

Guerzoni, Giuseppe, *Garibaldi* (Florence, 1882); *La vita di Nino Bixio* (Florence, 1875).

Luzio, Alessandro, *Garibaldi, Cavour, Verdi* (Turin, 1924).

Mack Smith, Denis, *Garibaldi, a great life in brief* (New York, 1956).

Mariani, Gaetano, *Antologia di scrittori garibaldini* (Rocca San Casciano, 1960).

Mario, Jessie White, *Della vita di Giuseppe Mazzini* (Milan, 1896); *Agostino Bertani e i suoi tempi* (Florence, 1888); *Garibaldi ei suoi tempi* (Milan, 1884).

Ministero della Guerra, Comando del Corpo di Stato Maggiore, Ufficio Storico, *Garibaldi Condottiero* (Rome, 1932).

Moneta, Ernesto Teodoro, *Le guerre, le insurrezioni e la pace nel secolo decimonono* (Milan, 1903).

Montanelli-Marco Nozza, Indro, *Garibaldi* (Milan, 1962).

Monti, Antonio, *La vita di Garibaldi giorno per giorno narrata e illustrata* (Milan, 1932).

Omodeo, Adolfo, *L'età del Risorgimento Italiano* (Naples, 1952).

Pieri, Piero, *Storia Militare del Risorgimento* (Turin, 1962).

Rosi, Michele, *Giuseppe Garibaldi* (Bologna, 1932).

Sacerdote, Gustavo, *La vita di Giuseppe Garibaldi* (Milan, 1933).

Valori, Aldo, *Garibaldi* (Turin, 1945).

Ximenes, Enrico Emilio, *Epistolario di Giuseppe Garibaldi. Con documenti e lettere inedite (1836–82)* (Milan, 1885).

Zangheri, Renato, *Lettere e proclami di Giuseppe Garibaldi* (Milan, 1954).

FROM PIRATES TO SOLDIERS

Assenzio y Ximenes, T., *Anita Garibaldi* (Rome, 1937).

Bandi, Giuseppe, *Anita Garibaldi* (Milan, 1952).

Bergés, Pedro, *La Légion française au siège de Montevideo* (Buenos Aires, 1936).

Biondi, Emilio, *Profili garibaldini* (Bagnacavallo, 1913).

Boris, Ivan, *Gli anni di Garibaldi in Sud America* (Milan, 1970).

Bourgin, Georges, *Garibaldi e la Francia in Uruguay 1840–48* (Milan, 1920).

Caillet Bois, Ricardo E., *Garibaldi en el Río de la Plata* (Buenos Aires, 1947).

Caronti, Luis C., *Legiones Italianas* (Buenos Aires, 1907).

Candido, Salvatore, *Giuseppe Garibaldi corsaro riograndese (1837–38)* (Rome, 1964); *Giuseppe Garibaldi nel Rio de la Plata 1841–48* (Florence, 1972).

Chiama, Letizia, 'La fuga di G. Garibaldi da Genova nel 1834' (in *Nuova Antologia*, 1916).

Coppellotti, Celestino, 'Garibaldi a Rio de Janiero' (in *Rivista Storica del Risorgimento*, 1932).

Corselli, Rodolfo, 'Anita Garibaldi' (in *Camicia Rossa*, 1942).

Cuneo, G. B., 'La Battaglia di San Antonio del Salto' (in *Camicia Rossa*, 1932).

Curatolo, Giacomo Emilio, *Anita Garibaldi l'eroina dell'amore* (Milan, 1932).

Del Cerro, Giulio, 'Intorno alla fuga di Garibaldi da Genova' (in *Rivista d'Italia*, 1907).

Dumas, Alexandre, *Montevideo ou une nouvelle Troie* (Paris, 1850).

Feraboli, Elsa, 'Il primo esilio di Garibaldi in America 1836–48' (in *Rivista Storica del Risorgimento*, 1932).

Garibaldi, Annita Italia, *Garibaldi en América* (Buenos Aires, 1930).

Giambruno, Cyro, 'Garibaldi nell'Uruguay' (in *Rassegna Italiana Politica Cultura*, 1953).

Gradenigo, Caio, *Garibaldi in America con diario della Legione Italiana di Montevideo* (Rome, 1969).

Lerroux, Alejandro, *Historia de Garibaldi desde 1807 a 1849, entresacadas de sui Memorias Autobiográficas y de los escritors de Alejandro Dumas sobre José Garibaldi* (Barcelona, 1904).

Luzio, Alessandro, *Carlo Alberto e Giuseppe Mazzini* (Turin, 1923).

Mackinnon, L. B., *La escuadra anglo-francesca en el Paraná* (Buenos Aires, 1967).

Maioli, Giovanni, 'Garibaldi in America; la battaglia di San Antonio del Salto narrata da una lettera ad Augusto Aglebert' (in *Camicia Rossa*, 1934).

Mariath, Frederico, 'O combate e tomada de Laguna' (in *Almanak Rio Grande Sul*, 1911).

Menghini, Mario, 'Francesco Anzani e sue lettere inedite' (in *Rivista di Roma*, 1907).

Milani, Mino, 'Inventario delle carte di G. Sacchi per i documenti della legione italiana a Montevideo' (in *Pavia Civica Istituti d'Arte e Storia*, 1963).

Mitre, Bartolome, 'Garibaldi nella regione del fiume Plata' (in *Patria degli Italiani*, Buenos Aires, 1904).

Passamonti, Eugcnio, 'Giuseppe Garibaldi e il moto genovese del 4–2–1832 secondo gli atti processuali' (in *Camicia Rossa*, 1934).

Rava, Luigi, *In memoria di Anita Garibaldi* (Bologna, 1931).

Virgilio, Varzea, *Garibaldi in America* (Rio, 1902).

A DREAM OF FREEDOM

Alba, November 1849 (Florence).

Anfossi, Francesco, *Memorie sulla campagna di Lombardia del 1848* (Turin, 1851).

Aporti, Ettore, 'Diario degli avvenimenti di Lombardia e di Roma (1848–49)' (in *Studi Garibaldini*, 1964).

'Atti e Memorie del XXVII Congresso Nazionale del Risorgimento Italiano' (Milan, 1948).

Baroni, Caloandro, *I Lombardi nelle guerre italiane 1848–49* (Turin, 1856).

Belluzzi, Raffaele, *La ritirata di Garibaldi da Roma* (Rome, 1899).

Beseghi, Umberto, 'L'indisciplina di Garibaldi a Velletri' (in *Camicia Rossa*, 1934); 'Garibaldi a Modigliana' (in *Camicia Rossa*, 1935); 'Lo sbarco di Magnavacca' (in *Camicia Rossa*, 1936).

Bollea, Luigi Cesare, 'Il contributo dei Lombardi alla prima guerra dell'indipendenza' (in *Risorgimento Italiano*, 1925).

Bonomi, Ivanoe, *Mazzini triumviro della Republica romana* (Turin, 1936).

Cadolini, Giovanni, 'I ricordi di un volontario. Il 1848' (in *Nuova Antologia*, 1909).

Capasso, Gaetano, 'La morte dei tre valorosi patrioti Dandolo, Manara, Morosini' (in *Rivista Storica Risorgimento Italiano*, 1914).

Cesari, Cesare, *La difesa di Roma nel 1849* (Milan, 1913).

Contemporaneo, 1848–49.

Corriere Mercantile di Genova, 30 June 1848 and September 1949 (Genoa).

Curatolo, Giacomo Emilio, 'Roma bombardata dai Francesi nel 1849' (in Rivista Storica Risorgimento Italiano, 1914).

Deiss, Joseph Jay, The roman years of Margaret Fuller (New York, 1969).

Demarco, Domenico, Una rivoluzione sociale. La repubblica romana del 1849 (Naples, 1944).

Detti, Emma, Margaret Fuller e i suoi corrispondenti (Florence, 1942).

Fiorini, Vittorio, 'Angelo Masina' (in Rivista Storica Risorgimento Italiano, 1895).

Forbes, Hugh, Manual for the patriotic volunteer on active service in regular and irregular war (New York, 1855).

Gabussi, Giuseppe, Memorie per servire alla storia della Rivoluzione negli Stati Romani (Genoa, 1852).

Giornale di Roma, 14 and 29 September 1849.

Goppelli, Zeusi (Giuseppe Zolli), La compagnia Medici e la difesa del Vascello (Montegiorgio, 1896).

Guerrini, Domenico, 'Il dissidio fra Mazzini e Garibaldi' (in Rivista Storica Risorgimento Italiano, 1909).

von Hoffstetter, Gustav, Tagebuch aus Italien 1849 (Zürich, 1851).

Hugo, Victor, L'expédition de Rome (Turin, 1849).

Koelman, Johan Philip, Memorie romane presented by M. Trebilian (Rome, 1963).

Leti, Giuseppe, La Rivoluzione e la Repubblica Romana 1848–49 (Milan, 1913).

Leone, Andrea, 'Reminescenze garibaldine a Velletri' (in Rivista Storica Risorgimento Italiano, 1909).

Loevinson, Ermanno, 'Garibaldi e la sua legione nello stato romano 1848–49' (Rome, 1902–7).

Macchiarelli, Andrea, 'Le vicende della Repubblica romana nelle memorie inedite di Pietro Gui' (in Camicia Rossa, 1941).

Maioli, Giovanni, 'La difesa di Roma e la ritirata di Garibaldi hel taccuino inedito di Pietro Fini' (in Camicia Rossa, 1934); 'Ancora la ritirata di Garibaldi da Roma' (in Camicia Rossa, 1935); 'I Bolognesi alla difesa di Roma' (in Camicia Rossa, 1941).

Mariotti, Temistocle, La difesa di Roma nel 1849 (Rome, 1892).

Michel, Ersilio, 'Ugo Forbes colonnello brittanico garibaldino' (in Atti del V congresso storico toscano nel Risorgimento, Lucca, 1953).

Milani, Mino, 'Appunti sull'origine del movimento garibaldino in Lombardia' (in Studi Garibaldini, 1962).

Miraglia, Biagio, Storia della rivoluzione romana (Genoa, 1850).

Monti, Antonio, Pio IX nel Risorgimento Italiano (Bari, 1928); 'Riflessi di eroismo e romanticismo, nella storia dei bersaglieri lombardi' (in Camicia Rossa, 1941).

Le Moniteur, 1849.

Morelli, Emilia, 'Episodi della difesa di Roma' (in Camicia Rossa, 1941).

Municipio di Roma, Mazzini a Roma (Rome, 1922).

Ortore, Bernardo, Ciceruacchio e i volontari della morte (Adria, 1879).

Pennacchini, Luigi Enrico, 'Dopo la caduta della Repubblica romana' (in Rassegna Storica del Risorgimento 1935–7).

Paladini, Luigi, La difesa del Vascello fatta dal commandante G. Medici (Rome, 1897).

Pisacane, Carlo, Guerra combattuta in Italia (Genoa, 1851).

Ritucci, Giosue', Memoria storica dell'attacco sostenuto in Velletri (Naples, 1851).

Rodelli, Luigi, La Repubblica romana del 1849 (Pisa, 1955).

Roselli, Pietro, Memorie relative alla spedizione e al combattimento di Velletri (Turin, 1853).

Rusconi, Carlo, La repubblica romana del 1849 (Capolago, 1850).

Sforza, Claudio, Ricordi della vita di Colomba Antonietti (Bologna, 1899).

The Times, January–June 1849.

Torre, Federico, Memorie storiche sull'intervento francese in Roma nel 1849 (Turin, 1851–1852).

Trevelyan, George Macaulay, Garibaldi's defence of the Roman republic 1848–49 (London, 1907).

Universo, 1848 (Rome).

Vaillant, Jean-Baptiste, Siège de Rome en 1849 (Paris, 1851).

Van Nuffel, Robert, 'Les souvenirs d'un garibaldien' (in Il Risorgimento, 1959).

von Willsen, Wilhelm, *La campagna del '48 giudicata da generale prussiano* (in *Documenti della Guerra Santa d'Italia 1851*, Turin).

Zaghi, Carlo, 'Nuovi documenti sul passaggio a Comacchio di Garibaldi e Masina' (in *Camicia Rossa*, 1933).

THE CACCIATORI DELLE ALPI

Adami, Vittorio, *Documenti relativi alle vicende del 1859* (in *Rassegna Storica del Risorgimento*, 1923).

Agazzi, Alberto, 'Breve cronistoria dei Cacciatori delle Alpi e ruolino dell'8 compagnia dei Mille' (in *Atti Ateneo Scienze Lett. arti Bergamo*, 1962–4).

Atti del XXXVIII Congresso di Storia del Risorgimento italiano (Rome, 1960).

Bertani, Agostino, 'I Cacciatori delle Alpi nel 1859, i loro feriti, i loro morti' (in *Politecnico*, Milan, 1860).

Brancaccio, Nicola, *L'Esercito del Vecchio Piemonte Vol. II* (Rome, 1925).

Cadolini, Giovanni, 'I Cacciatori delle Alpi. Ricordi del 1859' (in *Nuova Antologia*, 1907); 'Carte e Ricordi di Giovanni Cadolini' (Archivio Museo Risorgimento, Milan).

Camilla, Piero, *Como 1859 e la battaglia di San Fermo* (Como, 1959).

Cazzaro, Francesco, *I Cacciatori delle Alpi comandati dal generale Garibaldi nella guerra del 1859 in Italia* (Turin, 1860).

Chiala, Luigi, *Lettere edite e inedite di Camillo Cavour* (Turin, 1884–7); *Politica segreta di Napoleone III ed Cavour in Italia e in Ungheria (1858–61)* (Turin, 1895).

De La Verenne, Louis, *Les chasseurs des Alpes et des Appennins. Histoire de la guerre de l'indépendence italienne en 1859* (Florence, 1860).

Della Valle, Giuseppe, *Varese, Garibaldi ed Urban nel 1859 durante la guerra per l'indipendenza italiana* (Varese, 1863).

De Rossi, Eugenio, 'La cavalleria di Garibaldi nel 1859' (in *Rivista di Cavalleria*, 1905).

Gaiani, Emilio, *Garibaldi e i Cacciatori delle Alpi* (Citta di Castello, 1909).

'Garibaldi in Valtellina nel '59' (in *Bollettino Ufficiale Storico dello Stato Maggiore Esercito*, Rome, 1929).

Illustrated London News, 1859.

Luzio, Alessandro, *Garibaldi e Varese* (Varese, 1907).

Mack Smith, Denis, *Vittorio Emanuele II* (Bari, 1972).

Montale, Bianca, 'Le origini dei Carabinieri Genovesi' (in *Atti del Cong. Storia garibaldina*, Bergamo, 1960).

Omodeo, Adolfo, *L'opera politica del conte di Cavour* (Florence, 1940).

Ottolini, Angelo, *Le campagne di Garibaldi in Lombardia* (Milan, 1932).

Ottolini, Vittore, *I Cacciatori delle Alpi (1848–59)* (Milan, 1860).

Siboni, Pietro Pezzi, *La cavalleria nella campagna del 1859 per la liberazione della Lombardia* (Russi, 1959).

Stato Maggiore Esercito, *La guerra del 59* (Rome, 1910); *L'esercito e i suoi corpi* (Rome, 1971–3).

The Times, August–November 1859.

Westminster Review, October 1859.

THE THOUSAND

Abba, Giuseppe Cesare, *Da Quarto al Volturno* (Pisa, 1866); *Noterelle di uno dei Mille edite vent'anni dopo* (Bologna, 1880); *La vita di Nino Bixio* (Turin, 1905); *Ricordi garibaldini* (Turin, 1913); *Storia dei Mille* (Florence, 1904); *Maggio 1860. Pagine di un 'taccuino' inedito*, edited by Gino Bandini (Milan 1933); *Ritratti e profili* (Turin, 1912).

Agrati, Carlo, *Il primo dei Mille (Sirtori)* (Bari, 1940); *Da Palermo al Volturno* (Milan, 1937); *I Mille nella storia e nella leggenda* (Milan, 1933).

Agazzi, Alberto, *Le 180 biografie dei bergamaschi dei Mille* (Bergamo, 1960).

Almagià, Guido, 'Garibaldi in Sicilia nelle memorie di un Ammiraglio' (in *Bollettino dell'Ufficio Storico dello Stato Maggiore*, 1930).

Arzano, Aristide, 'Come morì Rosalino Pilo' (in *Memorie storiche militari*, 1913).

Atti del XXXIX Congresso Storia del Risorgimento, 1961.

Barbarich, Eugenio, 'Il Generale Cosenz' (in *Nuova Antologia*, 1910).

Barbetta, Roberto, *La Battaglia del Volturno* (Caserta, 1917).

Bartoli, Arnaldo, 'Garibaldi e le milizie nazionali nella guerra del 1860' (in *I.R.I.*, 1900).

Battaglini, Tito, 'Il diario dello Stato Maggiore borbonico in Palermo nel 1860' (in *Rivista Storica del Risorgimento*, 1938); *L'organizzazione militare del Regno delle Due Sicilie. Da Carlo III all'impresa garibaldina* (Modena, 1940); *La fine di un Esercito* (Rome, 1919); *Il crollo militare del Regno delle Due Sicilie* (Modena, 1938–9).

Belloni, Ernesto, *Scritti inediti* (Treviso, 1866).

Binda, Antonio, *Memorie garibaldine (1859–60)* (Milan, 1930).

Bixio, Nino, *Epistolario, edited by Emilia Morelli* (Rome, 1939).

'Rapporto Bosco sulla battaglia di Milazzo' (in *Gazzetta di Milano*, 1860).

Boyer, Ferdinand, 'Alexandre Dumas en Sicile avec Garibaldi (1860)' (in *Archivio Storico Messinese* 1956–7); 'La marine française et Garibaldi (mai–août 1860)' (*ibid.*; 1957–9); 'Les volontaires français avec Garibaldi en 1860' (in *Revue d'histoire moderne et contemporaine*, 1960); 'Souscriptions pour Garibaldi en France' (1860) (in *Rivista Storica del Risorgimento*, 1960); 'Les volontaires français de Messine à Capoue (1860) d'après les Souvenirs inédits d'Ulric de Fonvielle' (in *Archivio Storico messinese* 1962–3); 'Un garibaldien français: le général Bordone' (in *Rassegna Storica del Risorgimento*, 1971).

Bozzetti, Stefano, *La battaglia di Calatafimi; dai ricordi di uno dei Mille* (Alessandria. 1933).

Busetto, Girolamo, *Il generale Nino Bixio* (Fano, 1876).

Caldarella, Antonio, 'Combattenti stranieri nella campagna di Sicilia del 1860' (in *Sicilia e l'untita*).

Camardella, Pietro, *I Calabresi della spedizione dei Mille* (Ortona, 1913).

Campanella, Anthony P., 'Le memorie di un ufficiale svizzero volontario garibaldino nel 1860' (in *Archivio Storico Italiano*, Florence, 1967); 'La difesa di Palermo nel 1860 nelle memorie di Heinrich Wieland (in *Il Risorgimento*, 1963); 'La legione britannica nell'Italia meridionale con Garibaldi nel 1860' (in *Nuovi Quad. Meridione*, 1964); 'Le memorie di un regio soldato napoletano del 1860. Testimonianze oculari' (in *Il Risorgimento*, 1967).

Capello, Girolamo, 'Le aspirazioni di Nino Bixio alla vigilia della spedizione dei Mille' (in *Memorie Storiche Militazi*, 1911).

Cappellini, Antonio, *Nino Bixio, il secondo dei Mille* (Genoa, 1950).

Capuzzi, Giuseppe, *La spedizione di Garibaldi in Sicilia. Memorie di un volontario. edited by Ugo Baroncelli* (Brescia, 1960).

Caraguel, Clement, *Souvenirs et aventures d'un volontaire garibaldien* (Paris, 1861).

'I Carabinieri Genovesi nell'impresa del 1860' (in *Studi Garibaldini*, 1962).

Carosi, Salvatore, *La battaglia del Volturno* (Capua, 1905).

Casanova, Eugenio, *La Brigata Fabrizi da Palermo a Capua* (in *Bollettino dell'Ufficio Storico dello Stato Maggiore*, 1930).

Castellini, Gualtiero, *Pagine Garibaldine* (Turin, 1909).

Cesari, Cesare, 'L'artiglieria dell'escercito di Garibaldi nel 1860' (in *Bollettino dell'Ufficio Storico dello Stato Maggiore 1930*); *L'assedio di Gaeta* (Rome, 1926).

Chiodera, F., *Castel Morone. Ricordo patriottico del 1860* (Parma, 1893).

Corbellini, Pietro, *Diario di un garibaldino della spedizione Medici in Sicilia* (1860) (Como, 1911).

Corselli, Rodolfo, *L'opera di Crispi durante la spedizione dei Mille* (Palermo, 1920).

Corsi, Carlo, *Difesa dei soldati napoletani. Confutazioni alle 'Lettere del gen. Pianell e ricordi familiari'* (Naples, 1903).

Crispi, Francesco, *I Mille* (Milan, 1912).

Cuniberti, Felice, *Storia militare della spedizione dei Mille* (Turin, 1893).

Curatolo, Giacomo Emilio, 'Alessandro Dumas nel 1860' (in *Scritti e figure del Risorg. Ital.*, Turin, 1926); 'Paolo De Flotte' (*ibid.*).

D'Amia, Amerigo, *Fulgori ed ombre. L'impresa di Sicilia e l'armatore dei Mille G. B. Fauché* (Milan, 1961).

De Cesare, Raffaele, *La fine di un regno* (Citta del Castello, 1900).

De Donno, A., 'Un giudizio di Giacomo Medici sul trattamento fatto ai Garibaldini nel 1860' (in *Rassegna Storica Risorgimentale*, 1957).

De Feo, Achille Carlo, *Da Milazzo a Porta Pia. Lontani ricordi del mio lungo volontariato* (Scafati, 1901).

De Marco, Emmanuele, *La Sicilia nel decennio avanti la spedizione dei Mille* (Catania, 1898).

De Maria, Ugo, 'I Siciliani nella spedizione dei Mille' (in *Rassegna Storica Risorgimentale*, 1930); 'Il col. Nino Bonnet nei documenti dell'archivio Crispi' (in *La Sicilia nel Risorg.*, 1932); 'Ricordi della battaglia di Milazzo (20 luglio 1860)' (*ibid.*).

De Castro, Giovanni, *Giuseppe Sirtori* (Milan, 1892).

De Mayo, Guido, 'La crociera borbonica dinanzi a Marsala' (in *Memorie Storiche militari dello Stato Maggiore*, 1913); 'Il mancato sbarco a Marsala della brigata Bonanno' (in *Memorie Storiche militari*, 1914).

De Rohan Collection, Museo Centrale del Risorgimento, Rome.

De Sivo, Giacinto, *I Napoletani al cospetto delle nazioni civili* (Rome, 1967).

De Stefano, Francesco, 'Documenti militari relativi ad Enrico Fardella ed alla Brigata Milbitz (1860–61)' (in *Rassegna storica risorgimentale*, 1942).

XVIII Divisione Bixio, Archivio Guastalla, Milan.

Du-Camp, Maxime, *L'expédition des Deux Siciles. Souvenirs personnels* (Paris, 1861).

Dumas, Alexandre, *Mémoires de Garibaldi* (Paris, 1861); *Les garibaldiens. Révolution de Sicile et de Naples* (Paris, 1868).

Dunne, Giovanni, *Servizi presentati all'Italia nel 1860 dal generale brigadiere G. Dunne* (Turin, 1862).

Eber, Nandór, *Garibaldi a Palermo, narrato da un testimone oculare* (Livorno, 1860).

'Episodi della spedzione dei Mille nei ricordi inediti del generale Dezza' (in *Camicia Rossa*, 1930).

Fainelli, Vittorio, 'Da Marsala a Calatafimi secondo il carteggio La Masa' (in *Rivista Storica del Risorgimento*, 1956).

Falzone, Gaetano, 'Chiaroscuri della battaglia di Milazzo' (in *Archivio Storico messinese*

1959–61); *Ritratto di Luigi Tükory* (Palermo, 1938); *Legioni estere con Garibaldi nel 1860* (Palermo, 1961); 'Giovanni Corrao e la sua brigata nella campagna del 1860' (in *Camicia Rossa*, 1942); *Nicola Balcescu a Palermo* (Palermo, 1953; 'Memorie e tradizioni di garibaldinismo ungherese in Sicilia' (in *Rivista Storica del Risorgimento*, 1954).

Ferraris, Raffaele, *Da Sestri a Messina. Diario garibaldino del battaglione 'Cacciatori della Morte' della 2ª spedizione diretta dal gen. Medici* (Mortara, 1910).

Fonterossi, Giuseppe, 'Nuovi documenti sulle navi dei Mille' (in *L'Osservatore politico letterario*, 1960); 'La spedizione dei Mille nei ricordi inediti di un figlio di G. B. Fauché (Antonio)' (in *Camicia Rossa*, 1938).

Fucili, Angelo, *Augusto Elia, scudo di Garibaldi a Calatafimi* (Ancona, 1960).

Gasparini, Luisa, 'La verita sulle navi dei Mille' (in *Nuova Antologia*, 1950).

Giaracà, Emanuele, 'Lo sgombro delle truppe borboniche da Siracusa nel 1869' (in *Rivista Storica del Risorgimento*, 1918).

Giuffrida, Romualdo, 'Raffaele Rubattino e la spedizione dei Mille' (in *Nuovi Quaderni del Meridione*, 1970).

Giusti, Renato, 'Carteggio garibaldino' (in *Atti e memorie del Museo del Risorg. Mantua*, 1961); 'Giovanni Acerbi, Intendente dei Mille' (in *Studi Garibaldini*, 1961).

Godechot, Jacques, 'L'Europa di fronte alla spedizione dei Mille' (in *L'Osservatore politico letterario*, 1960).

Gotta, Salvator, *Camicie Rosse 1860* (Milan, 1959).

Grillo, Raffaele, 'Filippo Minutelli comandante del Genio dei Mille' (in *Bollettino del Ist. Storico e Culturale Arma Genio*, 1961).

Guardione, Francesco, 'Il contributo straniero nell'epopea garibaldina' (in *Rivista d'Italia*, 1911); 'Note sul fatto d'armi di Corriolo e sulla battaglia di Milazzo (in *Revista Storica del Risorgimento*, 1929); *Enrico Cosenz* (Palermo, 1900).

'Colonel Hicks and the American volunteers in praise of Garibaldi' (in *Herald*, New York, 18/11 and 9/12 1860, 26/1/1861).

Fonvielle, Ulrich, *Souvenirs d'une chemise rouge* (Paris, 1861).

Jászay, Magda, 'La campagna del 1860 nel carteggio di due garibaldini ungheresi' (in *Revista Storica del Risorgimento*, 1963); 'Un cronista ungherese delle gesta garibaldine: Ferdinand Eber' (in *Il Risorgimento in Sicilia*, 1967).

Illustrated London News, October–November–December 1860.

Kardos, Tibor, 'Valutazioni del Kossuth e di testimoni oculari ungheresi sulla spedizione dei Mille' (in *La Sicilia e l'unità*).

Koltay-Kastner, Jenö, 'Etienne Türr en 1860' (in *Il Risorgimento in Sicilia*, 1965); 'Kossuth e la Sicilia' (in *Rassegna Storica Risorgimentale*, 1928).

Kossuth, Lajos, *Souvenirs et écrits de mon exil. Période de la guerre d'Italie* (Paris, 1880).

La Masa, Giuseppe, *Fatti e documenti delle rivoluzioni dell'Italia meridionale del 1860 riguardanti i siciliani e La Masa* (Turin, 1861).

Landi, Guido, *Il generale Francesco Landi* (in *Revista Storica del Risorgimento*, 1960).

Lukacs, Lajos, 'Osservazioni sull'attivita del garibaldino Steffano Dunyov' (in *Revista Storica del Risorgimento*, 1967); *Garibaldi e l'emigrazione ungherese 1860–62* (Modena, 1965).

Magni, Alessandro, *Le vicende della spedizione Cosenz nella guerra del 1860* (Rome, 1902); 'La 16ª Divisione Cosenz nella campagna del 1860' (in *I Congresso Stor. del Risorg.*, 1906).

Maison, Emile, *Journal d'un volontaire de Garibaldi* (Paris, 1861).

Mario, Alberto, *I Mille, Biografie* (Genoa, 1876); *The Red Shirt* (London, 1865).

Mariotti, Temistocle, 'La seconda spedizione garibaldina del 1860 in Sicilia. Ricordi di un superstite del reggimento Malenchini' (in *Nuova Antologia*, 1909).

Markus, Stefano, 'Garibaldini ungheresi a Messina' (in *Archivio storico messinese* 1959–61); 'Il generale Stefano Türr e la Sicilia alla luci di nuovi documenti' (in *Atti del convegno siciliano*, Trapani 1962).

Marraro, Howard R., 'Il Risorgimento in Sicilia visto dagli Americani' (in *La Sicilia e l'unità*); 'Documenti italiani e americani sulla spedizione garibaldina in Sicilia' (in *Rivista Storica del Risorgimento*, 1957).

Medici, Giacomo, *Una pagina di storia del 1860* (Palermo, 1869).

Messineo, Giovanna, *I Mille e la spedizione garibaldina in Calabria* (Reggio Calabria, 1925).

Milani, Mino, *Garibaldi e Bixio nel diario di un garibaldino pavese (1860)* (in *Boll. Soc. Pavese stor.*, 1955).

Miraglia, Costantino, 'Battaglia di Milazzo' (in *Archivio storico siciliano*, 1960).

Miraglia, Rocco Vincenzo, 'Francesco Nullo e i suoi prodi' (in *La Martinella di Milano*, 1965).

Molfese, Franco, 'Lo scioglimento dell'Esercito meridionale garibaldino (1860–61)' (in *Nuova Rivista Storica*, 1960).

Mondini, Luigi, 'Ancora sulla difesa di Palermo nel 1860' (in *Il Risorgimento*, 1963); 'Dai Mille all'esercito meridionale' (in *Il Risorgimento*, 1960); 'I Mille. Note militari' (in *Bergomum*, 1961).

Mundy, Rodney, *H.M.S. Hannibal at Palermo and Naples, during the Italian Revolution 1859–61* (London, 1863).

Nardi, Carlo, *Benedetto, Enrico, Luigi Cairoli nella spedizione dei Mille* (Genoa, 1963).

New York Times, July and October 1861.

Orsini, Vincenzo, *Rapporto delle operazioni eseguite dall'artiglieria nelle azioni della campagna sicula-napoletana, diretto al luogotenente generale Sirtori comandante dell'esercito meridionale (1860)*.

Pecorini-Manzoni, Carlo, *Storia della 15ª Divisione Türr nella campagna del 1860 in Sicilia e Napoli* (Florence, 1876).

Piaggia di Santamarina, Giuseppe, *La campagna di Milazzo nella guerra d'Italia dell'anno 1860* (Palermo, 1860); *Dai fatti d'armi di Milazzo nella guerra d'Italia del 1860* (Palermo, 1910).

Pomelli, Giuseppe, 'Da Taormina a Teano' (in *Garibaldi e i garibaldini*, Como, 1910).

Pottino, Filippo, *Luigi Tükory* (Palermo, 1933).

Pouthas, Charles H., *La médiation de Napoléon III entre le roi de Naples, les Siciliens et le gouvernment piémontais* (in *Revista Storica del Risorgimento*, 1952).

Radice, Benedetto, 'Nino Bixio a Bronte' (in *Archivo Storico per la Sicilia orientale*, 1910).

Rava, Luigi, *N. Fabrizi, F. Crispi e L. C. Farini nella preparazione della spedizione dei Mille* (in *Revista Storica del Risorgimento*, 1931).

Rüstow, Friederich Wilhelm, *La guerra italiana del 1860* (Venice, 1861); *La Brigata Milano nella campagna dell'Italia Meridionale* (Milan, 1861).

Sardegna, Giuseppe Noto, *Luigi Tükory e l'impresa garibaldina* (Palermo, 1935).

Scaletti, Mario, 'Ippolito Nievo vice intendente generale dell'esercito garibaldino' (in *Studi sul Risorgimento in Lombardia*, Modena, 1953).

Sclavo, Francesco, *L'origine dei Carabinieri Genovesi e la parte avuta nelle guerre 1859–60* (Genoa, 1910).

Soriga, Renato, 'La brigata Sacchi e la prima spedizione garibaldina in Sicilia (8–17 agosto 1860)' (in *Rivista d'Italia*, 1912).

Telbizov, Konstantin, *Dati biografici sul colonnello garibaldino Stefano Dunjov, celebre eroe della battaglia del Volturno* (Sofia, 1965).

Tessari, Teodolfo, 'Genesi e Natura dell'esercito garibaldino del 1860' (in *Studi garibaldini*, 1961).

The Times, London, June–October 1860.

Trevelyan, George Macaulay, *Garibaldi and the Thousand* (London, 1909); *Garibaldi and the Making of Italy* (London 1911).

Türr, Stefania, *L'opera di Stefano Türr nel Risorgimento italiano (1849–1870) descritta dalla figlia* (Florence, 1928).

Türr, István, *Da Quarto a Marsala nel maggio del 1860. Appunti* (Genoa, 1901).

Vidal, Cesár, 'Gli studi francesi sul Risorgimento-Garibaldi et l'épopée des Mille' (in *Rassegna Storica Risorgimentale*, 1936); 'Garibaldi e les Mille' (*ibid.*, 1953).

Vigevano, Attilio, *La compagnia estera garibaldina nella campagna del 1860* (Rome, 1914).

Zibilli, Stefano, *Sulla conquista garibaldina di Milazzo* (Palermo, 1882).

Vigevano, Attilio, *La Legione Ungherese in Italia (1859–1867)* (Rome, 1924).

ECHOES AROUND THE GLOBE

Elia, Augusto, *Note autobiografiche e storiche di un garibaldino* (Bologna, 1898).

Herzen, Aleksander Ivanovitch, *Garibaldi a Londra* (Milan, 1950).

Milesi, Giuseppe Locatelli, 'Francesco Nullo il Fieramosca dei Mille' (in *Camicia Rossa*, 1934).

Mondini, Livio, 'L'Insurrezione polacca al parlamento italiano' (in *Studi garibaldini*, 1962).

THE GREAT DEFEAT

Adamoli, Giulio, *Da San Martino a Mentana* (Milan, 1892).

Baistrocchi, Cesare, 'Ricordi di un garibaldino di Bezzecca' (in *Camicia Rossa*, 1936).

Bortolotti, I., *La guerra del '66* (Milan, 1941).

Brentari, Ottone, *Garibaldi e il Trentino* (Turin, 1907).

Chiala, Luigi, *Ancora un po più di luce sugli eventi politici e militari dell'anno 1866* (Florence, 1902).

Corpo dello Stato Maggiore, *La campagna del 1866 in Italia* (Rome, 1875).

Cicconetti, Luigi, *Roma o Morte* (Milan, 1934).

Eyck, E., *Bismarck* (Turin, 1950).

Fonterossi, Giuseppe, 'Casa Ajani 25 ottobre 1867' (in *Camicia Rossa*, 1941).

Luzio, Alessandro, *Aspromonte e Mentana. Documenti inediti* (Florence, 1935).

Minghetti, Marco, *La convenzione di settembre, un capitolo dei miei ricordi* (Bologna, 1899).

Musini, Nullo, 'I settanta di Villa Glori' (in *Camicia Rossa*, 1941).

Di Nolli, Roberto, *Mentana* (Rome, 1965).

Rosi, Michele, *I Cairoli* (Turin, 1908).

Tosi, Raffaele, *Da Venezia a Mentana 1848–1867* (Forlì, 1910).

Vigevano, A., *La fine dell'esercito pontificio* (Rome, 1920).

Zanna, Piero, 'Pagine inedite su Mentana' (in *Camicia Rossa*, 1941).

Zanoja, Carlo, 'Diario della campagna garibaldina del 1866' (in *Studi garibaldini*, 1965).

RALLY ROUND THE GENERAL

Aroldi, Cesare, *L'ultimo dei vecchi garibaldini* (Viadana, 1973).

Beghelli, Giuseppe, *Le Camicia Rosse in Francia* (Turin, 1871).

Carlino, Ermete, *La spedizione garibaldina in Francia* (Bari, 1914).

Castellani, G. A., 'Una brigata e una bandiera' (in *Camicia Rossa*, 1937); *Legioni rosse. Memorie patriottiche di Ricciotti Garibaldi* (Milan, 1921).

Farlatti, Luigi, *La Brigata Lobbia nella campagna di Francia* (Venice, 1880).

Garibaldi, Ricciotti, *Souvenirs de la Campagne de France 1870–71* (Nice, 1899); *Da Digione alle Argonne – memorie storiche raccolte da Castellani* (Milan, 1915).

Garibaldi, Clelia, *Mio Padre. Ricordi di Clelia Garibaldi* (Florence, 1948).

Morando, F. Ernesto, 'Ritratto di Stefano Canzio' (in *Camicia Rossa*, 1936).

Socci, Ettore, *Da Firenze a Digione* (Prato, 1871).

Strocchi, Tito, *I garibaldini volontari in Francia* (Lucca, 1871).

The Times, October, November, December 1870.

L'Universo Illustrato March–April 1871.

THE THIRD GENERATION

Campolonghi, Luigi, *Amilcare Cipriani* (Milan, 1912).

Garibaldi, Ricciotti, *Le Camicie Rosse nella guerra dei Balcani* (Como, 1915).

K.A., *Oi Garibaldinoi en tò Hellenotourkikò polemò* (Athens, 1897).

Kerofilas, Costas, *La Grecia e l'Italia nel Risorgimento italiano* (Florence, 1919).

Lodi, Luigi, *Correspondence from the Garibaldini camp in Greece for 'Don Chisciotte'*, Rome, May–June 1897.

Rossi, Adolfo, *Alla guerra greco-turca (aprile–maggio 1897)* (Florence, 1897).

Spallini, Aldo, *La spedizione garibaldina in Grecia* (Forli, 1913).

Valiani, Leo, in *Rassegna Storica Toscana* 1965.

THE LAST OF THEM ALL

Giacchi, Nicolò, 'Il reggimento garibaldino nelle Argonne' (in *Rassegna Storica Risorgimentale*, 1931).

Camillo, Marabini, *La rossa avanguardia delle Argonne* (Milan, 1915).

The Times, January–March 1915.

Index

NEW ROCHELLE PUBLIC LIBRARY
B GARIBALDI   0090135966
Viotti, Andrea./Garibaldi : the revo

3 1019 02034952 1

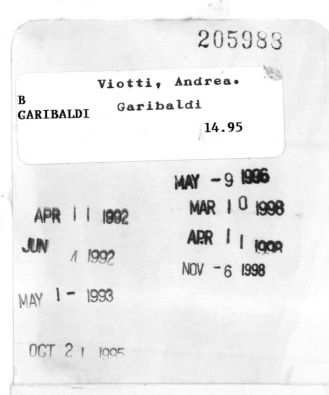

205983

B
GARIBALDI

Viotti, Andrea.

Garibaldi

14.95

APR 11 1992

JUN 4 1992

MAY 1 - 1993

OCT 21 1995

MAY -9 1996

MAR 10 1998

APR 11 1998

NOV -6 1998

NEW ROCHELLE PUBLIC LIBRARY

Library Plaza

New Rochelle, N.Y.   10801

632-7878

Please telephone for information

on library services and hours